The U.S. – China Issues
Trade +++

The U.S. – China Issues Trade +++

Mainstream and Organic Views

*****

Dr. Ifay F. Chang

ISBN: 0977159469
ISBN-13: 978-0-9771-5946-8
Library of Congress Control Number: 2019903615
TLC Information Services, Katonah, NY

Air Defense Identification Zone (ADIZ)
Air Sea Battle (ASB)
American Exceptionalism
Asia Pacific Economic Cooperation (APEC)
Arms Race
Asia Infrastructure Investment Bank (AIIB)
Asia Pacific Economic Conference (APEC)
Australia
Balance of Power
Belt and Road Initiative (BRI)(OBOR)
Bi-Polar
Brazil
Brexit
Cambodia
Causality Analysis
Chang'e (Space Missile)
Chinese Exceptionalism
Comfort Woman
Corruption
Communist Party of China Party Congress (CPCPC)
Comprehensive Progressive Transpacific Partnership (CPTPP)
Crimea
Currency Manipulation
Cyber Security
Defense Budget
Democracy
Diaoyu Islands
Dilemma
East China Sea (ECS)
Economy
Energy
Environment
Evolution
Financial Crisis
Global Warming
Gordian Knots
Hackers
Hacking
India

Inflation
Indonesia
International Code of Conduct (ICOC)
Islamic State of Iraq and Syria (ISIS)
Iran Sanction
Japan
Korea Penisula
Laos
Liuqiu
Malaysia
Multi-Polar
National People's Congress (NPC)
National Security
Naval Blockade
Network Security
North Korea
Nuclear Threat
Okinawa
One Belt One Road (OBOR)(BRI)
Pakistan
Paracel Islands
Philippines
Pivot To Asia
Pratas Islands (Dongsha Islands)
Prevention of Placement of Weapons Treaty (PPWT)
Rebalance
Recovery Day
Regional Development
Russia
Shanghai Cooperation Organization (SCO)
Shenyang POW Camp
Shouji (Cellphone)
Singapore
South China Sea (SCS)
South Korea
Space Technology
Spratly Islands
Stella Award
Taiping Island (the largest of Spratly)

Tariff
Term Limit
Terminal High Altitude Area Defense (THAAD)
Thad (Caring, Loving and Respectful)
Thailand
Thucydides
Trade Deficit
Trade War
Trans-Pacific Partners (TPP)->CPTPP
Trilateral Military Alliance
Trumponomics
Trump Phenomenon
Ukraine
Uni-polar
UN Educational, Scientific and Cultural Organization (UNESCO)
US-Mixico-Canada Trade Agreement (USMCA)
Vietnam
WW II
Xi Jinping
Yutu (Lunar Module)
Zhanguo Dynamics (Multiple Kingdoms in Chinese History)

Table of Contents

Acknowledgment

*****

I dedicate this book to my father Dr. Paul Chong Liang Chang who had served all his life in his government and pursued in the study of foreign affairs between China and the West.

I am blessed with six children and six grand children. Two of my children, Jerren and Jerray, are economics major, one reentered the John F. Kennedy School at Harvard for studying government policies and business administration, the other will study at the London School of Economics in coming months. Jerray selected London because his grandfather did his graduate studies in London University. We often talked about current events. Their honest discussions with me are fun, inspiring and helpful in helping me understand the generation gap and the huge gap between the American public and Chinese people.

The subjects of international relations, foreign affairs, economics, geopolitics and nation and global governance are too complex and dynamic for anyone to master in a limited time, in a few semesters studies or even with a life time. It requires not only historical information but also broad massive inputs from our societies at all times and from all places. School studies and research can enhance one's efficiency in collecting and comprehending a number of events or subjects, in making analyses and interpretations, and in extracting issues with the help of a few knowledgeable people. However, in the age of Internet marching from 4G to 5G technology era, massive information are generated in the real world by the minute and transmitted by the second. This information must be filtered and distilled as inputs supplementing the mainstream media and helping people making correct decisions. This book is such an effort on the U.S.-China Issues.

This is my fifth book on matters related to the United States and China. It collects and summarizes the columns I published in a number of Chinese newspapers in a few major cities in the United States, including Taiwan Daily, Washington China Daily News, Dallas Daily News, Southern Chinese Daily News, and Chicago Chinese News. I thank the US-China Forum for making the above newspaper media space available to me. I joined the forum because I firmly share and support its goal "to inform not only the American public about the U.S.-China issues (through its English website, **www.US-ChinaForum.com**), but also the Chinese Americans (through its bilingual website, **www.US-ChinaForum.org** as well as through the Chinese news media for those who prefer reading a paper)". The valuable print space offered by the above Chinese newspapers to publish my English columns is greatly appreciated.

There are so much misinformation and fake news in the mainstream media, thus, it is utterly important to bring the voices in the organic media like the Internet news lists, blogs and websites on foreign affairs to contrast with the mass media. The Asian Americans, especially their majority - Chinese Americans, have a special responsibility and a deep inner desire of bringing their homeland (the U.S. where they reside) and motherland (Asia where they or their ancestors emigrated from) to understand each other on issues rather than to let the so called experts or strategists create conflicts based on outdated information or cultural misunderstanding.

In our society, even among blood relations, people have generation gap. It is understandable that the U.S. foreign policy experts, (few being Asian or Chinese Americans), have huge gaps of misunderstanding with the Asian/Chinese Americans on the U.S.-Asia problems especially the U.S.–China issues. This book in short essay format is aiming at bridging the gaps, the generation gap (between immigrants and their children born in the U.S.) and the cultural gap (between immigrants of different ethnicity), in the understanding of the U.S.-China issues.

I especially like to acknowledge the great help from my colleagues in the US-China Forum, English editors, Richard Chen, Paul Tung and Nelson Ma , Chinese editors, Prof. Wenji Chang, Thomas Fann, Paul Shui and Sam Chen, Forum Directors, C. Y. Kao, Bill Chou, Frank Chang and Ambrose Wang as well as the Forum Web Master, Betty Tsang. Many our forum readers have given us guidance and kept us going in our endeavor: monitoring and analyzing the daily events and intriguing issues happening between China and the United States. Without their encouragement, it would be very difficult for us to continue our work and for me personally to publish my writings as long as I have.

Finally, my deepest appreciation goes to my fans, whose response and correspondences are source of my nourishment and inspiration; Please do continue to send me comments, newspaper cuttings and controversial articles from both mainstream and organic media. As I said above, distilling information is very important; everyone has such a duty in the era of information explosion.

Preface

"One of the key problems today is that politics is such a disgrace, good people don't go into government."
~ President Donald Trump
"One of the key problems today is that mass media is such a disgrace, good people don't go into Journalism."
~ Dr. Wordman's Paraphrase

The mass media like to pick on President Trump's 'famous' quotes, mostly in a negative tone. The above quote attributed to President Trump is an honest statement even though some have extended the statement to imply that Trump is not one of the good people. In all honesty, the above quote is not only true today but also can be extended to today's mass media: One of the key problems today is that mass media is such a disgrace; good people don't want to go into journalism. Mass media seems to be controlled by conglomerates showing biases and favouritism. So, the author would like to declare that this book is written independently with no financial assistance from anyone and no strings attached to any institution, especially any commercial media organization

The author has written four books previously; they are entitled as: 1. U.S.-China Relations (2015), 2. Understanding the U.S. and China (2016), 3. Two Changing Giants - the U.S. and China (2017) and 4. New World Order–The Bipolar View (2018). The author has spent quite a bit of time in naming the present book. As book writing advisors say, some people decide a title first then write the book and some will complete the book then decide on a title. This book belongs to the latter. After the book chapters were completed, the author browsed through the book chapters and flipped through their contents then decided on a title. This process is explained below.

There were numerous topics covered in this book since there were numerous events happened between the U.S. and China recently. First, there is the East China Sea Issue involving Taiwan, Diaoyu Islands and Liujiu. The Taiwan issue alone contains the Taiwan Travel Act, recent election result, Xi's speech on Taiwan and the question of a peaceful or forceful reunification of Taiwan. Then there is the South China Sea (SCS) issue where freedom of navigation is a controversy between the U.S. and China and China's fortification of SCS small islands are progressing too rapidly since the U.S. has announced her pivot to Asia policy. SCS involves nearly all countries in South East Asia (ASEAN countries) but Australia and Japan whose foreign policies on SCS are also changing. Of course there is the North Korea problem consuming a lot of attention from world leaders but a peace treaty and denuclearization is still not insight despite of the leaders' summit meetings.

China emulates the U.S. and sees the signs of problems like wealth gap, inequality and public debt which are the same problems the U.S. faces but yet the arguments never ends on national governance system and economic development model between the two nations. There are many more issues between the U.S. and China like puzzles with no clue (why the issues must exist?!), such as competing in space exploration – why must the U.S. and China compete instead of collaboration? Is China a real threat to the U.S.? Or is the U.S. pushing China to stop her de-poverty effort and engaging her in arms race? It appears that travelling to China is a good thing for Americans to know the real China. The vast increase of Chinese travellers to the world certainly helped Chinese to understand the world and appreciate the fact that environmental issues are important and the civil manners were in their ancient culture which can be revived in their society along with prosperity.

The trade imbalance is a real issue but it is snowballing to a much bigger size than trade issue alone. The statistics of trade imbalance is not as a big deal as they are interpreted with implication far beyond trade. The tariff war has been more lip service than actual action, but the extended issues surrounding trade are far more alarming. Demanding extradition of a CFO of a nearly trillion dollar corporation from Canada without formal charges and concrete evidence is leading the world to worry and resent the long legal arm of the U.S. The CFO of Huawei, being a female, was arrested and detained for weeks not only creating a diplomatic hot potato for Canada who made a hasty arrest but also making the U.S.-China trade negotiation more complicated. China has launched the Belt and Road Initiative (BRI) as a platform to drive global economic development. Despite of nearly half of the world embracing BRI, the U.S. is opposing it and some even accusing it as a new colonialism. All these complications happened along with the U.S.-China trade issue.

Therefore, the author named this book as The U.S.-China Issues – Trade +++.

Introduction

This book is a collection of essays related to the U.S., China and their conflicts including more than the trade issue, a book principally containing discussions on current events occurred between the two countries. This is the 5th book of the series of Mainstream and Organic Views in the domain of national and international affairs. The conflicts between the U.S. and China are rooted in the differences of political ideology and governance system that the two countries believe in and practice on. In the previous books, the author had discussed the definition of ideology and democracy. The Western world has over emphasized the democracy rather than accepting the fact it is ideology that human society should pursue, modify and transform to fit the society. Democracy is just a means for selecting and transforming ideology. There is no guarantee that through democracy a perfect ideology can be selected and executed well. In the following, a couple of old ideas are presented here; the first one offers the idea that there is not that much difference in ideology between the U.S. and China, each country is transforming to meet their citizens' needs, such as better living condition, improved environment, adequate healthcare, sufficient jobs, etc. The second idea explains and emphasizes that there is really no need to export democracy, especially after witnessing the fact that two third of the top twenty prosperous nations with GDP above $20,000 do not have a democratic governing system. Therefore, there is no valid reason that we must promote or export democracy, certainly not at the expense of war and human casualty. The author hopes that the readers after reading this introduction will have a stimulated mindset to delve into the chapters included in this book. Although the US-China trade issue is discussed more in this book, however, the two countries have other confrontational issues such as technology competition, military interference and even cultural clash. Hence this book is entitled US – China Issues – Trade +++ but the author believes that these issues are solvable.

Ideology, Democracy and Promotion of Democracy

In our modern world, the members of a society or a nation need to have adequate political knowledge in order to define and appreciate their preferred ideology and to have the skills to apply a method in the political system to uphold and realize the goals of their desired ideology. A common mistake even among scholars is that the word 'democracy' is used as a term of 'ideology' rather than as a term of 'methodology'. This confusion can be understood when one hears ideological phrases such as liberal democracy or social democracy which really means liberalism or socialism using a method, democracy, to uphold the goals of the ideology. Liberalism or socialism are ideologies just like conservatism, capitalism, communism, imperialism and colonialism which define a belief and philosophy about setting up a framework for a human society or a nation in which what and how resources, materials and properties each society member could use, create, own and share are prescribed. Nations may adopt different or mixed ideologies and employ different methods to uphold and achieve the goals of their ideologies. An authoritarian government can pursue liberalism just as well a democratic government can pursue socialism. The adaption of an ideology is not a one-time affair; it may require modification and constant reform to evolve an ideology to fit a particular human society.

In fact, democracy is a method employed almost by all societies of different ideologies and practiced more or less at different levels. Democracy is the strongest and at the same time most vulnerable (to chaos) when each society member has the same power and authority in terms of one man one vote for everything. Democracy is less strong and less vulnerable when society members share varying degrees of power and authority as exhibited by a party system and/or a hierarchical representation system. Democracy is nearly nil in a dictatorship where society members have very little power and authority and the dictator's conduct has nothing to do with sharing authority. Today, in every country, no matter what ideology or multiple ideologies are embraced, the method of democracy is employed but somewhat differently. Even a government of monarch employs the method of 'democracy' at some levels in its political system.

Since human had history, many ideologies evolved, some hoping to converge to an ideal one for all people on earth. Democracy as a method existed even longer than some ideologies and yet to be refined to function effectively in all ideological systems. In ancient China, the emperors had great power but democracy was employed but practiced only in their courts, the emperor usually cannot arbitrarily enact a law, say taxation, without the consent of the majority of his ministers.(The ministers suppose to look out for the welfare of the people) So did the practice of democracy in the Roman Empire's Senate. In ancient times, the study or development of 'methods' such as democracy were hampered by the emperor's power but there were plenty of ideologies as represented by philosophers in the East and West with rich conservative, liberal and socialistic ideas, as represented by Confucianism（孔子思想）, Laoism（老子思想）and Moaism（墨子思想）(not to be confused with Maoism which is a blend of socialism and communism) and liberalism (John Locke and before) and socialism and communism (Karl Marx, Vladimir Lenin, and Mao Zedong. Although Mao had never set foot to the west except Moscow, Maoism had followers beyond China, including people like Mandela from Africa. Over more than two centuries, the Western ideologies blossomed along several revolutions including the industrial revolution which eventually divided the world resulting in a long drawn Cold War with capitalism/liberalism fighting against communism/socialism. Although the Cold War ended with the collapse of the Soviet Union, one cannot conclude that capitalism/liberalism is absolutely superior to communism/socialism; perhaps it is the 'method' employed to practice ideology that had made the difference, if one compared China's economic success over Russia's.

Socialism had a deep root going back to the French Revolution and it blossomed in the next two centuries. Starting from 20th century, we have seen socialism emerged in different countries expanding in different degrees. In Northern Europe, Sweden and Denmark adopted socialism coupled with democracy even though an emperor system still existed in each country. Unfortunately, the media often refer their system as a social democracy, but correctly it is a socialism adopted to fit their political systems with the method, democracy, practiced at the citizens' level not at the King's court level. Socialism in more or less degree has propagated throughout the Europe and elsewhere in Asia, Africa and America.

On the other hand, liberalism as an ideology had several centuries of history, but its champions were the French and the Americans. The United States declared her independence with the liberal principle that all men are created equal then after a few years, through French Revolution, with a slogan, liberty, equality and fraternity, the French overthrew her monarch. The French Revolution had an impact beyond France reaching Worldwide. Both Americans and French people adopted democracy as a method to safeguard liberalism. France, in 1789, was the first Nation that granted all her male citizens voting right, the fundamental tool of democracy. The United States through Jackson's movement on democracy in the 1820's gradually granted voting rights to white males, then black males (1870) and eventually to women on August 18, 1920. So the adoption of the method, 'democracy' was much later than the adoption of ideologies, liberalism and capitalism. It took more than a century for the United States to fully embrace democracy as the method to uphold her ideologies be it liberalism, socialism, capitalism or conservatism in an amalgamated form.

The collapse of Soviet Union did not mean the death of communism since it shared many common principles with socialism which not only persisted in socialist countries but propagated into liberal countries like France and the United States. That entry meant to improve the capitalism and liberalism rather than to replace them for the benefit of the human society. Conversely, liberalism and capitalism have crept into many socialist and some former communist countries, where marked differences in economic growth were seen. These diffusion of ideologies produce very different economic results in different countries owing to many factors unique to each country but not so much dependent on the method or how strong a 'democracy' was employed. Greece, functioning under a strong democracy with liberal socialism, went bankrupt whereas China, functioning under a tailored democracy in a principally one party system, created a near miracle in economic development.

Culture, tradition, resources, geopolitical conditions, citizens' knowledge and political leaders' ability are all part of the factors influencing the diffusion process of ideologies and their interpretation. The method of democracy may accelerate the changes or interpretation of ideologies but it comes with an inherent vulnerability. This vulnerability may be represented by a U shape function of the strength of democracy. The strongest and the weakest democracy create the biggest vulnerability (chaos and tyranny). Currently, the United States is going through a transformation with forces of different ideologies (liberalism, socialism, capitalism and conservatism) propelled under a strong democracy; yet her government is vulnerable to chaos owing to a dysfunctional congress with government shutdowns due to budget crisis or grid lock in Congress. Americans must spend more energy in debate to converge their ideologies to avoid chaos; whereas China is also going through a transformation with forces of communism, capitalism and socialism to define an ideology for her citizens under the leadership of the Chinese Communist Party.

The Chinese citizens may ultimately desire to have a stronger democracy, but they may be wise to focus on converging their ideologies and weigh on the strength and the vulnerability of democracy to find an optimum point on the U curve before throwing out their current limited but effective democracy under the one party (CCP) system. Judging on the political and economical issues the United States and China each faces, the two countries may not have any serious ideological conflict at all as each is transforming with time; hence, in the US-China relationship there is no reason to target each other as an enemy. Each country would be better served by immediately stopping their hostile foreign policy towards each other and focusing on each country's transformation on ideology.

The U.S. has been the defender of democracy as well as the promoter of democracy. History tells us though; the success of economic development has no direct correlation with the democratic system. Statistics show us that the wealth and the share of world economy of the U.S.-led West has declined. Political scientists, Adam Przeworski and Fernando Limongi, have found that democracy does not work in poor countries and only countries with a GDP per capita above $14,000 are reliably secure. This proves that democracy cannot guarantee prosperity, only culture, tradition, resources, geopolitical conditions, citizens' education/knowledge and political leaders' ability working together can influence the diffusion, adoption, and transformation of a suitable ideology which can then lead to a successful economic development for prosperity. Therefore it does not make sense to export to or promote democracy in developing countries. Insisting having democracy before having economic success is like putting the cart in front the horse. As discussed above, in such a case, democracy may bring chaos. So we may conclude that democracy is only a method of decision making which can be adopted and practiced at different levels under suitable conditions.

The U.S. and China being geographically on opposite of the earth need not feel insecure in any way. The two countries have a lot of similarities, size, rich resources and a diverse population, despite of their different political systems. China and the U.S. have followed a different path of nation building but they are facing very similar challenges. It is apparent only collaboration and friendly competition will benefit the people of two countries and the whole world. In time, a slow but steady convergence of ideologies will occur as each is trying to maintain a good living condition for her citizens. With today's rapidly advancing communication infrastructure and technologies, it is very easy for the Americans and Chinese to understand each other and deal with differences. It is only ignorance that will drive the two people apart.

Author Information
Ifay Chang. Ph.D.
Producer/Host, Community Education - Scrammble Game Show
Columnist, www.us-chinaforum.org -Dr.Wordman
Trustee, Somers Central School District
President, IPO2U.COM, Inc. and TLC Information Services
Retired Professor, Polytechnic University (Now Part of NYU)
Retired Scientist, TJ Watson Research Center, IBM
Published books:
US-China Relations (4/2015)
ISBN 0977159426   ISBN 13: 9780977159420
Understanding the U.S and China (4/2016)
ISBN 0977159442   ISBN 13: 9780977159444
The Changing Giants – The U.S. and China (4/2017)
ISBN 0977159450   ISBN 13: 9780977159451
Two Lovely Space Stories (12/2017)
ISBN 1981611576   ISBN 13: 9781981611577
New World Order – The Bipolar View (4/2018)
ISBN 1981506942   ISBN 13 9781981506941
Publisher
TLC Information Services
3 Louis Drive, Katonah, N. Y. 10532-3122
All Available from Amazon.com and Other Retailers and Kindle
http://www.amazon.com/U-S-China-Relations-Mainstream-
Organic/dp/0977159426 Search Example
Facebook.com/ifaychang Websites: www.tlcis.uswww.ipo2u.com
Twitter: ifaychang@drwordman.com, DrWordman@scrammble.com
Email: DrWordman@gmail.com

Chapter 1

Three Connected Dilemmas in the East China Sea and Rational Solutions (I)

*****

Abstract

This two-part article discusses the three dilemmas in the East China Sea, namely the Diaoyu Islands, Liuqiu Islands and Taiwan Islands. Through a detailed historical review, the three dilemmas are shown to be connected. The human actions that created these dilemmas are discussed. Only by recognizing the historical background, hints for rational solutions for these dilemmas may be found.

There are three dilemmas in the East China Sea that not only post diplomatic difficulties for China, Japan and the U.S. to develop friendly relations but also create dangerous hotspots in Asia Pacific that may be ruptured into extensive military conflicts dragging three nations into a devastating war. The three dilemmas are: 1. Both China and Japan claim sovereignty rights to the Diaoyu Islands and the U.S. uncomfortably maintains a neutral position on the issue. 2. The U.S. wishes to maintain and expand a military base in Liuqiu but meeting strong local resistance and the resistance is becoming more concerned with political (independence movement from Japan's illegitimate occupation of Liuqiu and desire to establish a friendly relation with China or even return to China for protection) than social issues (crimes committed by the U.S. military and Japan's treating Liqiuans as second class citizens below Japanese). 3. Taiwan needs to be united with China under the One China policy which both the U.S. and Japan recognized and committed to China but apparently unwilling to see it happens for different and complex reasons.

These three dilemmas are connected as I shall discuss in this two-part article. I shall make a thorough review of the relevant history and offer an explanation of how the above dilemmas were created and connected. Only through understanding of the history and the human actions taken place that caused these dilemmas, then these dilemmas may be resolved rationally and the justice may be served in the end peacefully.

The Diaoyu Islands are a group of uninhabitable tiny Islands, some like barren rocks above the ocean surface. The five larger islands have area size averaging between 800 square meters to 4.32 square kilometers. Historically, these islands and the surrounding ocean, called black water trench (trough)(dark water color due to its depth) dividing the thirty six islands belonging to "Liuqiu Islands" on the North-East and the Taiwan islands (including the Diaoyu Islands and other islands surrounding Taiwan) on the South-West. Historical maps and records showed clearly that the Diaoyu Islands were part of Taiwan, in fact as a part of Yi-Lan Xian (county) of Taiwan according to old official documents. The Chinese have been fishing there for centuries. A piece of history involving an American diplomat, Charles Le Gendre, offers an illustrative background on the Diaoyu Islands issue. Gendre was a diplomat stationed in Xiamen port of China. In 1872, on his return journey to America passing through Japan, he was hired as a consultant by the Japanese government. He proposed a theory that Japan can take control of the islands surrounding Taiwan as no-man's land. Japan as an aggressive island nation accepted his proposal and enhanced Japan's 'pirate like' foreign policy further to attack Taiwan, Diaoyu Islands, Liuqiu and other surrounding islands. Gendre might have acted as an individual not on a diplomatic mission, but nevertheless, he planted a seed of embarrassment and dilemma for the U.S. that still troubles today.

Based on many documents, Taiwan had clearly been under China's sovereignty at least from the Ming Dynasty (1368-1644). Timeline of China's sovereignty over Taiwan can be roughly categorized in four periods: China sent expedition to Taiwan (230, East Wu Kingdom and 607, Sui Dynasty) and partial control of islands surrounding Taiwan (1263, Yuan Dynasty). 2. Arrival of sailors from Portugal, Spain and Holland in 16th and early 17th century establishing trade but then the Western visitors surrendered to Zheng Cheng Gong (1662, son of Zheng Zhi Long, Ming's general retreated to Taiwan seeking to recover failed Ming Dynasty). Later Qing Dynasty defeated Zheng (1683) and included Taiwan and surrounding islands into her sovereignty. 4. Japan practiced her 'pirate' foreign policy to expand her island territories especially eyeing Liuqiu, Taiwan and surrounding islands, initially in secrecy till she was militarily strong enough to take on China. Japan defeated China in the first Sino-Japanese War in 1894. Taiwan was ceded to Japan thus Taiwan was ruled by Japan for 50 years (1895-1945) and became separated from Mainland China till today due to China's civil war and external interference, namely from the U.S. and Russia. The U.S. supported the KMT-ROC even after it retreated to Taiwan. Russia supported CCP-PRC and it succeeded in taking over the entire mainland China. ROC went through a political transformation ended the one party KMT rule, experiencing the expected multi-party power struggles dividing the island into multi-parties factions. On the other hand, since 1960's PRC departed from Soviet style of communism and experimented on her own socialism, initially with disastrous results and lately adopting some capitalism with amazing accomplishments. The U.S. had recognized PRC in 1979 and honored the one-China policy, but she was reluctant to see the reunification of Taiwan with Mainland China creating a diplomatic dilemma. One must ask is it long overdue for the U.S. to adopt a new China policy to recognize China as she is today and not hinged on a legacy strategy. It may not be so obvious to the Americans that the U.S. had created this Taiwan dilemma and erred on the side of injustice because herr failure of recognizing the history behind these dilemmas.

Japan's pirate behavior started in later part of Ming dynasty, attacking China's coastal cities (for example, Hangzhou and Ningbo, 1550-1570) and Korea (1593, but was defeated by China, Korea was China's Protégé State). When the Western powers came to Asia, Japan like China was mistreated. China was defeated by the British in the infamous Opium War (1839-1842) and was forced upon her an unequal treaty in 1842. Japan also suffered with an unequal treaty from the U.S. in 1858, but Japan as a small nation underwent a drastic and successful reform of its political and military system adopting a constitutional monarchy system patterning the island nation Great Britain and copied the West earnestly in modernizing its industry (good for Japan), strengthening military (problem for neighbors) and practicing colonialism (more evil than the Western powers thus sad for Asians). This transformation period is known as Japan's Meiji Restoration Period, from 1868-1912. When Japan grew stronger militarily, she became more imperialistic and desired to practice colonialism; Japan set her sight on China as China was obviously weakened by the seven powers descended upon her from the West. Japan first tried to secretly (without alerting China) encroaching Liuqiu (invasion in 1872), then attacking Taiwan (1874, invading Taiwan and its surrounding islands in the East China Sea and forced Liuqiu to be Japan's protégé State) and then Korea peninsula in the North (1875, Japan invaded Korea).

In 1879, Japan annexed Liuqiu Kingdom and kidnapped the king despite of China's effort in asking the former U.S. President Ulysses Grant to intercede. Japan triggered the Sino-Japanese War in 1894. China's defeat resulted in a devastating settlement by ceding to Japan: 1. Taiwan (Japan ruled Taiwan from 1895 to 1945 until Japan surrendered to the Allies), 2. Liaoning Peninsula (later returned to China under pressure from Russia and other European powers)., 3. Korea, pronounced to be an independent State (essentially letting Japan to dominate Korea, later Japan annexed Korea in 1910), and 4. War

Reparation, equaling to more than seven times of Japan's annual national budget. Since then Japan accelerated her military expansion and developed a plan to conquer China and to rule Asia. This plan was later obvious to the world and the U.S. especially after Japan attacked Pearl Harbor (1941) in order to realize her plan. (to be continued in part II)

Chapter 2

Three Connected Dilemmas in the East China Sea and Rational Solutions (II)

*****

Abstract

This two-part article discusses the three connected dilemmas in the East China Sea, namely the Diaoyu Islands, Liuqiu Islands and Taiwan Islands. After digesting the detailed history and the human actions that created these dilemmas, clues leading to rational solutions for these dilemmas are suggested.

Liuqiu was an independent Kingdom maintaining a peaceful relationship with China as a suzerain State during the Ming and Qing dynasties. Liuqiu was seized by Japan in 1879. During WW II, the U.S. navy recovered Liuqiu from Japan and Liuqiu was a major base in the Asia theater supporting US military's island-hopping strategy against Japan with the goal of reaching Japan's four main islands. Even though Liuqiu was ruled by Japan by several decades, the Liuqiuans maintained their culture despite of Japan's 'Japanization' effort which was forced upon on all Japanese occupied territories including Taiwan. Sadly during WW II, more than one hundred thousand Liuqiuans were killed by the Japanese Imperial Army and some by the U.S. military, as spies for the other side. After the war, the U.N. gave the U.S. the administrative authority over Liuqiu and the Diaoyu Islands. The U.S. regarded Liuqiu as a strategic location for her global anti-communist foreign policy stopping the expansion of the communist Soviet Union and its encroaching over China and Japan. Liuqiu then became a stepping stone for the U.S. into Asia, as it had been in WW II and later during the Korean War.

The Liuqiu military bases were used for testing and storage of nuclear, chemical and biological weapons as well as air force and naval bases for equipments and planes. The US governance of Liuqiu Islands was riddled with social problems caused by the presence of large US military. Liuqiuans became resentful and hostile towards the US military and intolerant to the frequent crimes committed by them in Liuqiu. The U.S. contemplated (1969) and formerly returned (1972) the Liuqiu Islands to Japan to govern along with the administrative rights of the Diaoyu Islands, without a justified procedure involving Liuqiuans or China or the U.N. Liuqiuans expected that Japan would help Liuqiu's economy and the US military bases would diminish and disappear. As time went by, neither expectation was realized. Japan, for purpose of strengthening her Mutual Defense Treaty with the U.S., allowed the U.S. to maintain her large military presence in Liuqiu. The livelihood of Liuqiuans was not improved. When the U.S. wished to move and expand her military base to Henoko, Liuqiu (Okinawa, Camp Schwab), strong opposition from local Liuqiuans took place. The elected governor of Okinawa, Takeshi Onaga, wanted to close down the US military bases. Liuqiuans view the bases as a threat to their security rather than as a guaranty for peace. Today, the democratic elections in Liuqiu indicate a strong sentiment for expelling the U.S. military bases, seeking independence and even desiring a friendly relation with China like one and half century ago. Again, the U.S. is in a dilemma: Continuing her unwelcomed presence in Liuqiu for the sake of military purposes (for Japan's defense?) with outdated political goal (Is China a Soviet style communist country threatening the U.S.?) or right the wrong of the past - violating Liuqiuans' rights for self-determination. Will the U.S. be willing to get out of this dilemma for international justice?

The creation of the above three dilemmas is largely the making of the U.S. foreign policy. Without understanding or considering the history, the U.S. in 1972 unilaterally without even the U.N.'s approval process, offered the administrative rights of Liuqiu Islands and Diaoyu Islands to Japan. It appeared like the U.S. was tossing a hot potato to Japan so the U.S. would not have to deal with the anti-US protests for expelling military bases and seeking independence and social justice. However, this decision only pleased Japan (History showed that Japan had always wanted to occupy Liuqiu as its territory) but angered the Liuqiu people (whose rights was ignored), provoked China (ignoring Japan's pirate like foreign policy and aggressive behavior in the past history and deliberately strengthening Japan worry China) and embarrassed Taiwan (whose fishing rights in the East China Sea were compromised as the U.S. gave the administrative right of the Diaoyu Islands to Japan). One can vividly recall the protests over the Diaoyu Islands issue happening worldwide from 1970's onward, in Taiwan, Hong Kong and major cities in the U.S. and Europe, demanding the recognition of the historical evidence that the Diaoyu Islands were a part of Taiwan, China. Although, the U.S. stated a position of neutrality on the sovereignty issue of the Diaoyu Islands for quieting down the protests; however, that was a cop-out move getting more blames. China and Japan diplomatically tabled the dispute but in 2012 Japan reneged that promise by orchestrating a property buy back of three small Diaoyu Islands sold illegally to private citizens in 1970's, a devious scheme to claim ownership. Thus, the Diaoyu Islands issue was activated again by Japan's ambition of expansion and return to its past imperial 'glory'. However, the Diaoyu Islands is one issue both PRC and ROC (except a small group of pro-Japan Japanese descendents in Taiwan) are on the same page. It seems that the U.S. cannot use neutrality to shield herself from facing historical evidence, international justice and potential military confrontation. The U.S. needs to honestly correct the mistakes made and promote a rational solution.

Today, the Diaoyu Islands became a hot spot in the East China Sea because China and Japan had increased their military patrol of the area with chances of breaking into war (Recalling history: The Imperial Japanese Army nearly always were the one triggering an incidence for excuse to initiate a premeditated attack, for example, Mukden incidence (9-18-1931), Marco Polo Bridge incidence (7-7-1937), …, Pearl Harbor attack (12-7-1941)). The U.S. faces a dilemma to risk engaging in a war for some uninhabitable rocks for the sake of endorsing Japan's aggression. The legitimate position of Liuqiu Islands is another hot issue in East Asia. The Liuqiuans deserve to have their say in governance. The U.S. and Japan should not use force to control the ultimate outcome regarding the support of the US military bases in Liuqiu . The indefinite delay of the reunification of Taiwan with Mainland is brewing another trouble in Asia Pacific. China is rightly running out of patience in expecting a peaceful reunification. The U.S. and Japan have no justification to interfere but yet tied to the small anti-China activities in Taiwan.

The current US awkward positions regarding these dilemmas all hinge on the fact that the U.S. is aligning with an aggressive Japan (eager to revise its Pacifist Constitution and strengthening more its military power) against a hypothetic enemy, China. Therefore, the U.S. and Japan established a Mutual Defense Treaty, under which Japan was eagerly building her military on the pretense of self-defense and defending the U.S. In fact, such treaty's initial intention is for the U.S. to help defend Japan from the encroaching communism. No American can believe that such treaty is necessary today since Japan has developed the strongest Navy in Asia once again. China with her successful economic reform and her independence from Russia is the least belligerent or threatening nation in Asia compared to Russia and Japan. Perhaps, Americans should entertain an alternate scenario: What if the U.S. is wrong to assume the hypothetic enemy to be China. A U.S. - China Mutual Defense Treaty may be more beneficial to the security of the U.S. and world peace, if the enemy is another aggressive nation or international terrorism. When Japan's economy was the envy of the world, Liuqiu citizens might have had false hope that they would be benefitted from Japan's economy, but it did not happen. Now that China has overtaken Japan to become a much larger economy with successful policies to trade with the whole world, not surprisingly some Liuqiu citizens, intellectuals especially, will reminisce the peaceful and prosperous days when Liuqiu was a suzerain State of China. Similarly, the people in Taiwan will recognize the benefit of reuniting with motherland China.

The above historical account and analysis should lead Americans to think outside of the box to revise the US foreign policy, especially her China policy to solve the three dilemmas with rational solutions.

Chapter 3
Australia's Logic and Illogic thinking in Foreign Policy

*****

Abstract

Australia is a large and remote country with little national security threat until the arrival of 'Pivot to Asia'. Australia has a small military force, Australia Defense Force (ADF) compared to many Asian nations' defense forces. Australia published defense white papers in 1976, 1987, 1994, 2000, 2009, 2013, 2015, 2016 and a Foreign Policy white paper in 2017. The increased frequency of publication signifies Australia's increased concern for her national strategic security. Australia together with New Zealand has a security agreement with the U.S. (ANZUS), but Australia has a mixed concern with the future impact of the 'Pivot' and the apparent waning influence of the U.S. in Asia. This paper makes observation and analysis of such a concern expressed by Australians.

Bloomberg View (February 3, 2018) has published an interview article, entitled, What Happens When China Eclipses the U.S. in Asia, a provoking title triggered by an Australian political essay, Without America: Australia in the New Asia. Through email, Tobin Harshaw and Daniel Moss of Bloomberg View interviewed Hugh White, the author of Without America, a labor party member and professor at the Australian National University in Canberra in Australia. White had worked for Bob Hawke, former Australian prime minister (1983-1991), and Kim Beazley, Hawke's defense minister and later served as Australian ambassador to the U.S. from 2010-2016. Both politicians were among the most pro-American figures in the Australian Labor Party.

The interview was triggered by White's essay, Without America, published in the Australian Publication, Quarterly Essay on 11-28-2017 and a concerned 'rebuttal', entitled, China Hasn't Won the Pacific (Unless You Think It Has), published in Bloomberg View on 1-5-2018 by Hal Brands. Brands is the Henry A. Kissinger Distinguished Professor at the Henry A. Kissinger Center for Global Affairs at Johns Hopkins University's School of Advanced International Studies and a senior fellow at the Center for Strategic and Budgetary Assessments. Brands' quick response to White's essay and the subsequent email interview of White by Bloomberg View clearly indicate the importance of these essays.

White's view is somewhat persistent based on his earlier Quarterly Essay, Power Shift: Australia's Future between Washington and Beijing, 2010 and following up in 2012 with another **essay,** The China Choice: Why America Should Share Power. White's main point in Without America is that 1. The U.S. and China are engaging a classic power politics. 2. The American leadership in the West Pacific held prominently since WW II is eroding. 3. In New Asia, China will be dominating. 4. Australia got into the habit of seeing the world through Washington's eyes that must change or will risk failure in foreign affairs. White argues that Australia can now stop talking about power sharing because, in their contest for regional supremacy, America will lose and China will win. White has few allies but more opposing debaters in Australia. However, the Australian Foreign Policy White Paper just released about the same time as White's essay acknowledges that China's growing strength will shift the regional power balance and hints that Washington has become a less reliable regional leader, essentially endorsing White's view. Certainly, White's new essay must have caught attentions from many American political analysts. Hal Brands is a representative one.

Brands in his article, China Hasn't Won the Pacific, published in Bloomberg View on 1-5-2018, expressed concerns with perceptions like Hugh White described; such a view may become self-fulfilling prophecy. Brand citing his new book, "American Grand Strategy in the Age of Trump", counters that the U.S. is still too powerful for China to match; the island chain will be effective to curtail China's expansion by encouraging Japan, Taiwan and Philippines to acquire anti-access /area denial capabilities. Brands also holds the view that China will have difficulties as limited by her model. The U.S. and her allies can slap sanctions on China, although Brands does acknowledge that the measures are risky and offering no guarantee. He also admits that White's essay is simultaneously essential and dangerous, meaning that the U.S will be foolish to ignore and dangerous to accept White's thesis.

However, White, in his defense, brushed away the idea that his article was trying to get the U.S. to beef up her strategic position in Asia. In fact, White states that "the U.S. strategic position is eroding so quickly that even sharing the region with China isn't really a valid option any longer, America's allies in Southeast Asia and Australia say they don't want to choose between the U.S. and China, but underneath those platitudes, nobody in the region wants to make an enemy of Beijing. All the more so because officials increasingly doubt the U.S. will be there in the end." In the interview, White further clarifies that Allies must begin to adapt a post-American regional order. Australia's future depends on how well we (Australia) understand China knowing that in the longer trend the U.S. will be edged out by China and the U.S. will become like European countries who will invest in Asia but with no strategic presence.

After reviewing the above two essays and the interview, the author agrees with White's analyses but questions his logic and his thinking of what Australia should do in terms of her national strategic security. First, China's rise or her effort in expanding her influence in the Pacific started at least two decades ago as pointed out by White's earlier essays. The balance of power shift has been gradual. Australia and her Asian Allies should not have been surprised by the current situation whether Obama or Trump ever accelerated the eroding of the U.S. strategic presence in the Pacific. Over the decades, the strategic security in Asia Pacific has not changed for the worse at least for Australia other than the verbal security arguments and showy military exercises which were more like gestures made through the Pivot to Asia policy of the U.S. The North Korea's nuclear threat is entirely another matter to which China, the U.S. and Australia are on the same page. Australia's **legacy concern** for 'security' and continued reliance on the U.S. to provide 'security' had been a debate issue for years before the Soviet Union collapsed in 1991. After that Australia has grown accustomed to the presence of the U.S. in the Pacific and developed the habit of seeing the world through Washington's eyes as acknowledged by White.

The fundamental question is what and where is the security threat coming from, in particular, for Australia?! If the U.S. and China would engage in a Collaborative Bi-Polar World Politics rather than a confrontational one, then there would be no strategic threat or any need to pick side between Washington and Beijing for and by Australia or anybody else. White's mentioning of "for Australia to build her independent military and even go nuclear" is totally illogical and absolutely wrong! Engaging in arms race especially nuclear weapons will for sure raise the danger level of national security for a scarce populated and remote Australia. As Sun Tze said in his world famous book, a diplomatic effort - promoting the U.S. and China to lead a collaborative bi-polar World Order - would be far superior to any military strategy - preparing for war and hope to survive it. Any nuclear threat like the one from North Korea can only be resolved by the U.S. and China acting collaboratively.

In White's essay, a statement unintentionally revealed a racial tone caught my attention;White said, "Australia is heading for an unprecedented future, one without an English-speaking Great and Powerful friend to keep us secure and protect our Interest." Indeed, Australia was a colony of the Great Britain and is a dependent ally of the United States, but there is no reason that Australia cannot get along with a Chinese-speaking nation as former Prime Minister (Labor Party) Kevin Rudd could personally testify. I am not saying that Australians must master Chinese, as Mr. Rudd has, to be friends of China. Australian does have to feel confident to get out of the crib and walk on her own. Diplomacy is by far the better tool than military power to deal with neighbors, great powers and international bodies.

.

Chapter 4

Thoughts After Reading Senator Feinstein's Letter on Taiwan Travel Act

*****

The Taiwan Travel Act if passed is a political statement from the U.S. Congress to influence the U.S. Administration's China Policy. The US-China Forum (UCF) is formed by a group of Chinese Americans caring about the unification of Mainland and Taiwan and the future welfare of Chinese people. The majority of the forum supporters live in California but the readers of the Forum are nationwide and gradually becoming worldwide. The members of UCF sent a letter to Senator Feinstein to urge her to vote no on the Taiwan Travel Act and they received a reply letter from Senator Feinstein as published in this forum. I am impressed and moved by Senator Feinstein's taking the time responding quickly to UCF's letter. Even though more Chinese Americans live in the State of New York, I have not seen New York Congressmen or Senators responding to Chinese Americans so promptly on their political concerns.

As a New Yorker, I read and like to respond to Senator Feinstein's letter, in my column, hopefully I can reach the other Congressmen and Senators about the Chinese Americans' view on this issue of One China Policy. The major points in Senator Feinstein's letter are 1. "The U.S. must maintain a policy of engagement with China.", 2. "Not call into the question of the above policy every time we have controversial issue or differences.", 3. "I also support One China Policy. ..The One China Policy has worked well. ...Taiwan has become a model of fledgling democracy.", and 4. "I fully support the development of a democratic Taiwan and the absolute necessity of a peaceful resolution of its differences with China." The following is my comments.

Senator Feinstein is so right on her first point. The U.S. and China are two greatest powers on this planet today. We must engage in a collaborative manner for mutual benefits as well as for world peace and prosperity. The Uni-Polar World Order never existed and will remain as an illusion as past imperialistic foreign policy of any past world power had demonstrated.

However, the key word, 'collaborative' not confrontational must be in the engagement policy to be productive. Senator Feinstein is also right that whatever issues the U.S. wishes to influence China should not call into the question of the U.S. standing policy of engagement with China and One China policy. Rather, the U.S. should engage in a positive diplomacy not a negative diplomacy to engage China on the world stage. The U.S. must maintain a 'consistent' not a 'convenient' foreign policy especially on the China Policy.

It is so great to hear from Senator Feinstein to say that I also support One China Policy. It implies that many Senators do support One China Policy. China agrees with the U.S. to a peaceful reunification with Taiwan so long Taiwan is not seeking separation or independence. This is easily understandable. For example, if a group of Californians promote and declare independence of California, don't the rest of the U.S. have the right to oppose such a ridiculous attempt. In fact, the Catalonia independence episode in Spain is a real case. The U.S. and many EU States are supporting Spain unification, even though it is Spain's domestic issue. So on the Taiwan issue, the U.S. must take a honest position in supporting the One China Policy. Encouraging Taiwan government to seek independence even resisting reunification is an inconsistent even hypocritical "engaging China" "One China Policy".

Senator Feinstein is right about not to call into the question of "engage China" and "One China" policies. Human rights, political freedom, security issues and Taiwan reunification with Mainland must be dealt with on their merits under the One China Policy. We have witnessed day and night change on human rights, political freedom and security issues over the years; conservatively, more than 500 million Chinese had been brought above the poverty line, 12.6 million in 2016 alone. It took us 150 years from Independence Day to give women voting rights. In China, democracy is used as a tool in many levels and many places but not touted as an ideology, a correct political science point of view. Democracy can take different forms to serve ideology just as Robert's rules can be applied differently in different institutions such as unions, corporations, town governments, school boards and Congress.

We all have genuine concern for the welfare of People in Taiwan. Most of the world (majority of UN members) believes in One China Policy and its ultimate benefit to the Taiwan people. "A fledging Democracy" does not mean that a ruling party should prosecute the opposing political party, deny constitution, and engage in separatism among its citizens, does it? The Mainland China legislated clearly that the reunification will be peaceful unless Taiwan seeks independence. Therefore, it is obvious, if the U.S. believes in One China Policy, She should legislate laws or declare resolutions to encourage Taiwan and Mainland China to move to reunification peacefully, for example, participating in Olympics under One China (like the two Koreans courageously did in 2018 Winter Olympics) or joining The WHO under One China Policy for the health benefits of all Chinese people. Taiwan government politically refuses humanitarian aid from Mainland China when a 6.4 degree earthquake hit Hualian to make a political statement is beyond our comprehension.

Knowing that Senator Feinstein will closely monitor our foreign policies is assuring. I thank her office paying attention to Chinese Americans' concerns. I hope the other senators and Congressmen will be as conscientious in dealing with China Policy.

Attachment – Senator Feinstein's letter

Dear Richard:

Thank you so much for writing to share with me your concerns regarding U.S. policy towards the People's Republic of China and Taiwan. I appreciate hearing from you and welcome this opportunity to share with you my views on this important issue.

I believe that the United States must maintain a policy of engagement with China. It is my view that in order to positively influence China in the areas of human rights, political freedom, and security issues, the United States must not call into question our standing policy of engagement with China every time a controversial issue or disagreement arises.

I also support the "One China" policy that we have upheld since the signing of the Shanghai Communique in 1972. This policy is based, in part, on the understanding that China will seek to resolve its differences with Taiwan through peaceful means. The "One China" policy has worked well: the United States and China have been able to conduct normal relations befitting two great powers, the U.S. and Taiwan have developed extensive economic and cultural ties, and Taiwan has prospered and become a model for fledgling democracies.

I fully support the development of a democratic Taiwan and the absolute necessity of a peaceful resolution of its differences with China. Please know that I will continue to closely monitor the situation between Taiwan and China and should legislation regarding this issue come before the Senate, I will be sure to keep your views in mind.

Again, thank you for writing. If you have any more comments, feel free to visit my website at http://feinstein.senate.gov, or contact my office in Washington, D.C. at (202) 224-3841.

Sincerely
yours,

Dianne Feinstein
United States Senator

Further information about my position on issues of concern to
California and the nation are available at my
website,feinstein.senate.gov. And please visit
my YouTube, Facebook and Twitter for more ways to communicate
with me.

Chapter 5

Safeguarding Freedom Is Right but Profiling and Bullying Are Dead Wrong

*****

Abstract

Three news headlines, the U.S. sending Navy ships to SCS protesting island construction activities there, the violent shooting in Florida school and the irresponsible profiling remarks against Chinese Americans expressed by FBI Director Christopher Wray, seemingly unrelated events, triggered serious thoughts on the attitude of Americans and the U.S. government officials about safeguarding freedom, racial profiling and bullying. The three events will be reviewed and discussed around this 'attitude' issue.

Three news headlines have shocked the world. The first is an international incidence concerning Freedom of Navigation in South China Sea (SCS) raising new tension of confrontation between the U.S. and China. The second is a violent shooting in a Florida school killing seventeen persons adding another shocker to the American people. The third is FBI Director's racial profiling of Chinese students and academicians as spies for China, raising fear and anger among Chinese American citizens. These three news events have no connection from geography point of view, one in SCS of the Pacific Ocean and the other two in the U.S. The shooting took place in the State of Florida on the Atlantic coast tens of thousands miles away from SCS. There is also no direct political connection of the three events, since one is a US foreign affair and the other two are US domestic issues. However, as rational people, when news like these flooded the media and reached the public, they become inter-connected as the public began to talk, listen, digest and develop their opinions about these events. In the process, the connection of these events emerges in our attitude towards safeguarding freedom, racial profiling and violent bullying. Understanding these connections may be very significant in understanding our social problems and foreign policies.

There is no question that the shooting in Marjory Stoneman Douglas High School is a tragedy. The 19 year old Nicolas Cruz apparently is a disturbed young man, crazy about guns and knives, as vividly shown by his Instagram pages. How can Cruz easily purchase an AR-15 semi-automatic assault rifle calls into serious questions about our society's definition and value of freedom. We cannot get any meaningful gun control legislation passed because we are obsessed with our freedom. In our society, we are supposed to be condemning racial profiling as Blacks, Hispanics and Asians have often been profiled by law enforcement and even by general public. When Nicolas Cruz was tipped to the FBI long before the tragic event, why didn't FBI take any action to prevent this horrible school shooting? Cruz is a Hispanic name and we do have a Senator Ted Cruz, a powerful politician with Hispanic background. The FBI did not act on the tip, was it because that FBI was concerned with possibility of being accused to be profiling or simply being negligent?

No, the FBI, at least its Director, Christopher A. Wray, is not afraid of being accused of profiling. In fact, Wray was openly profiling Chinese Americans in the Senate Intelligence Committee Hearing answering Senator Marco Rubio's very pointed question. "The counterintelligence risk posed to U.S. national security from Chinese students, particularly those in advanced programs in the sciences and mathematics," Wray responded. How dare a senior government official openly profiling Chinese Americans who contributed so significantly to science, technology and many other academic and business fields? Is it because there was no powerful Chinese American Senators like Hispanic American Senators, e.g. Ted Cruz and Marco Rubio? Now, there are protests calling Wray's resignation because of FBI's inaction on a tip on Nicolas Cruz as well as his profiling remarks labeling Chinese Americans as spies for China. The latter issue is Wray's serious personal mistake which is more reason for making him unfit to serve in the US government. The anger of the Chinese Americans can be seen from the (like a person carrying a weapon to school) press releases issued by United Chinese Americans (UCA 2-14-2018), Congressional Asian Pacific American Caucus (CAPAC 2-15-2018) and Committee 100 (C100 2-16-2018).

Why are the above social issues related to our foreign policy matter such as our demand of Freedom of Navigation in the SCS? The connection is in the attitude towards freedom, racial profiling and bullying. Demanding Freedom of Navigation in open sea is justified and politically correct. However, it is neither correct nor justified to demand freedom by bullying. The U.S. Navy, the most powerful one in the world, always enjoyed the freedom of navigation around the globe. The only incidence when the U.S. Navy was challenged, for example, by Russian navy, was when the Russians felt their national security being threatened, for instance in the Arctic Ocean or Black Sea near Russia. Therefore, the U.S. Navy must be careful about the legal boundaries of 12 sea miles surrounding a nation's sovereign boundary. Following this guideline, there will not be any freedom of navigation issue.

The SCS and the Pacific Ocean are vast areas for maritime activities. There is no freedom of navigation issue for American vessels military or commercial. There are territorial disputes in the SCS but they are largely handled by bilateral negotiation by the concerned nations. The recent dispatching of U.S. military ships to the SCS passing through or close to the 12 sea mile region of the claimed small islands is very much like a bullying action (like a person carrying a weapon to school) since no one would stop the U.S. Navy vessels if they were just passing by. When the U.S. on the one hand declares that she is not going to get involved in any territorial dispute and on the other hand she sends military vessels to the region to show force, it is very hard to shed the image of a bully. If the infrastructure development of these small islands by China, Philippines and Vietnam etc were violating any international law or truly interfering with freedom of navigation, the only logic action would be bringing the issue to the international court. The U.S. should not be the one to play judge and calling names. Naming China for wrong doing is similar to profiling Chinese Americans as spies without proof, an unacceptable attitude and practice. One wonders whether the FBI Director's profiling remarks and Pentagon's SCS behavior are mutually enforcing out of a common attitude?

We know weapons are dangerous. Too much freedom in weapon acquisition leads to more possibilities of weapon abuse. Abusive use of weapon is an act of bullying. Bullying leads to violence. Regardless of motive, the Florida school shooting is an excessive act of bullying. A troubled young man used a deadly weapon; a semi-automatic rifle on unarmed students caused the death of seventeen persons. In SCS, the U.S. Navy is showing force to China, what does Pentagon expect to accomplish? Is the end result an intimidation, violence or total war? We can't imagine Pentagon to behave like a troubled young man carrying a powerful weapon to bully the students without any concern for consequences. The smart generals in Pentagon must have studied the Sun Tze Bin Fa, diplomacy is always superior to battle in settling issues. Not bullying does not mean weakness. Poised diplomacy can be more effective than military exercises. In today's world, total war means total mutual destruction. An attitude change is necessary, even for the most powerful nation on earth, to deal with international affairs. Bullying must be replaced with rational thinking, intelligent analysis and skillful diplomacy to deal with international affairs and to lead the world.

Chapter 6

Focusing on Term-Limit Is Missing the Mark on China's Constitution Revision

****

China's Constitution Revision prepared and submitted by the Central Committee of the Chinese Communist Party (CCP) to be ratified by China's 13th National People's Congress (NPC) in its first plenary session (March, 2018) is dominating the Western press. Before we examine the details of this amendment and its implication, let's review the history of the constitutional amendments of the U.S. to provide a comparison and discussion.

National Constitution, ratified by the people and/or its representatives, is the document prescribing the structure of the government, the rights of the people and rule base for governance and serving the people. Every country is founded on its Constitution which can be amended as needed by a due process defined in the Constitution. The U.S. declared its independence in 1776 but its Constitution was first written and ratified in 1787 during the Philadelphia Convention. Subsequently to this day, there were 11,539 proposals for amendment but only twenty seven being approved by the Congress. The First twelve (ten of which are the bill of rights defining people's freedom and rights) were approved by the Congress in 1789 and sent to the States for ratification. By December, 1791, the ten Bills of Rights of people were ratified including freedom of religion, speech, press, assembly, bearing arms, security and personal effects, protection from search and seizure, warrant for arrest with due cause, guarantee of proper indictment, speedy public trial with jury, prohibition of double jeopardy and any rights not specified by the constitution and all powers not specifically granted to the government.

The fourteenth amendment (1868) is a significant one offering a clear, simple definition of citizenship with all enjoying equal treatment. The 22nd amendment is also significant concerning the presidency's term limit. The 27 amendments endured a long debate process till Congress approved them in 1992 for State ratification. To this date, six of 27 have not been ratified by the required number of states; two were closed and four were still pending. This signifies that Constitution Revision is a very serious matter and highly dependent on the procedure requirement in the original Constitution.

China's Constitution like many others defines the country's people's rights and duties, the structure of the State and the government hierarchy including the NPC and its formation and duties. What is different and unique in China's Constitution is the Chinese style of Communism prescribed as a socialistic economic system with public ownership of the means of production (such as land). Like the U.S. Constitution, China's Constitution consists of versions of 1975, 1978, 1982 (amended through 2004), 1988,1993, 1999, and 2004 amendments, 2007 resolution on amendments, 2012 revised constitution and the latest 2017 resolution on amending the Constitution yet to be ratified by the 13th NPC this month.

The proposed revision and amendments by the Central Committee of the CCP can be summarized concisely in terms of definition, clarification and energizing the functions and effectiveness of the socialistic political and economic system with Chinese characteristics. The total 21 revisions can be grouped in four categories: 1. Adding words to clarify the direction, method and focus of China's future development to include Xi's thoughts and to anticipate new era, emphasize scientific development, and clarify win-win peaceful development under a 'Human Common Goal'. 2. Adding phrases to sustain reform, achieve Great Rejuvenation (Great Chinese culture and dignity), and cultivate patriotic attitude (e.g. oath on the Constitution to take office), racial and minority harmony, and socialistic values as well as paying attention to environmental improvements. 3. Establishing organizational change by emphasizing law-based (治) rather than system-based (制) governance, giving more power to NPC in election and supervision, restricting NPC representatives and members to serve in administrative or monitoring and supervising roles in other branches of government, empowering NPC to elect the chief of the new monitoring and supervising branch (監察) separated from the executive branch. (Noteworthy point: this branch was uniquely described in China's founding father, Sun Yat Sen's Book, Three Principles of People, which has been practiced by KMT under Chiang Kai-Shek till today in Taiwan as a watch dog on the government.)

The revision of Article 79 in China's Constitution, removing the second sentence in "The term (of President and Vice President) is the same as the NPC's term. They shall serve no more than two consecutive terms." Implies that the Chinese leader can serve without term-limit. This has been the focus of the Western Press with numerous articles cautioning the world leaders that they have to deal with a smart and powerful Chinese leader for his life time. However, this implication is highly speculative. We can examine the term limit issue in the U.S. and China's Constitution and offer a far more rational interpretation and implication analysis.

In the original U.S. Constitution, there was no term limit set on the Presidency. When George Washington resigned after serving his second term, he essentially established a convention that the U.S. President will serve only two terms, eight years. This practice persisted over 152 years till President Franklin Roosevelt, served four terms and died in his 4th term (1933-1947). Roosevelt was a capable President and the U.S. was facing the threat of World War II, the US Congress and the American people supported his Presidency extending to third and fourth term to lead the nation in war. When Roosevelt died in 1947 after the war was ended, the Congress approved the 22nd Amendment to limit the Presidency to two consecutive terms, based on the speculation that the US bi-partisan system may not be able to return to the two-term convention establish by Washington. Of course, such a speculation had no real evidence.

The supreme leader Mao of China served for his entire life (1949-1976 in Power) with great achievement in uniting the nation but also with devastating social programs sunk China in misery. When Deng Xiao Ping emerged as the strong leader (1978-1992) with an agenda for reform and focused economic development, he was the de facto leader till his death even holding no official position from 1982-1992. It was Deng who restored the figure head position of Presidency and divided the power between the party Secretary General and the Premier (head of State Council, the Executive Branch); all three led by the paramount leader Deng. Deng instrumented the two-term limitation (1982) in order to prevent the formation of a convention of life-long leadership like Chairman Mao. The two -term limit was practiced during Deng's era (1982-1992) through Hu Yao Bang (1978-1987), Jiang Zemin (1992-2002), Hu Jintao (2002-2012) and Xi Jinping (2012- Present). From Jiang to Xi, they all have had the three positions, General Secretary of CCP, Chairman of the Military Commission (of CCP and National) and the President of China but Xi is the only one now holding all three positions concurrently.

Though the Western press is speculating the removal of the two-term limit on the Presidency as a possible sign for more authoritative power and life-long service for President Xi; personally, I believe that this move may just be Xi's design to figure out a way to ensure a sustainable law-based governance with smooth transition so that the long-term objectives of China's national rejuvenation can be accomplished. China's rapid rise is envied by her neighbors including great powers like the U.S. and Japan targeting China as a security threat. Xi's past performance adequately demonstrated his ability as a great leader not only for China but also for the world. The Chinese people by and large support his tenure extension beyond second term. One might even draw parallel to Franklin Roosevelt's term extension discussed above, considering Xi in a critical time with a critical task to fulfill (including the grand scheme of One Belt and One Route, OBOR). The more pressure the other nations are putting on China thwarting her peaceful rise and limiting her leadership in pursuing a 'Human Common Goal', the more support the Chinese people and third world nations will offer to Xi demanding his leadership beyond his second term.

President Xi and the NPC have a lot of options and leeway to structure a transition scheme with structure and term limits redefined for the future round of Chinese leaders. One can observe some hints from the detailed revisions presented to the 13th NPC. Focusing on the term limit and making wrong interpretations is missing the mark of assessing China's Constitution Revision.

Chapter 7
Past, Present and Future of China

*****

The subject title is big for books, thus difficult to discuss in a limited space. However, the subject is so fitting to think about while China is holding its 13th National People's Congress (NPC). Therefore, I shall make an attempt to discuss the past, present and future of China in a broad notion. Hopefully, this discussion will draw more in-depth dialogue to follow.

The past of China is of course a long history, but only her recent past and history relevant to her present and future will be discussed. China is a unique nation, longing for peace and survived numerous times from external invasions including the meditated Japanese invasion which ultimately became WW II. Following the world trend of revolutionary movement, China endured a treacherous path and suffered from interventions by Western powers and of Russia and Japan. Although China had her glorious past in terms of prosperity (GDP), she missed and ignored the industrial revolution which created the Western powers and Imperial Japan and Russia.

The past of China about a century ago can be characterized as an ignorant and sleeping lion indulged in her own governance with no clue and later no energy and no skill in diplomacy as a big nation. China was basically an agriculture country with nearly 80% rural population illiterate. The peasants live a poor life subject to the mercy of nature. A Chinese phrase, 看天吃飯 (pray meals from heaven), described well the Chinese farmers' lives. There was hardly any industrial base then. Whatever manufacturing existed was largely labor based, inefficient and depended on foreign technology. For example, although Chinese made very significant contribution to metallurgy centuries ago, the steel production of China in 20th century was less than Germany's in 1871. When Western powers invaded China, Chinese people lost her self-confidence. Chinese thought everything foreign being superior as revealed in the language created at that time, such as 洋(釘nail, 火 match, 油 oil, 裝 suit, 車 car, etc). Adding the word 洋 (foreign or western) means superior quality.

China's Present is now represented by amazing achievements accomplished in the recent decades. When Communist Party of China (CPC) established PRC in 1949 and KMT led ROC retreated to Taiwan, China, though divided, had the same time period of truce without war. The Chinese on both sides of the Taiwan Strait had an opportunity to focus on economy. The CPC went through two decades of experimentation of hardcore communism with obvious obstacles and failures, but its later reform strategy embracing part of capitalism and engaging planned economy (since Deng's retaking the CPC party leadership in 1978) paid off handsomely. China is now the number two economy of the world beating Japan and Germany. China's purchasing power based GDP is actually world's number one.

China can be proud of her economic achievement of bringing more than half billion people out of poverty and giving better life to 1.4 billion citizens. Today, China is no longer an ignorant or illiterate nation; China graduates more than eight million college students every year, twice as many as the U.S., a daunting achievement. China not only has become industrialized but also has become the manufacturer of everything for the world and world's biggest trading power. China's steel production is the number one in the world drawing US tariff against her steel export (a merely 2% of the total export to the US). China's infrastructure development outshines every nation with multi-tier cities across the country. The peasants no longer pray their meals from heaven. The new phrase, 知天吃飯 （know nature and harvest come) now describes the knowledgeable peasants lives. The social life of Chinese people is elevated with self-confidence as exhibited by their traveling to every part of the world. Gradually, people understand the difference between the deep and rich Chinese culture and the shallow and simple civility. Foreigners recite Tang Poetry; Western society begins to appreciate the long Chinese history and civilization. Chinese self-confidence is reflected by the Chinese language absorbed into English vocabulary from food to other subjects,炒麵 chowmein, 餛飩 wonton, 豆腐 tofu, 茅台酒 Mao Tai jiu, 餃子 Jiao zi, 長衫 changsan 祺袍 Qi Pao 功夫 kongfu 太極 Tai Ji 武術 wushu 武俠 wu xia 少林 Shao lin 麻將 Mahjong 風水 feng shui 漢字 Hanzi 拼音 pinyin, 你好 Nihao, 陰陽 Ying Yan 氣 Qi 道 dao 上海 shanghai 北京 Beijing, 丁 ting, J particle, 嫦娥 chang'e, space vehicle to the moon 武器 wu qi, weapons, so many Chinese phonetic words familiar to the common Westerners.

China's future is uncertain. The rising China is not a threat to the world but she will change the world for sure. The Western powers have tried to lead the world as a uni-polar world order with Western rules giving little voice to the rising giants, China, India, Brazil, etc etc. The World has changed and the productivity comes from knowledge workers, just China and India alone, millions of knowledge workers joining the work force each year. Peasants will become knowledge workers too. Food production will become a stable element in the economy. The phrase 經營糧食 （food production and distribution management) will describe the 'peasants' lives. Continuous technology advances and innovation is the only way to lead the world. China will likely become a principal manufacturer of auto-driving pollution-free 'autoporters' as well as robots that producing them.

The uncertainty about China's future is really the uncertainty of the world's future. Will the legacy Uni-Polar World Order yield to a bi-polar or multi-polar world order by stopping arms race and engaging in genuine collaboration? China has risen militarily as well, by external foreign pressure not by her own design. If the Western powers and Japan continue their irrational military confrontation with China, China has no choice but to respond, leading the world to inevitable world war. If China were not targeted as an enemy, then the world's future is rosy and China will continue to contribute to world prosperity and peace. The One Belt One Route (OBOR) program will be one beneficial program to the world.

With the U.S. and her allies still having a hostile China policy, China obviously must be prepared for the worst scenario with the following possible strategies:

1. Militarily, China will continue to invest in military capability and preparedness unless the world powers can reach a sensible conclusion to urge all parties to stop the ever-increasing military development for more economic development. Hopefully, China's advances in space program, missile and nuclear weapons, and satellite communication may induce a genuine arms truce treaty among the superpowers.

2. Economically, China will continue to invest in OBOR like win-win programs to stimulate world economy. Hopefully the benefitted countries, especially the developing nations will collaborate with China, in turn influence other nations to join in.

3. Diplomatically, China will likely exercise constraint but be assertive on the side of justice. China will not pursue military base proliferation but will focus on defense measures. China will engage fully with the U.N. and various multi-nation institutions and conferences to seek diplomatic solutions as done before.

4. Culturally, China will exert emphasis internally on the rejuvenation of the Chinese culture, peace loving philosophy and ideology of world harmony and externally on making the world to understand the Chinese

culture. Chinese is an efficient language and Chinese history and literature are rich with wisdom. Through cultural exchange to promote world harmony is likely China's soft-power Strategy. Early signs indicate that such a strategy is effective for gaining mutual acceptance and confidence.

The current trend of Chinese language adoption by the West and more people are learning Chinese as a second language are good omens for China and world harmony. Chinese words and phrases, for example, 人民幣 Renminbi, 支付寶 Zhifubao, 元 yuan, 胡同 hutong, 春節 chun jie, etc are exemplary words found in the Cambridge Dictionary. When the number of foreigners learning Chinese increases from millions to tens of millions, the value of Hanzi and the Chinese literature and culture will be widely appreciated. Then the natural integration of citizenship, smooth convergence towards one harmonious nation, and those Special Administrative Regions (SAR) influenced by external forces preferring Chinese influence will take place as China act effectively on the world stage. When China unites peacefully, the world will be more assured that China will continue to contribute to world prosperity.

Chapter 8
Can Trump-Xi Solve North Korea Problem Through Trump-Kim Talk?

*****

The North Korea (NK) nuclear threat has a long history with NK being on and off and off and on in signing the Nuclear Non Proliferation Treaty (NPT). The recent years accelerated pace of nuclear testing and missile launching by NK invited strong reaction from the U.S. Japan and South Korea, harsh exchanges of words, increased military exercises and heightened economic sanctions placed on NK approved by the U.N. However, the North Korea nuclear threat has already reached a dilemma: North Korea has demonstrated possible capability of launching and delivering a nuclear armed continental ballistic missile, showing off by flying one over Japan (4475km, capable of reaching the U.S. if calculated with a shallow launching angle). The U.S. has installed The Terminal High Altitude Area Defense (THAAD) system despite of the objections by China and Russia as a counter measure. This mutually claimed touché obviously did not dissolve the real nuclear threat.

The confrontation and exchange of harsh words and threats between the NK and the U.S. are exemplified by the speech the Minister of Foreign Affairs of NK, Ri Yong Ho, delivered at the U.N. on September 23rd, 2017. Ri attacked President Trump for his tweets calling the North Korea leader Kim Jong Un a rocket man. Ri accounted historical events and labeled the U.S. as the aggressor, being First used nuclear weapon, First brought nuclear weapon to Korea Peninsula and First possessed the largest amount of nuclear arsenal. Ri regarded Trump's actions as on a suicide mission which will invite the inevitable arrival of nuclear missile to the U.S. homeland. According to The Times report, the Chinese Foreign Minister, Wang Yi, brokered a meeting between Rex Tillerson and Ri Yong Ho with an implicit agreement that the U.S. will cease military exercises with South Korea (SK) and Japan in exchange for NK's suspension of nuclear tests. This meeting did not realize a real hope for opening a dialogue until the Winter Olympic events involving two Koreas took place.

The president of SK, Moon Jae-In (born 1-24-1953), has taken an initiative since taking office (5-10-2017) to engage NK despite of the hesitation of the

U.S. and the serious opposition from Japan. Moon dispatched an envoy to NK eventually leading to the outcome that NK embraced the Winter Olympics (held in Pyeong Chang, South Korea) by sending a high-level envoy led by Kim Yong Nam, head of parliament, accompanied by Kim Yo Jong, younger sister of Kim Jong Un and a sizable Olympic team with cheer leaders to the Winter Olympics games. North and South Korea hockey teams played together in the Winter Olympics which wrote a special chapter for the Olympic history.

This Olympic encounter with NK delivering a personal invitation from Kim Jong Un to President Moon of SK appears to be the diplomatic act thawing the ice between the two Koreas. Actually behind the scene, Kim's rude manner and not meeting the special Chinese envoy in November, 2017, led by Soon Tao, intending to brief Kim a traditional update after the 19th Chinese Communist Party (CCP) Congress, angered President Xi to the point that China cut off all avenues of supplies of oil and gas to NK knowing the arrival of a bitter Winter. In this column, we have always held the position that the NK problem can only be solved by a synchronized joint plan endorsed by the U.S. and China. China's move to support the sanction as a message to Kim and Xi's vivid anger over Kim's irrational behavior turned messages to punishments. This punishment apparently triggered the softening of NK, delivering an Olympic Oliver branch to SK, and seeking a direct dialogue with the U.S., hence the possibility of a Trump-Kim meeting.

With what happened between NK and SK, The U.S. has little choice but goes along with the wishes of the two Koreas of meeting and talking, whether the North is sincere or not. On March 9, President Trump agreed to meet with Kim Jong Un to discuss how to realize the denuclearization of Korea Peninsula. This was a big news and considered a big win for Kim since the U.S. had never agreed to have direct talks with NK before. Soon, Kim was invited to make a State Visit to China which happened on March 28. Then on April 27, Kim Jong Un and Moon Jae In held a summit meeting at the two-Korea border creating an historical event with embrace, kind words and planting a 'peace tree'. The U.S. is putting the preparation of Trump-Kim summit in high gear focusing on setting a date and location for the meeting. On May 4, President Trump announced that he had a date and place in mind for his meeting with Kim. Then on May 8th, Kim made a secret visit to Dalian, China with a purpose of having a personal dialogue with President Xi and thanking him for his years of support in resolving the Korea Peninsula issue through dialogue. Then on May 10th, Trump tweeted that the Trump-Kim Summit will take place at Singapore on June 12th. Seemingly, the summit event was sure to take place.

Following the above announcement, a series of dramatic development, which ultimately led to President Trump's cancellation of the summit meeting, was so bizarre and intriguing that might be made into a movie someday. At this time, we can only string together a few things happened and reported in the media connecting to the cancellation of the Summit: (1)NK not entirely happy about Singapore being the meeting place unilaterally decided by the U.S. (2)NK threatened to pull out of the meeting because the U.S., Korea and Japan were still to hold military exercises. (3) National Security Advisor John Bolton suggested that Libya (Gaddafi was killed) could serve as a model for persuading NK to give up its nuclear weapon program. (4) Kim's top aide Choe Son-hui regarded VP Mike Pence's remark, "NK may end like Libya" stupid and call him a political dummy. (5)Pompeo's meetings with NK did not go well resulting in NK not communicating with the US officials.

All the above indicate the possibility that NK will call off the summit, thus Trump decided to call it off first and sent Kim a letter. President Trump had agreed to meet with Kim Jong Un for talks in May 2018 then postponed to June 12; in between Kim made a second visit to China obviously seeking some diplomatic consultation. The U.S. got into the summit agreement without a solid plan. Trump's staff should have focused on preparing a game plan than uttering rhetoric destroying instead of building trust. At this point, though the June 12th meeting is once called off, all sides, the U.S., NK, China and SK all left doors open thus reassured the reopening of a Trump-Kim meeting. We sincerely hope that Trump and Kim will not focus on scoring personal credit and glory but concentrate on getting a peace treaty and making the Korean Peninsula free of nuclear weapons. China has been consistent and sincere in her position and effort to solve the Korea Peninsula issue through dialogue. We believe that a Trump-Kim meeting will be fruitful if Trump-Kim can build trust through China, reaching a mutual understanding. We will emphasize a view we have expressed before, that is the nuclear threat in the Korean Peninsula may be completely resolved if the North and South Korea can be united. If the Korean War in the 1950's was ended with a peace treaty allowing the two Koreas to unite like East and West Germany did at the end of the Cold War, there would be no nuclear threat in Korean Peninsula. The unification of West and East Germany should be used as a history lesson for negotiating a peace treaty between the U.S. and the two Koreas. Trump and Xi should work out a mutual understanding on the pre-conditions for exercising the reunification of two Koreas thus achieving denuclearization.

From the historical perspective of the U.S., the Korean War, the defense treaty with SK and the problem of NK nuclear threat are all rooted in the legacy strategy of deterring the spread of communism. Ignoring differences in party and election politics, China's own socialistic ideology today is not communism and is more leaning towards the socialism practiced in the U.S. A united Korea Peninsula co-existing with China will stop the spread of communism and contribute to world peace.

Chapter 9
Correct Measures Are Not Trade War
for Trade Imbalance and Job Loss

*****

As a Presidential candidate, Trump rightly touted the issues of huge US trade deficit and loss of jobs in the U.S. as serious problems requiring fixing. When Trump won the election, rightly he wanted to fulfill his campaign promises by fixing those problems. During the campaign, Trump attributed the loss of manufacturing jobs in the U.S. to imports, claiming US jobs been stolen by China due to her exporting inexpensive goods to the U.S. This might be a catchy campaign rhetoric raising voters' attention on but hardly a fair statement. Many economists had analyzed the job loss issue over the three decades, the most plausible explanation was that jobs were displaced by technology advances and/or skill obsolesces. Trump threatened to tear up the 'unfair' trade agreements (such as NAFTA and other bilateral agreements) and to renegotiate them with 'America First' Principles. The American people resonated with Trump's messages, voted for him and expected him to solve the problems.

After victory, Trump accelerated investigation on trade imbalances. Secretary of Commerce Wilbur Ross has concluded a number of investigations. On February 16, The Commerce Department reported the following facts on steel and aluminum imports:

On steel: 1. The import is four times of export. 2. Six oxygen and four electric steel furnaces were closed since 2000 (US production decreased 35% since 1998). 3. World production increased 127% to four billion tons exceeding demand. 4. Global excess production, 700 million tons, seven times of US annual consumption (China's excess is greater than US production capacity). 5. China's one month production is greater than US annual production (only one electric furnace left in the U.S.) and 6. As of 2/15, one hundred and sixty nine anti-dumping (AD) orders were issued, 29 against China and 25 under investigation. The Commerce Department's recommendation is to apply 24% tariff against all steel import countries and 53% against Brazil, China, Costa Rica, Egypt, India, Malaysia, S. Korea, S. Africa, Thailand, Turkey and Vietnam causing global concern of eruption of a trade war.

Similarly on aluminum: 1. Import has increased to 90% of demand (up from 60%) since 2012, 2. For 2013-2016, employment in Aluminum industry dropped 58% (six smelters retired, only two out of five operating at capacity), 3. US military needs high quality aluminum but insufficient to support the aluminum industry (only one company remaining capable of producing high quality aluminum) and 4. As of 2/15, two AD orders are issued against China and four more investigations ongoing. The Commerce Department made the following recommendations: 1. Applying 7.7% tariff on all aluminum imported or 2. Applying 23.6% tariff on all products from China, Hong Kong, Russia, Venezuela and Vietnam and all other countries subject to a quota limited to 100% of their 2017 imports or 3. Setting a quota on all imports from all countries to 86.7% of their 2017 exports to the U.S. Each proposal is intended to raise production of U.S. aluminum from the present 48% average capacity to 80%, a level that might provide the industry with long-term viability.

President Trump slapped steep multi-year tariffs on imports of washing machines (20% deceasing to 16%, parts 50% to 40% in 3 years) and solar energy cells and panels (30% to 15% in 4 years) on January 22nd by the recommendation of the U.S. Trade Representative (the Trade Policy Committee and the U.S. International Trade Commission) based on a rule used since 2002. (Last time when the U.S. used such a tariff rule on steel import during Bush Administration in 2002, the World Trade Organization ruled against the U.S.) While Trump's tariff is intended to protect domestic production of washing machines and solar cells, some industry analysts estimate that the solar tariff may cost 23,000 jobs in installation, engineering and project management this year and may result in cancellation or postponement of billions of dollars in solar investment. The long term impact of solar tariff may affect one third of the 260,000 American workers in the solar industry. As for washing machines, we can certainly expect an increase in prices affecting a large number of American consumers, potentially causing inflation.

Following the above Commerce Department's reports, on 3/22nd, President Trump ordered a 25% tariff on imported steel and a 10% levy on imported aluminum to take effect in 15 days (with exceptions granted to Canada and Mexico, a NAFTA consideration, and possibly to other U.S. allies). While this measure was intended to protect the US steel and aluminum industries but will it stimulate them to be globally competitive is uncertain. When world production is far exceeding global demand (127%), the competition will force down the price. The effect of tariff may squeeze out a few foreign suppliers but may not necessarily help domestic producers with enough profit to increase production unless price is hiked up sufficiently high. The U.S. needs a major update in infrastructure (roads, bridges, air and sea ports and buildings) where steel and aluminum are major resource materials needed. Maintaining high price on steel and aluminum will cost the U.S. far more in infrastructure upgrade, not a very desirable situation. On the other hand, taking advantage of global over supply (depressed prices on steel and aluminum) will be very helpful to the updating of the U.S. infrastructure. Money saved on infrastructure upgrade can be strategically used to support key manufacturers and/or stockpile of strategic resources.

The above tariff 'fixes' may start a trade war as many economists warned and may offer little help in job creation. Past history showed us, tariff has always led to retaliation, eventually escalated to counter retaliation, resulting in a lose-lose trade war. Therefore, it is wise to analyze thoroughly what is the root cause of trade deficit and job loss to find rational solutions for these problems. The McKinsey Consulting Company's McKinsey Global Institute (MGI) had published a report in May 2012: Trading Myths: Addressing Misconceptions about Trade, Jobs, and Competitiveness. Though this report is five years old, its findings are still quite relevant to our current concerns.

MGI analyzed the performance of mature economies' trades and found that "reality is often at odds with conventional wisdom." Policy makers often wish to increase investment and net export and focus on manufacturing with a perception: Their countries are losing ground to developing countries and emerging markets. They take measures such as tariff to stimulate manufacturing and exports but raise risk of protectionism. It was found that the trade balance and net export of mature economies had remained stable or even improved comparing to emerging economies over the past decade (2002-2012). Primary resources (average -3.3% GDP) not manufactured goods (average +0.5% GDP) contributed to trade imbalance in mature economies. Specifically, the knowledge intensive manufacturing made a surplus (average +1.6%). Changes in the composition of demands and ongoing productivity increases caused job loss in mature economies. MGI found that trade or off shoring were only responsible for 20% of the 5.8 million US manufacturing jobs eliminated between 2000-2010. Although, we have no more recent data to extend the MGI claims, it is reasonable to assume that the advances in automation, data integration and artificial intelligence are the major contributors to the loss of manufacturing jobs in the U.S.

Far from applying tariff measures, we agree with MGI study to recommend that the U.S. instead of applying tariff and protectionism should liberalize trade in services especially knowledge intensive services, support attractive and competitive stages of global value chains rather than creating or sustaining non-competitive manufacturing and most importantly investing in education, infrastructure and innovation to create advantageous high-value jobs.

Chapter 10
Incredible View by a China-Basher on US-China Trade War

*****

Trump's presidential campaign and his victory to a large extent banked on the 'America First' message which resonated with voters frustrated with declining US prestige on the world stage, stagnating US economy and disappearing Jobs thus quality of life. The ineffectiveness of US government under an impotent or paralyzed bipartisan Congress induced American citizens to demand a change. Trump, being an outsider of Washington DC, has chosen the strategy to blame the country's problems to incompetency of the previous administrations and delivered the most inciting campaign rhetoric calling for policy changes in defense (reversing the declining defense budget and strength), diplomacy (employing unpredictable actions and negotiations to get results), trade (tearing up existing agreements and renegotiate in favor of the U.S.), environment (retreating from international commitments on environmental control) and immigration (building American 'Great Wall' to stop illegal immigrants and overhauling immigration laws). Trump won the election as a dark horse over nearly a dozen finger-pointing politicians with little exciting proposals other than Sanders' unreasonable proposal of granting free tuition for all college education, which energized some young people for obvious reason.

It is perfectly understandable that the Trump Administration in its first year or so is focusing on making visible deliverables on Trump's campaign promises whether his team had completely understood the complex issues at hand or developed thoroughly considered solutions for the problems. Recently, Trump announced a set of orders to place tariff and quota on imports based upon the recommendation of the U.S. Trade Representative (on wash machines and solar cells) and the Commerce Department (on steel and aluminum imports and a list of imports amounting to $60 billion). Trump's action on the above mentioned imports appeared to be principally targeting at China since exemptions were offered or granted to selected US Allies.

Trump's actions triggered a global fear of trade war. The Wall Street reacted with a number of sharp falls accumulated to 1149 points on Dow Jones Index over two days (3/22-23). Most reactions in the press are negative. Worldwide economists are expressing concerns about the consequences of these tariff measures leading to retaliations which will escalate to a mutually damaging trade war and possibly a global recession. The Nobel Laureate (2001) and former Chief Economist of the World Bank (1997-2000), Professor Joseph Stiglitz of Columbia University has expressed his views on trade war in a number of public forums and most recently at China Development Forum in Beijing on March 24, 2018. His main opinions can be summarized as follows: 1. "The U.S. is constrained to act .... as the U.S. depends on low-cost imports. Tariff increases cost of living making Fed to raise interest." 2. "China has more ability to direct some parts of the economy ... to shift to domestic consumption". Colin Grabow of Cato Institute also expressed his concern: "China may retaliate by not buying American.....Trump will pay the price." These remarks seemed to be reasonable, even though it is too early for anyone to predict what events may take place in days to come.

When comes to China policy, there is no shortage of either 'pro-China' or 'con-China' analysts in the U.S. voicing their opinions. However, on the trade issue, I found an incredible view expressed by Gordan G. Chang in his article, Why China Will Lose a Trade War with Trump, published in Daily Beast, on March 26, 2018. Gordon is best known for his book *The Coming Collapse of China* (2001) predicting the fall of China in 2011. Gordon repeatedly made the 'collapse' prediction (The Coming Collapse of China, 2012, e-Edition Foreign Policy; China's collapse is coming, more so than ever, 2016) eventually receiving criticism from peers (Chang's Predictions of China's Collapse destroy his own credibility, Shen Dingli, 1-5-2016 Global Times). Gordon in his Daily Beast article disputed Grabow and Professor Stiglitz's analyses and again made a prediction that China will lose the trade war to Trump. By now, we can say that Gordon Chang is somewhat a 'China Basher' as evidenced by his publications. Time has proven him wrong; so far, not only China has not collapsed but instead has grown stronger to the point that the U.S. is feeling threatened. If China would collapse easily as Gordon persistently wished, there shouldn't be any China threat, should it?

Gordon repudiates experts' views on "China holding more leverage (than the U.S.)" by arguing the following: 1. China is more dependent on the U.S. because China maintained a trade surplus for decades, China's trade surplus related to US trade increased from 68% in 2016 to 88.8% in 2017. 2. The U.S. economy, $19.39 trillion, is greater than China's $12.84 trillion in 2017. 3. The U.S. economy is more stable than China's; China has more debt and capital flight problem. Gordon further disputes Stiglitz's first point stated above by using his wife, Mrs. Chang's shopping experience that China is no longer the most low-cost goods supplier. Taking apparel as example, Gordon argues that Americans will buy from other Indo-China and Latin American low cost suppliers. On this argument, a consumer's observation can be considered as one data point but it is hardly a crucial point to cover up the fact that China has been conscientiously upgrading her products to higher technology and higher value added goods. In addition, China has made significant investment in Indo-China and Latin American countries in their manufacturing sectors.

Gordon does not believe Stiglitz's second point nor Grabow's prediction. Gordon said: " Stiglitz has misunderstood China's economy......China is not a consumption driven economy but an investment driven one. ...China cannot create growth by investing because of her debt problem." Gordon brushed off the possibility of losing Boeing airplane and US soybean sales to China. I think it is Gordan who failed to understand that for trade items like the two above, China and the U.S. are mutually tied because they are the biggest buyer and the largest seller respectively. Since the U.S. has no monopoly on airplanes or on soybeans, the biggest buyer sure has more leverage than the seller. It is difficult to predict how the domino effect of tariff and counter tariff will play out. However, South Korea, a smaller trader, seems willing to make a modest if not fake concession to the U.S. For getting waived from the US steel tariff, South Korea would take a voluntary quota of 70% of the **average** steel export to the U.S. over last three years (A   modest concession considering sales was declining) plus doubling American car import quota to 50,000 units. This may appear as a big win for Trump, but whether or not the Korean consumers would change their long held bias preferring Korean to American cars is a big question.

At this point, China's Ministry of Commerce on March 23rd took a small step to announce tariffs of 15 percent and 25 percent on almost $3 billion of American products in 128 categories in retaliation for Trump's Section 232 tariffs on steel and aluminum products. China is yet to respond to Trump's tariff on $60 billion of Chinese import based on the 301 Trade Act of 1974. Whatever measures China will take, they sure will make some impact on US economy. The U.S. needs steel and aluminum at low prices for her infrastructure upgrade. There is no advantage for jacking up prices by tariffs. I firmly agree with the warning from the majority of experts that tariff or trade war is not a solution to balancing trade or to creating jobs. Let's hope the two major trading partners in the world will find ways to negotiate out a compromise.

Chapter 11
Travel to China Is A Good Thing for Americans

*****

There is an old Chinese saying, "Read ten thousand books are not as good as travel ten thousand miles." The original source of the above saying is attributed to Liu Yi (刘彝 1017-1086, born in Fuzhou, a scholar and artist), recorded by an author (董其昌) in Ming Dynasty. The original inscription on Liu's painting was "Read ten thousand books, travel ten thousand miles, (You will) remove the dust clustered in the chest (your brain), natural scenery will register and cities and places will form (in your mind). From an artist's point of view. Liu's words were interpreted as 'emphasis on absorbing true natural imagery for artistic paintings'. From a scholar's point of view, his words were interpreted as 'reading and traveling are complimentary', reinforcing facts through personal experience.

Later, Liu's original statements were further expanded with realism and philosophy   as: "讀萬卷書,不如行萬里路,行萬里路,不如閱人無數,閱人無數,不如名師指路,名師指路,不如跟著成功人士的腳步,跟著成功人士的腳步,不如走自己的路!" The first phrase makes the comparison that reading ten thousand books are not as good as traveling ten thousand miles, a philosophical statement emphasizing personal experience more valuable than (heresy even written words) in books. The latter phrases expand further philosophically: traveling ten thousand miles are not as good as meeting and knowing numerous people, which is not as good as getting pointers from well known scholars, which is not as good as following the footsteps of successful people, which is not as good as persistently taking one's own chartered steps." Obviously, the above sayings were injected with a lot of wisdom.

In today's world, the above saying stood the test of times but with added new reality. Ever since the Chinese invented the paper and printing technology, books became available and valuable, hence reading books broadens one's knowledge. But traveling still gets you the true facts as "Seeing is believing." When human civilization is advanced further with broadening information source beyond books, humans supposedly are benefitted by the abundance of information through multimedia including books, movies, television, radio and Internet, containing all kinds of digital information. Unfortunately, with increasing amount of misinformation, humans are harmed by the media as well. This is a serious issue deserving explanation.

Everyone must have heard three modern terms: soft power, media power and fake news. These three terms explain why we are living in a dangerous time, why we still have killings and wars and why human societies are not in harmony! We sure recall the centuries of colonialism when the Imperial powers invaded and conquered other countries by using their superior military and economic strengths. Thank goodness, World War II ended with the Imperial Japan and Germany defeated by the Allies, but the Cold War persisted. It is during the Cold War that one has realized the mighty force of soft power. Essentially it is the soft power that collapsed the Soviet Union since the Soviet had possessed a strong military power rivaling that of the U.S.

Soft power is non-coercive, consisting of economic power (technology, finance and trade) coupled with media power (News, television, movies, books, magazines and all digital communication over the Internet) delivered through cultural, social and political influences. The Soviet Union was collapsed by soft power. The media power had established the liberal value system which many countries were pursuing. There is nothing wrong by using the media power to promote liberty, democracy and a fair value system, however, it is wrong to cover up their faults and failures and negate any positive effect of other political and economic system.

Since the collapse of the Soviet Union, the Cold War is only nominally ended. The confrontations between nations persist, creating an unstable world. The NATO not only had not gone away but instead had gained members. With the advancement of Internet, the media power was exploding in the world reaching every corner and everyone. The media power has become so strong that they can cause 'color' revolutions, influence elections and topple governments; worst of all, they divide people, create hatred and confuse facts, even the President of the U.S. would charge the media for creating fake news and American people distrust them.

The simple definition of fake news is false news or spinning the News to create a false impression. The media are controlled and orchestrated in a subtle way by money hands to selectively report News and interpreting News. Take the recent trade war initiated by the U.S. against her trading partners, in particular targeting China, as an example. How much truth there was when news on "China Threat" was reported in the media? Why does the media only report 'bad' news about China? (Over 95% of News on China is negative) If there were no good news about China, how could China rise so fast? Tens of millions of people were lifted above the poverty line in every two years? How can the U.S. strengthen her competitiveness if the US media would not report China's success stories? Why is the US media so polarized in reporting politics and foreign affairs? Do we want to turn the media power into a monster destined to create hatred and division, mounting wars?

We accuse China for suppressing media freedom. It is true that China does not allow US political websites appearing on China's networks, nor YouTube or Facebook. Can we really blame China if China is concerned with Western media power spreading color revolution turning their social progress back to turbulent societies? Can we blame China for her concern of pornography and drugs poisoning their citizens' morality or her concern of violence spreading into their harmonious society? I now perfectly understand why Americans, who travelled to China, come back with a very positive impression. They see the advanced infrastructure in China's first and second tier cities providing Chinese citizens comfortable working and living conditions. The Chinese people seem to enjoy more freedom and opportunities pursuing personal goals and success. This can be seen from the energy they exhibit.

Ironically, the Chinese people have been (and still are) influenced by the Western media. They had been brainwashed for decades to adore the Western value system. However, as the Chinese gain more wealth and opportunities to travel, they get to see a true world. They begin to realize watching Western movies and reading American books do not necessarily give them a true picture of the Western world. For instance, New York City held a magic spot in the minds of Chinese until they traveled there and compared with their own mega cities like Beijing, Shanghai, Chongqing, etc. No wonder, the Chinese youths with traveling experience have gained so much self-confidence and a broader worldview.

It is true, China still has millions of citizens living poorly unable to travel, but they are given a promise, by 2030, everyone will be lifted above the poverty line, thus an opportunity to see the world. As an American, I am concerned that our focusing on negative reporting on China will only deprive Americans opportunities to engage with the changing world. Blaming others for our failures or wishing others to fail or destroying others' success is also destroying the American spirit. I encourage Americans to visit China to get "seeing is believing" experience about what kind of society China is shaping up. Americans can make America great again only by thinking and acting positively.

Chapter 12
Feel Like Living in a Dictator State

*****

The U.S. is touted as the promoter of democracy. The U.S. had granted voting rights to women on August 18th, 1920 (Congress ratified the 19th Constitution Amendment), thus making her a truly democratic nation for ninety eight years. (all citizens, male, white, black and female, having voting right) The U.S. had parted from Great Britain as a colony since 1776; she is a 242 year old independent nation. The New York State was one of the earliest States joining the independence movement and she joined the federation on July 26, 1778 (ratified). Another big State, California was admitted to the federation on September 9, 1850, 168 years ago and the last two states, Alaska and Hawaii were admitted on Jan 3rd and August 21, 1959 respectively, merely fifty nine years ago. So, historically speaking, the U.S. is a young nation and her practice of democracy (one person one vote) as a decision tool to elect the officials of the tri-branch government, executive, legislative and judicial branches, is less than a century old.

Each state has a similar tri-branch government system with key officials elected by a democratic voting method. Thus governor, mayor or leader of local government in the executive branch, the legislators in the legislative branch and in some cases, various court judges in the judicial branch are elected by the citizens, and in other cases, judges are nominated by the head of executive branch and approved by the legislative branch. What the U.S. promotes is not so much as the tri-branch government system (since they have existed in history with varying degree of independence between branches) but the democracy – a method of selecting the officials by citizens' votes. Presumably the direct voting method, one person one vote, will create a more independent tri-branch system and that is what the U.S. is promoting in the world. However, the citizens' voting rights whether exercised directly or by delegation are influenced by political parties which unfortunately are increasingly controlled or dictated by money power through the political party machinery, the political elites and the media. If multiple political parties truly existed advocating different ideology without influence from money power, then we would expect that the citizens could exercise their choice to elect a set of government officials according to their preferences to serve in an effective tri-branch government system. Well, life is not so simple, is it?

I have lived in New York State for fifty years since I completed my graduate studies. Fifty years in New York means 20% of its 246 years history in the independent U.S. (Some of my cotemporary friends living in California and Alaska or Hawaii for fifty years can claim 30% and 84% respectively, a very significant portion) Politically, I was not active initially, growing up from little political interest to be an independent, then leaning towards conservative Republican in terms of political ideal. New York State has been governed by a divided government since mid seventies up to 2018, 44 years. A divided government means that the governor and the two legislative branches, the Senate and the Assembly, are not controlled by the same political party and unfortunately they don't work very well together. Prior to 70's since WW II, New York State was governed by a 'trifectas' government, three government branches all controlled by the same party. There was no rigorous research studying the effectiveness or economic outcome of New York State throughout the years mentioned above. However, from a citizen's point of view, many New Yorkers including me feel that the State has been going downhill during the past four and half decades under a divided government. Industries and manufacturing are disappearing and people are migrating to other states.

Like the U.S. federal government, New York State has two legislative houses. The Assembly members are elected from 150 districts of population average about 128,652 per district. Since mid 70's, the NY Assembly has always been controlled by the party of Democrats (D) with a large margin mainly supported by the population in New York City. The NY State Senate has 63 districts of geographic regions. The Republican Party (R) barely has control by having 32 seats or by coalition of caucuses to gain effective control. The devastating performance of New York government with high taxes, deteriorating infrastructure, high cost of living and inadequate services can only be attributed to the dysfunction of a divided government. The Assembly has always been locked by Democrats elected by the large liberal NY City population.

Taking a look at another big state, Texas, it had a trifectas government (either D or R) from 1874 to 1994 except when Bill Clements, a Republican, served as governor intermittently from 1979-1982 and 1987-1990 all with a Democrat legislature. From 1995 to 2000, George W. Bush (R), served as Governor and turned the Texas Senate Republican during his tenure. Then Rick Perry (2001-2014) and Greg Abbott, both Republicans served with a Republican legislature, followed a trifectas government. Without rigorous research data, one can only say that Texas State has not done badly under a trifectas government either with Democrats or Republicans.

Taking another look at the State of California, it also had mostly a trifectas government since 1849 to 1942 with only a few times of divided government. From 1943 to 1982, California continued trifectas government with both Republican and Democrat governors. When George Deukmejian and Peter Wilson, both Republicans took over from Governor Jerry Brown (D), they both had a Democrat Legislature thus a divided government. Greg Davis (D) served a full term with Democrat legislature but Arnold Schwarzenegger (R) had a Democrat legislature. Currently, Jerry Brown (2011-2018 D) is back with a Democrat trifectas government. It would be extremely interesting for political science students to do research comparing the government effectiveness of a Republican, a Democrat trifectas government versus a divided government for California so that California voters can appreciate the benefit of a trifectas government and which party did it better.

Even though I am living in a town with more conservative people with a majority voters registered as Republicans, I felt like living in a dictator State controlled by an ineffective divided government. My vote is powerless to change Albany into an effective trifectas state government. The large population in New York City locks the State Assembly. Essentially, the single city is controlling the fate of the entire New York State which is decaying day by day. Yes, New Yorkers have the freedom to move to Texas or Carolinas or California but the same phenomenon is appearing at the national level. That is, our federal government is working poorly as a divided government. My hunch is, with increasing frequency of divided state government happening in more states, the fate of the U.S. is very much like that of New York State. Thus, no matter where you go you feel like living in a dictator country except the dictator is a party courting and controlling votes of the populated cities and states. It is damn hard to change that trend.

If one person one vote is the true democratic method we use to construct our government, then fair to say, it is trending to a divided government as population grows and clusters. When a divided government is locked in for decades by one party, we can say that we have a dictator government except it is an ineffective one. Sad to admit it, I feel like living in a dictator state! Do you feel the same?

Chapter 13
Is G2 Relation a Trap, a Shame or a Perfect Match?

*****

Politics is not a science with hard principles. International politics are more complex to follow causality principles. For example, although credit has often been given to Ronald Reagan for ending the Cold War, the collapse of the Soviet Union was not predictable even at the year it happened. Richard Nixon in his book had clearly indicated so. Therefore, no matter how one strategizes, there is no sure way to foresee the outcome of world politics. However, from hindsight, one sometimes may do a plausible causality analysis to explain some international affairs.

After the Soviet Union collapsed, some would conclude that the collapse was due to its economic failure not the inferiority of its military power. On a closer examination of the Soviet Union's economy, one might suggest that losing China as an economic partner was likely the biggest contributing factor to its failure. China didn't do anything directly to the Soviet, rather it was because the U.S. had strategically selected China to export her capitalism and accepted China into the US led global economy allowing China to industrialize. The U.S. didn't expect China to become the No. 2 world economy decades later surpassing Japan; but her strategy of isolating the Soviet Union worked.

The Soviet Union collapsed sooner than anyone could have predicted. Comparing to the U.S. economy and her standard of living, the Soviet communist system produced disaster, evidently explained the Soviet Union's collapse in 1989. China on the other hand realized her mistakes in economical development, hastened her departure from the Soviet style communism and sought her own ways of nation building. Hindsight again, China's reform and selective piece-meal adaptation of capitalism and industrialization starting from coastal region gradually but rapidly made her the largest trading partner with many countries in the world. China's total GDP reached close to 12 trillion US dollars.

Occasionally, one may see a chain of events or signs of a consequential development in world affairs; when that happens, it is usually too late to stop it, thus viewed more as a natural course rather than a man made plot. The ending of Cold War may be an objective of the U.S. Strategy but the way and the timing of the collapse occurred more naturally than intended. After all, some still consider that the Cold War has never ended judging on the confrontation continuing between the U.S. and Russia and through the new pivot to Asia Pacific strategy the U.S. is contemplating. It appeared that the U.S. was targeting China regretting that she had become the biggest economic competitor to the United States.

Even though China is not as potent a military power as the Soviet, the U.S. is again allying with Japan and other nations to contain China as she did to the Soviet Union. This time the U.S. is even luring India, a normally non-align nation, to join the U.S. security partnership by encouraging India to rival China militarily. Whether or not it was motivated from the lesson learned from the collapse of the Soviet Union is not important. What is apparent is that the pivot to Asia policy seems to follow the legacy strategy. Would the strategy work with China to collapse like Soviet Union, no one can tell for sure.

The World has become more complex as more countries have developed vying for the limited resources Earth can provide. Thus, world politics becomes more complex for any single nation to manage and control the consequences of world affairs. The world is constantly changing challenging mankind with unpredictable results. Nations must be concerned with the Earth Planet as a whole rather than bickering as rivals fighting for a superior leadership position. No single nation was able to dominate and lead the world for a long time before and none likely in the future, all owing to the complex global issues involving nature such as climate change, dwindling resources like energy and water as well as man-made situations such as nuclear and terror threats, financial crisis and even waste management.

The U.S. has become the superpower after the WW II. She has maintained her military superiority but her economic might has proportionally changed from 40% to less than 20% of the world economy. The U.S. now needs strong economic partners to deal with world crises both from natural challenges and man-made affairs. For example, the world is expecting the U.S. and China the two biggest economies to work together to remedy the threats of climate change as well as nuclear threat such as from North Korea, Iran and terrorism spreading throughout the world. The advantage of the U.S. and China working together as partners rather than adversaries has become obvious.

G2 was a concept first proposed by C. Fred Bernstein in 2005 to describe an economic relation between the U.S. and China. Later in the beginning term of the Obama Administration, Zbigniew Brzezinski, broadened G2 into foreign policy arena to advocate a G2 relationship between the U.S. and China in a speech given in Beijing (Jan/2009) celebrating 30th anniversary of US-China diplomatic tie. Initially, China was lukewarm to the G2 idea concerning that it may be a trap to force China onto the world stage prematurely to bear more financial burden coming from world affairs and obligations. As China continues to maintain her 6-7% economic growth while the U.S. can hardly maintain her 2-3% growth rate, the political sentiment changed in the U.S. When Donald Trump ran for the U.S. Presidency in 2016 and won on the thesis of a failed Obama Administration making the U.S. weak, Trump's slogan was 'America First and Making America Strong'. Trump blamed the US domestic and international problems on China, G2 became a derogatory term, seeing accepting G2 as a 'shame' for the No. 1, the U.S.

In reality, the U.S. is facing numerous problems that cannot be fixed without working with a strong economic partner. China is the perfect partner for the U.S. because of her size and a prospering economy, a huge market of 1.4 billion people with GDP per capita only $8123 (2016). The trade deficit with China can be easily fixed by selling more goods, technologies and services to China than say to Japan or any other country. The current US policy of restricting high tech sales to China is somewhat cowardly and applying high tariffs on Chinese goods can only hurt the U.S. economy and her standard of living. China has become a competitor but never an aggressor. It would cost the U.S. more to curtail China's development than to prosper with China's growth. Through a G2 Relation, the U.S. can solicit China's help in solving nuclear and terror threats more effectively and can stimulate the U.S. economy. If the U.S. were to engage China to raise her per capita GDP by $1000 through lifting her standard of living via consumption, it means $1.4 trillion dollars goods and services needed. Why is the U.S. with per capita GPD $57466 (2016) so afraid of engaging in the 'Chinese dream' to bring Chinese out of poverty into a better life? China could provide a tremendous opportunity for the world if anyone would partner with her. The British is the first to recognize that, then the EU, Brazil, India,why not the U.S.?

The U.S. holds an advantage over China in many aspects. The U.S. must have confidence that she can maintain her lead in the G2 relationship. Yes, there will be competition but that is inevitable in global economy, as exemplified by Japan, Korea, and Brazil. Competition is motivation for progress. A healthy G2 Relation with China is a win-win situation for both. Under a healthy G2, other big neighbors India, Russia, Japan, Brazil, Mexico and Canada would more likely to co-exist peacefully with the U.S. and China. Therefore, the U.S. and China should accept a G2 Relationship. The world would be better off for it.

Chapter 14
Frenemies Friend Each Other And Rivals Unravel Issues in Asia

*****

April 27-28, 2018 may go down in history as a very significant weekend in Asia with consequences impacting the whole world. Coincidentally, on this weekend, the two most populated countries in the world, China and India, will have an informal summit meeting between the two strong leaders, President Xi Jinping and Prime Minister Narendra Modi while the Supreme Leader Kim Jong-Un of North Korea (NK) is meeting President Moon Jae-In of South Korea (SK), both meetings expecting positive results.

The two Koreas were separated since the Korean War in the 1950's (6/25/1950- 7/27/1953). The Korean War involved the United States and China. The U.S. adamantly practiced the anti-communism foreign policy by resisting the spread of the Soviet Union led communism in Asia and Europe. China, as a communist country heavily depended on Russia for aids in her recovering from WW II, had little choice but engaged in Korean War. The Russian Army would willingly cross the Chinese northern border to fight the Americans in Korea Peninsula if China would not help NK. China did help NK and paid a hefty price in human casualties. The Korean War ended with a truce in 1953, dividing Korea in two by an artificial line known as 38 degree line. The truce, not a peace treaty, was signed on July 27, 1953 by Lt. Gen. William Harrison representing the U.S. and United Nation Command and Gen. Nam I'll, representing Korea People's Army and Chinese People's Volunteers. In 1954, During the Geneva Conference, Chinese Foreign Minister Zhou En-Lai proposed to sign a peace treaty for the Korean Peninsula, but the U.S. Secretary of State, john Foster Dulles rejected it, a big mistake leading to today's nuclear threat. SK and NK were eventually admitted to the U.N. on August 8th, 1991.

The ideological divide in two Koreas persisted seven decades. SK is a constitutional republic consisting of an executive branch led by an elected President and an elected legislative branch with elected legislators. SK's road to democracy has not been smooth as exhibited by the fact that several presidents were either assassinated or murdered or jailed throughout the seven decades. SK remained as a strategic partner of the U.S. having US military presence of 23,468 (2017) American soldiers, sailors, airmen and Marines (USFK) which has Title 10 authority; meaning that USFK is responsible for organizing, training and equipping U.S. forces on the Korean Peninsula so that forces are agile, adaptable and ready. Recently, the U.S. installed the Terminal High Altitude Area Defense (THAAD) system in response to NK's nuclear threat. This has not only annoyed China, Russia and NK but also raised protests in SK, a possible trigger for NK and SK to hold peace meetings today.

Different from China who has departed from the Soviet style of communism since the 1960's, The Democratic People's Republic of Korea (DPRK) was established in 1948 when **the** United States and **the** Soviet Union divided control of **the** peninsula after World War II. **NK** has maintained an authoritarian secretive communist system with present Supreme Leader Kim Jong-Un inherited the leadership from his father, Kim Jong-Il. NK pursued nuclear weapon development as a leverage for maintaining security of the regime. NK's success in long range nuclear missile development not only has caused concern of SK, Japan, and the U.S. but also irked China since China has always advocated a nuclear free Korea Peninsula.

NK's nuclear threat has been a thorn on the north side of Pacific causing uneasiness all over the world. The recent development of the leaders of two Koreas meeting each other at the military demarcation line is welcoming News. The two leaders stepped over the line to symbolize a visit to the other side and they planted a tree of peace. Both leaders showed warmth and worked hard to exhibit their sincerity towards the goal of achieving denuclearization on the Korean Peninsula and signing a peace agreement to permanently end the Korean War. Although the two rivals may still have a long way to unravel their issues, this meeting really opened a new era despite of some rhetoric still appeared in the U.S. media. President Trump seems to be genuinely welcoming this development. As an American citizen desiring peace, I don't mind President Trump claiming the credit for promoting this historical event. Going a step further, I would even encourage The Nobel Prize Committee to award Kim, Moon, Trump and Xi a Nobel Peace Prize, if a denuclearization and peace treaty could be achieved prior to or at the Kim-Trump meeting in May or June.

During the same weekend, the Chinese President Xi and Indian Prime Minister Modi are meeting at Wuhan, China for an informal Summit. India and China are regarded as frenemies, a word presumably created to describe a relationship of friendly enemies. Narendra Damodardas Modi (67) was the Chief Minister of Gujarat from 2001-2014 and became Prime Minister since 2014, a strong leader standing for reelection in 2019. At the request of Modi for a friendly get-together, the two leaders agreed to meet over the weekend at a relaxing spot in China favored by Chairman Mao. Although the meeting is informal with no official agenda, the leaders are expected to touch a few issues in a relaxed informal manner reminiscing Xi's visit to Modi's home in Gujarat in 2014, sitting on a swing with Modi.

In 2017 China-India relations took a dive, when a border braw happened at Doklam with military stand-off lasting two and half months. China was building a road at the border with Bhutan also nearing China-India border. India was overly concerned with the Chinese influence over Himalayan states and South Asia in general. The stand-off was resolved before the BRICS Summit in September of 2017 in Beijing, but the mistrust between the two nations deepened, nevertheless, on top of India's boycotting the Belt and Road Initiative (BRI) Summit in May in Beijing where even Japan and the U.S. attended as well as India's joining the Quadrilateral Security Dialogue (QUAD) with the U.S., Japan and Australia which is another contributed factor to the cooling of relations between the two nations.

In the 1980's India's and China's GDP were comparable, but now China's GDP is about five times of India. Out of the $84 billion trade between the two nations today, China enjoys a trade surplus about $15 billion. India is concerned with this trade deficit but the economic cooperation is hampered by political relationship such as the above issues as well as by India's attitude towards Dalai Lama and China's position regarding designating Jarsh-e-Mohammed chief Masood Azhar as a global terrorist.

Over all, the mistrust between India and China, although long rooted but is not irreparable. If India and China, the two largest nations in Asia, could cooperate, it would bring more benefits to the two nations, Asia and the whole world. At this juncture, the U.S. is initiating a tariff war on trade; it creates a tremendous opportunity for India and China to focus on trade and economic cooperation. The political issues might be hardened by further deeds of mistrust but could also be resolved by mutual benefits derived from economic cooperation. Based on News reports and tweets, Modi and Xi had a heart to heart conversation aimed at removing the 'frenemies' image and making friends with each other for the benefit of the two largest nations on earth and their people.

Chapter 15
The US-China Trade War and Beyond - A Fair Analysis

*****

The US-China Relation is a complex one. The recently hyped trade war is by no means the single issue nor the most important issue. The complexity of the two-nation relationship is not because of their size but because of their biased views towards each other, causing serious misunderstandings and ill-considered actions and policies in handling competition. China is very different from Russia. China's threat is from competition, a fair competition under nationalism and global regulations. China does not really pose military threat since her military capability is more defense oriented comparing to Russian military. The fact that the U.S. will send a trade negotiation team consisting of Peter Navarro, author of "The Coming China War" (2006) and "The Death by China" (2012 book and documentary), and the wildest anti-China economist with no other American economist agreeing with him, is a bizarre diplomatic event. No wonder the negotiation team rushed back in two days emptyhanded. Now that Trump has made an about-face statement regarding cutting off crucial supply to ZTE and expecting President Xi's special envoy, Vice Premier Liu He to visit Washington to continue the trade talk is intriguing to say the least.

1. (A) China's economy is the world's second largest. China's ambition is to dominate the world. China is gaming the system to grow her economy at the expense of the U.S. (B) The U.S. is the No. 1 economy of the world. She is already dominating the world. She sets the rules for her self-interest. She sanctions and controls what she wants to export and imports goods at low costs taking advantage of the hardworking developing countries. (C) COMMENT: the above statements seem to be fair and harmless assessments so long as free competition and free trade is honored.

2. (A) China desires to become a leader in hi-tech industries. China trades her market for technology, letting foreign companies to do business and make profits in China for introducing technologies into China. (B) The U.S. is the most advanced leader of hi-tech industries. The U.S. leverages her market for capital, absorbing foreign capitals to invest in the U.S. funding her hi-tech developments and industries, financial products and imports of cheap goods and services. (C) COMMENT:

Each country is planning for one's self-interest and objective. The growing size and changing nature of the Chinese market seems to support China's desire and goal. The stagnant and saturating US market seems to lose its leveraging power to attract capitals to the U.S. - a US concern.

3. (A) China's military strength is ramping up with a budget increasing over 10% per year, focusing on naval force and modernizing all her combat capabilities. China is able to sell some of her weapons at competitive price to regional small countries. (B) The U.S. maintains her superiority in military strength in all areas with both offensive and defensive nature. The U.S. maintains a large number of military bases all over the world explicitly targeting Russia and China. She fosters alliances with many countries, recently cultivating an additional tie with Japan, Australia and India targeting China. (C) COMMENT: China's defense budget is set about 2% of her GDP ($175B 2018) a reasonable figure for her geographic size, fourteen neighbors and over 8530 miles of coastlines. Her military development is apparently more defense in nature. Whereas the U.S. maintains a defense budget at 3.3% of her GDP with an absolute figure about $650B. (2018) The U.S. is the No. 1 arms seller. Russia is No. 2 and China is a distant third.

4. (A) China has a mounting debt mainly produced by her provincial and lower governments, a potential financial problem, but China holds over one trillion dollars of US debt, pressuring the U.S. (B) The U.S. has persistently maintained a deficit budget mounting a huge national debt. The interest and principal payment of the debt is maintained by selling Treasury Bills. The U.S. has the largest pool of liquid assets relying on printing money and selling T-bills to finance her deficit spending at the expense of other countries' hard earned dollars. (C) COMMENT: Both the U.S. and China are vulnerable under a debt financing scheme to run their governments, but the U.S. is in worse shape far more depending on a controllable dollar. China's large holding of the US Treasury Bills becomes vulnerable with dollar currency fluctuation uncontrollable. China would like her RMB to become an international trading currency so that she will have control on her trading balance sheet. This is understandable except the U.S. sees RMB as an international trading currency posting a threat to the US dollar and her ability to manage her debt financing.

5. (A) China's Belt and Road Initiative (BRI) is seen by the U.S. as China's means to bind other countries with China through trade. Other countries are happy to accept Chinese funds to finance economy-boosting projects. (B) The U.S. is seen to bind other countries through military alliances. Other countries under security threat accept the military protection from the U.S. The U.S. is accused to be stirring up

more security issues in the world. (C) COMMENT: China has made tremendous investment in her basic infrastructure development, not only lifting her country's transportation, communication and commerce (economy) as well as her capability of exporting infrastructure development technology to other nations. China seems to be more willing to engage in solving international conflicts through the U.N. actions.

6. (A) China's leader Xi Jinping is called a dictator especially after the Chinese Communist Party amended the constitution to permit Xi to assume leadership position without term limit, but Xi's performance received wide support from the Chinese people and the respect of the international leaders. (B) The U.S. President Trump won the election as a dark horse. His style of leadership bewildered not only the American political elites but also the international political arena. (C) COMMENT: Xi came up the ranks through harsh life and career experiences seemingly understanding the poor people and their dream of being middle class. He seems to be leading with a sincere goal, call it Chinese dream. Trump was born with a silver spoon and made a fortune through wheeling and dealing in the complex US real estate business. His business skills seem to be foreign to the diplomatic world. Trump puts the world on an edge which may or may not be good for the U.S.

Trump Administration is only into its 17th month, but a turbulent change of his cabinet personnel and White House appointees has occurred. Currently, Trump seems to surround him with people more hawkish against China, some like Navarro beating the drum that China has taken the US jobs and the two are destined going to war and some others like 'Pentagon generals' believing in military power. The combination of these people driven by Trump's "Make America Great" slogan is not a good plot for the U.S. since both 'bias attitude' and 'legacy strategy' just do not make sound policy. At this point, Trump seems still acting independently, possibly able to learn on his own and call his own shots. He claims that he has a good personal relationship with Xi. Let's hope the two leaders will guide their relationship onto a sensible mutually beneficial path rather than into a deadend alley by 'fake common perception'.

Chapter 16
Who Took Away American Jobs and How to Fix It?

*****

Thomas Loren Friedman, three times Pulitzer Prize winner and a columnist and author, once wrote an article (NY Times, Opinion, 3-20-2010), "America's Real Dream Team", attributing the success of America to her brilliant immigrants. A well known Chinese historian and political analyst, Ms Zi (資中筠 88），has referenced Friedman's article recently to answer her own query article, what is the reason making America so great? (4-27-2018, Knowledge Search 知識探索）She said that American talents made America great and China's education did not produce talents for China but sent them to the U.S. becoming their talents. She pointed out that the U.S. has been able to attract bright students from all over the world and many of them become America's talents. China must create a condition conducive to attracting talents to come to China (not just offering money) to stay in education and work place. These two articles all shared a view, that it is people or talents that make a nation great.

It is puzzling though while pondering on the above two scholars' profound articles I repeatedly heard the American President saying that China has stolen the jobs away from America (hence making the US economy and export trade weak?) President Trump won his presidency on the slogan, 'To Make America Great Again'. Indeed, since his inauguration, he has been focusing on his campaign promises. Trump has been tough on illegal immigrant issue even affected the legal immigration process. He blames China for US domestic problems such as losing manufacturing industry and companies move abroad. But are we really dealing with a situation that the U.S. has talents but lost jobs Or more seriously the U.S. has lost both jobs and talents or there is a serious mismatch of skills and jobs? Are these problems really caused by China while record number of Chinese students coming to the U.S. to study? A rising unfortunate sentiment, which was fanned by the media, was charging all Chinese Americans as potential industrial or military spies for China and suggesting restriction on Chinese students and faculties engaged in hi-tech researches in the U.S. Recalling Friedman's above article, this type of sentiment is not only unfair and discriminating but is also harmful to the core value of immigrants making this country great. This is the reason the title subject must be discussed in this column.

History show us, China as a principally agricultural nation had a strong economy leading the world for many centuries. The industrial revolution brought machine and energy systems to human society that made the Britain the world's strongest nation deserving her name, Great Britain. While the industry revolution brought the invention of automobile, but a short-sighted British Law to limit automobile speed to be comparable to horse carriage to protect the coach and buggy drivers' jobs essentially gave the auto industry away to Americans and later also to Germans. The engines played a significant role in Second World War. The victory of allies in WW II made the U.S. militarily strong, but it is the computer revolution and its resulting automation really made the U.S. the number one economy in the world, not only made Americans rich but also sustained her military superiority. China on the other hand was a victim of foreign aggression throughout most of the nineteen and the twentieth century thus barely could provide food for her citizens.

Post WW II, the U.S. almost led in every field of agriculture, manufacturing, science and technology. While many Western countries including the defeated Germany and Japan were helped by the U.S. recovering from the war damage, China was artificially divided into two parts across the Taiwan Strait thus having a slower recovery. It was not until the U.S. recognized Mainland China for the purpose of rivaling the Soviet Union, only then China systematically embraced capitalism under a Chinese defined communist system to accelerate her economic development. Like Japan and many other fast developing countries who took the coattail of the U.S. in industrialization and computerization copying and overtaking the U.S. from low tech to mid-tech, while the U.S. was able to keep up with the innovation and advances in hi-tech industries, China was trailing behind them in a low-key but methodical manner. What amazed the world was China's rapid speed in development, a double digit growth in economy and a fast-forward in embracing technology and innovation.

We are living in a very competitive world. The advance of information technology and Internet made the world a fairer playing field. Countries with large population backed with easy access of education like India and China can exert their competitive power. It was never easy for any country to maintain at the No. one spot forever. Seventy years ago, the size of US economy was 40% of the world economy and today she is less than 20%. Taiwan at one time had a GDP comparable to Mainland China's but now at 5% or less. No matter what political system a country has, it needs great leaders to make the country great. President Trump is a very unusual leader. He recognizes the problems of the U.S. and is trying to figure out how to fix them fast. Rhetoric, bluffing and threats are always part of the international politics, but at the end of the day, great leaders must make intelligent decisions based on facts learned.

Japan, Europe and China did not steal American jobs. The U.S. had chosen or let her economic development to shift away from labor intensive and/or low profit industries to brain intensive businesses, partly because of computer/automation advances which striped away many physical jobs and partly because of the ease of making a fortune in financial industries with Information technologies. Even the government became more and more dependent on creating and selling financial instruments to pay for its operation. The US education was the envy of the world but the U.S failed to recognize and match the rapid change of job/skill requirements in the industry and marketplace. Creative minds need to know where creativity is required. Only physical hands-on experience can give one the immediate clue to apply one's creativity. Americans cannot get more jobs because of skill obsolescence and failure to engage life learning to anticipate job changes and new skill requirements. Most US colleges were too liberal allowing majority of faculty and students pursuing teaching/learning with no career planning in mind. The foreign students usually came with career in mind and they cherry pick the best schools, the best course and the best faculty to study under. If they chose to stay that would be advantage to the U.S. If they chose to go back that would be US loss.

Many scholars, economists and educators do understand the above scenario, but education reforms and life philosophy changes take time. Life-long learning takes generations to form into a professional habit. Rapid rises in China and India swept Americans off their feet but the U.S. is a big and strong nation. There is no doubt that she can compete in this world by making fundamental changes in education system, life philosophy and learning habits. One must realize that in 21st century by throwing one's military weight around or bullying can only hurt each other. Judging from the rapid changes of pace in the US-China trade negotiation from hostility/confrontation to discussion/compromise, hopefully, our leader President Trump and his good friend President Xi have understood the real challenges and will lead the two great nations onto the right path for mutual prosperity and world peace.

Chapter 17
Memorial Day Thoughts

*****

Memorial Day is not just a holiday or sales day. Henry Carter Welles of Waterloo, New York was credited for suggesting a national memorial day. Although Henry was a well known druggist at the time, he would probably be forgotten today by all but his descendants if he did not make a comment to his townspeople in the summer of 1865. At a social gathering, Henry suggested that a day should be set aside to honor the dead of the Civil War. The next year, he repeated his suggestion to **General John B. Murray**. The two men and a group of local citizens gained the support of the village, and on May 5, 1866, the first complete observance of **Memorial Day** took place in Waterloo, NY. The Centennial Committee, formed in Waterloo for the 100th observance in 1966, found the newspapers of the time credited Henry for suggesting the first Memorial Day which was nationally proclaimed by General John Logan of the Grand Army of the Republic by the famous 'general order 11' issued on May 5th, 1868. The Memorial Day is observed now on the last Monday of May. One of the most impressive images of WW II photographed by Joe Rosenthal (Associated Press), five marines and a navy corpsman raising the American Flag on top of Mount Sunbachi during the battle of Iwo Jima is often associated with Memorial Day. But this image, made into a statue (referred to as Iwo Jima Memorial), was actually representing all Marines, now located near the Arlington National Cemetery.

Besides thinking about the history of Memorial Day, what I would like to share with all patriotic Americans today is the following thoughts:

Today, we solemnly remember the patriots who fought for our freedom and died for our country, we pay respect to our veterans who served our country to protect us so we may have peace and we salute our service men and women who protect our land and sea so we may have our American way of life freely pursuing prosperity and having justice for all.

As the world is growing and developing, we are facing more challenges today, not only from human affairs but also from nature but we must also remember that our success comes from American ingenuity and hard work. Americans coming from all over the world and settling down in the U.S. are peace loving people. On Memorial Day, As an American citizen, I would like to cite a few quotes from our great leaders to reflect on history and encourage ourselves about the future:

First from the 32nd President, Franklin D. Roosevelt (Democrat):
"This country seeks no conquest. We have no imperial designs. From day to day and year to year, we are establishing a more perfect assurance of peace with our neighbors. We rejoice especially in the prosperity, the stability and the independence of all of the American Republics. We not only earnestly desire peace, but we are moved by a stern determination to avoid those perils that will endanger our peace with the world."

From another great President, John F Kennedy ((Democrat):
"Mankind must put an end to war before war puts an end to mankind." He also said: "Forgive your enemies but never forget their names."

From a great heroic President, Dwight D. Eisenhower (Republican):
"In the councils of government, we must guard against the acquisition of unwarranted influence, whether sought or unsought, by the military-industrial complex. The potential for the disastrous rise of misplaced power exists, and will persist." He also said: "Together we must learn how to compose differences not with arms, but with intellect and decent purpose."

Let's examine our world today and reflect on the above quotes. Today, sadly we see the world is moving to peril and mutual destruction, the continuous regional wars, the nuclear threat and terrorism around the world on top of natural disasters caused by humans' abuse of our environment. In our country, it seems that there is 'the invisible military-industrial complex' President Eisenhower so warned us about is busy at work nonstop. It pays lobbyists and retired government officials "to bay for war incessantly on K Street, in the Dirksen Senate Building and in election campaigns in regions where the manufacturing of weapons provides the only substantial jobs." (excerpt from Henry Harris, the Rise of American War Lord by Emanuel Pastreich, an American scholar with BA degree from Yale University, MA from University of Tokyo, PhD from Harvard University, presently mainly active in Korea, an

associate professor at Kyung Hee University and director of The Asia Institute
(A Think Tank) in Seoul, who writes on both East Asian classical literature
and current issues in international relations and technology.)

Unfortunately, the invisible military-industrial complex is apparently driven by
profits from selling weapons, building ships and warplanes, not so much by
noble cause. It creates war threat stories to justify the expansion of military
budgets and development of weapons and it induces the world to compete in
arms capabilities so that the sales of weapons flourish. Since the end of Cold
War, the U.S. instead of a long peace, she has been involved in several wars.
The worst scenario, of course, is that our government is too easily persuaded
by the "invisible complex" to enter war and send our service men and women
into harm's way.

On this Memorial Day, we must reflect on history and the lives that American
soldiers sacrificed. Indeed as President Kennedy said, we must not forget the
names of our enemies but we must also remember President Eisenhower's
words that we must learn how to compose differences not with arms, but with
intellect and decent purpose. American citizens must pay attention on what is
going on in the world, to see through the invisible forces and speak out openly
to warn our government. Let's hope that the leaders of our country will hear
from us, common folks, not just the lobbying voices. We also hope that the
leaders of this world will ponder on the above words spoken with experience
and wisdom, especially on how to compose differences with intellect and
decent purpose, not with arms and guide our world in peace and to prosperity.

Chapter 18
An American ThinkTank Scholar's Objective View on Pivot to Asia (I)
*****

Pivot to Asia has been a key component of the U.S. foreign policy since Obama Administration. With Asian countries rapidly rising economically, such a policy is logical. However, the interpretation and implementation of the policy is subject to question on its true purpose and ultimate objectives. The current tension in the South China Sea, Korea Peninsula and Iran and over all intense relationship with and among China, India, Japan and Russia begs answers on what does the U.S. really hope to accomplish with her Asia Pacific foreign policy. The actions and their consequences up till now have left Asia in stress against Asian countries' desire which is to achieve prosperity through economic development. The U.S. seems to have made a wrong assumption or taken the wrong actions leading to unexpected outcome.

The 'Pivot' or 'Rebalancing' term was introduced in the Fall of 2011 During the Obama Administration, but the core of its strategy of shifting emphasis to Asia was a continuation from the G. W. Bush government and the early stage of Obama's first term, such as strengthening ties with existing allies in Asia, redeploying or balancing troops and increasing naval presence in Asia, signing free trade agreement with South Korea and engaging with TPP development as well as cultivating partnership with India and Vietnam. Obama's formal announcement on 'Pivot' and taking actions in military sphere such as new deployment of troops and equipments to Australia and Singapore certainly had alerted China worrying what is the real purpose of the 'Pivot'.As a Congress Research Report, authored by seven social scientists (Mark Manyin et. al.) on March 28, 2012, stated, the "pivot" is a conviction (benefit) that the center of gravity for U.S. foreign policy, national security, and economic interests is being realigned and shifted towards Asia, and that the U.S. strategy and priorities will be adjusted accordingly. However, the report noted the risk of 'pivot' being its 'cost' which may cause a significant reduction of U.S. defense spending elsewhere, a reduction in U.S. military capacity in other parts of the world,

and may jeopardize the Congressional plan to cut Navy spending. Additionally, the perception among many that the "rebalancing" is targeted against China could strengthen the hand of Chinese hard-liners thus deteriorating US-China Relation and making it more difficult for the United States to gain China's cooperation on a range of issues. Moreover, the report warned that the pivot's prominence would have raised the 'costs' to the United States if it (Obama) or successor administrations (Trump) failed to follow through on the 'pivot' plan. One key assumption, that for years 'many' countries in Asia have encouraged the U.S. to step up its activities to provide a counter balance to China's rising influence, is later proven not exactly correct. The Asian nations, seemingly changing more so lately（with Japan as an exception perhaps）, want a peaceful environment for economic development rather than a stressful confrontational atmosphere brought on by 'pivot'.

There are many essays written about 'Pivot'. From a nice early assessment made by Kenneth Lieberthal, The American Pivot to Asia - Why President Obama's turn to the East is easier said than done, Foreign Policy 12/21/20111, to a latest PhD research work, The Case of the Pivot to Asia - System Effects and the Origin of Strategy, by Nicholas D. Anderson and Victor D. Cha, Professor at George Washington University and former Ambassador to South Korea (SK), Political Science Quarterly, Vol. 132, no. 4, 2017-18, one can see that there is a lot of issues concerning how the 'Pivot' was executed and what was accomplished. After researching these 'pivot' studies, I have found one article by Emanuel Pastreich (53), an American academic, very revealing about the intriguing intention of the 'Pivot' program and how the US military establishment is really in control of it. Pastreich was born in Nashville, TN, (10/16/1964), attended Lowell High School in San Francisco and began studies in Yale University and obtained a B.A. degree in Chinese (1987, during college he also studied abroad at Taiwan University), then obtained a M.A. degree in comparative literature from Tokyo University (1991, dissertation in Japanese language) and completed his PhD in East Asian Studies from Harvard University (1998). So Pastreich is an American scholar with a deep understanding of Asia.

It is necessary to go into Dr. Pastreich's background to appreciate his views on the U.S. foreign policy on Asia. Academically, he served as assistant professor at the University of Illinois at Urbana–Champaign, George Washington University, and Solbridge International School of Business. He is currently an associate professor at the College of International Studies, Kyung Hee University. Previously he served as an international relations and foreign investment adviser to the governor of Chungnam Province (2007-2008), SK, as an external relations adviser at the Daedeok Innopolis research cluster, and was appointed to serve on the committee for city administration (2010-2011) and for foreign investment (2009-2010) for the city of Daejeon. Pastreich also served previously as the Director of the KORUS House (2005-2007), a think tank for international relations housed in the Korean Embassy in Washington D.C., and as the editor-in-chief of *Dynamic Korea*, a journal of the Korean Foreign Ministry that introduces Korean culture and society. Prof. Pastreich is no doubt an expert on Asian affairs well versed in Asian languages and having working experience in SK, Japan and Taiwan, Asian allies of the U.S.

Recently, Professor Pastreich published a lengthy opinion in the Korea Times (5/12/2018), entitled, From the Prison Cells of Guantanamo Bay to Embassy in Seoul - Harry Harris, the rise of an American warlord. His opinion is certainly very explicit in criticizing the inappropriateness of appointing General Harris as the ambassador to SK, while NK and SK are attempting to make peace and the U.S. is trying to negotiate with NK for denuclearization. But more importantly, his arguments for against Harris's appointment touch upon the strategy of 'Pivot' and who is guiding it into a wrong path. In my analysis, Pastreich had made an astute observation and his opinion deserves US mainstream media coverage and clarification as well as our serious reflection. Thus, after presenting a brief history of 'Pivot' and Professor Pastreich's scholarly background above, I am ready to use the next column to discuss Prof. Pastreich's essay in detail. The arguments against and the inappropriateness of General Harry Harris's appointment as ambassador to SK (after Australians expressed displeasure to his appointment as Ambassador to Australia), a detailed account of General Harris's Navy career rising like a warlord (including his role as the Commander of Quantanamo Prison Camp and rapid promotions to become the Commander of Pacific Command) and what factional groups existing in the U.S. military will be discussed, analyzed and interpreted in relation to the U.S. 'Pivot to Asia' policy as part II.

Chapter 19
An American ThinkTank Scholar's Objective View on Pivot to Asia (II)

*****

Admiral Harry Harris, commander of the US Pacific Command in Hawaii, was slated to start work as ambassador to Australia in May. Suddenly, out of the blue, the Trump White House announced on April 24 that Harris would be assigned to South Korea. Australian Prime Minister Malcohm Turnbull was not able to control the opposition to Harris in control even in the more conservative business community. The fact that Harris was born in Japan to a Japanese mother was not a reason for Pastreich's objection to his new appointment, even though in general Koreans remember deeply the savage invasion and crude ruling of Korea by Japan. Pastreich raised multiple salient reasons for his objection. Pastreich reasoned his objection on several levels. First, assigning a military officer as ambassador to Korea when SK and NK are trying to develop peaceful ties and the world is anticipating the U.S.-NK to hold a summit meeting to discuss denuclearization is extraordinary. Second, as a US military officer having a close ties with the far-right faction in Japan and receiving an award, 'the order of rising sun' at the same moment, Harris's appointment is odd.

Furthermore, as the previous Commander of then the controversial Quantanamo Prison Camp (3/2006-6/2007), Harris had received a series of promotions ultimately to be the Commander of Pacific Command without any public scrutiny was also extraordinary while Gina Haspel, appointed as the director of CIA, and Mike Pompeo, the former CIA Director and the New Secretary of State, both had to answer questions about their involvement with Quantanamo. The book, Murder at Camp Delta, authored by Joseph Hickman with six years of research has described in detail the overdosing of prisoners with anti-malaria drugs with known psychoactive effect whereas Harris publicly claimed those death cases as suicide events. John Kiriakous, former CIA employee was sentenced to jail for revealing to the public the human experimentation at the Quantanamo prison camp. Pastreich certainly has given enough grounds to raise objection to Harris's ambassador appointment whether it is a promotion or demotion or not, but his story of Harris may be linked to the 'Pivot' policy deserves our attention.

Pastreich's essay went far deeper than Harris's career, his analysis of the shifting of strategy on national defense security as dictated by the US military establishment is very profound and to large extend explains the evolvement of 'Pivot to Asia' up to its current status. It was no surprise that the US military has factions broadly named by 'war on Iran', 'war on terror', 'war on China' with their emphasis on preparing for war and focusing on obtaining sufficient defense budget to make more battleships, aircrafts and submarines. I was surprised by learning that there were groups, mainly working level experts, believing in a far more important national security threat by climate change and land and ocean environment. This group is gaining strength in the Pacific Command with a history over a decade long. They are concerning with the threat of climate change and its impact on the effectiveness of US military, thus they are focusing work on electric batteries, alternative energy infrastructure and forming new alliances.

The above faction on climate change and new alliance rose to a peak when the Pacific Commander, Admiral Samuel Locklear delivered a speech at Harvard University (3-9-2013) claiming climate change as the primary long-term security threat in Pacific region. In a documentary movie, entitled, 'the Burden', made by military veterans (2015), it showed the serious effect of fossil fuels not only on climate change but also on military effectiveness. (The US military is overly dependent on oil)Thus it makes sense to work on batteries, alternative energies and forming new alliances, especially collaborating with China. This type of thinking was reflected in Obama's declaration with Xi at the Hangzhou Summit (9-3-2016) about dealing with climate change.

However, the 'new alliances' group posed direct threat to the 'war on China' group (and their traditional or legacy military alliance system – island chain surrounding China) who wanted to stick to anti-China strategy, seeking more overpriced ships and fighter planes and rewarding defense contractors and generals with cushy retirement packages. Admiral Locklear's speech triggered a fast strike back by the right-wing for-war groups and military industrial complex. (K Street lobbyists and far right organizations) Cecil D. Haney as the Commander of Pacific Fleet was replaced by the right-wing hardliner Harry Harris (10/16/2013) who then was nominated within a year for promotion to replace Admiral Sam Locklear as the Commander of Pacific (9/2014). The nomination was confirmed by the Senate in December, 2014 but the ceremony was delayed to May due to a Navy internal investigation. Harris had been very vocal while in Command of the Pacific Fleet and Headquarter making anti-China rhetoric and demanding defense budget increase to the point of annoying the White House (Condoleezza Rice and Obama) on occasions.

The rapid changes in Naval command and Trump Administration's staff turn-over certainly does not help in clarifying and executing the US Pivot to Asia policy. In 2012, the US Navy invited Chinese Navy to participate in the 2014 Rim of the Pacific Exercise (RIMPAC). Recently, the US Navy is uninviting China to the RIMPAC 2018, citing reason that the previous invitation had not served the purpose of deterrent to make China de-escalating the buildup of her navy. This is obviously a right-wing statement. It seems clear that the right-wing is gaining control of the US military (Pentagon and Navy) and the civilian Administration (Defense Secretary, General James N. Mattis, White House Security Advisor, John Bolton, Secretary of State, Mike Pompeo and CIA Director, Gina Haspel mentioned above), together they are waging a confrontational position towards China. With Trump mixing national security issues such as the NK and Iran nuclear threat and trade and commerce problems such as trade balance with China, EU and others in the same pot, stirring the pot with anti-China sentiment as the sole ingredient is definitely not a good recipe for solution. Peter Navarro (Pro-Tarriff and anti-China), Assistant to the President, Director of Trade and Industrial Policy, and the Director of the White House National Trade Council, a newly created entity in the executive branch of the U.S. federal government, was rumored to move up to head the National Economic Council (NEC) but ultimately Larry Kudlow got the job which may signal that a trade war is avoidable..

The assumption that many Asian countries welcome the 'Pivot' program could be erroneous with China's Belt and Road Initiative (BRI) gaining momentum. The fact that Australians showed no welcome to Harris's ambassadorship to Australia and the possibility of signing a new free trade agreement among China, Japan and SK as well as the recent private Summit of Indian Prime Minister Modi and China's President Xi contemplating closer relationship could be interpreted as a no-confidence vote on the US 'Pivot' policy on its current course. Therefore, the Trump Administration is better advised to redefine the 'pivot' policy to produce win-win results for the U.S. and Asian countries including China rather than targeting China creating a stressful Pacific.

Chapter 20
Economic Development, Income Inequality and Wealth Gap

*****

The most challenging problem in economics is not in the understanding of the theory or the model of economic development which is evidenced by the fact that many nations' GDPs have been steadily increasing as various economic development models are applied. The real challenge lies in the finding of a solution to limit the wealth gap created by the economic development. The wealth gap in a society is invariably the consequence of economic growth. All economic development models based on the principle of getting uniform return across all the society members seem to be fruitless. A few as practiced by the communist countries have proven to be a failure when compared with other economic development models based on capitalism.

There seem to be two fundamental factors producing the above outcome. First, capital is a necessary ingredient for economic development and it must be applied strategically, selectively and timely to development projects to yield optimum return. Second, Human Resources are necessary for economic development but they must be selected based on human intelligence and talents, trained with right skills and knowledge and motivated by a driving force to devote energy and time in economic development projects. The above first condition also depends on talented humans to manage the capital under a management system ranging from a totally free capital system to a totally government controlled capital system with varying degree of man-made regulations. The second condition usually can be met by a competitive education system and a talent selection scheme. The motivation, however, is rooted in human nature, that is human's desire for material or asset possession and a self-defined life style, which ultimately leads to wealth accumulation. We might term this model as 'capital-talent' model for later reference. Under this model, wealth has become the most effective and consequential motivation factor for talented humans to engage in productive economic projects. Even in the charity organizations and religious institutions, this materialistic motivation factor cannot be ignored. That is why successful charity organizations pay their executives millions of dollars in salary and all successful churches pay their pastors with full range of amenities including housing, cars, phones, salaries above average parishioners' income and cushy retirement benefits.

There are ample successful examples of nations as well as private corporations applying the capital-talent economic development model. Just following post WW II world economic development, the U.S., Germany, Japan, and the four little dragons in Asia all can offer solid 'case' examples to support the above conclusions. China, after switching from an unsuccessful socialistic economic model to a 'capital-talent' model, albeit knowing the wealth gap issue and willingly letting a small group of smart people to drive their economy and getting rich, has shown us an non-debatable success story of economic development. So did many other nations and global corporations succeed in building their enterprises under the above principle. China's rapid rise in economy or her GDP growth is accomplished with the consequence of the above capital and human driven economic development model producing the wealth gap phenomenon, a small number of people possess a large portion of the national wealth.

The U. S. is the wealthiest nation on earth as far as her national GDP and total assets is concerned. The U.S. is a capitalist country and is a beacon for the world coming to pursuing capitalistic economic development. However, the wealth gap problem in the U.S. is likely the most severe case. The wealth gap of course is produced and compounded yearly by income inequality (income gap). In 2015, the bottom 90% of people in the U.S. had an average income of $34K and the top 10% had an average income of $312K, nearly ten-fold difference. What is more shocking is that the top 1% average income was $1.36M and top 0.1% was $6.75M, 200 times greater than the average income of 90% of population. It is clear that income inequality will produce a larger wealth gap, since the majority of U.S. citizens are not making enough money to save or build assets. Based on the data from Internal Revenue Service and Congressional Budget Office, since 1979, the before-tax incomes of the top 1% of America's households have increased four times more than the bottom 20% population's income. The after-tax incomes of top 1% has increased on average 192.2% since 1979 -2013 whereas the corresponding before-tax income of top 1% has increased on average 186.8%. This shows that the tax system does not cure the income inequality problem and its consequential wealth gap issue. The U.S. has used welfare program to boost the income of the bottom 0-40% of the population, but the above data indicates that so long as the economic development operates under the 'capital-talent' model and its principles derived from human nature, the income inequality and wealth gap will persist. Even in the top income population, the same problem exists; the highest 0.1% income earners have seen their income rise much faster than the rest of top 1%. (The top 400 earners doubled their earning from 1992 to 2002) The seriousness of the wealth gap can be illustrated by the following statistics: In 2013, the top 10% of family holdings held 76% of the national wealth whereas the bottom 50% of the families held 1%, a rapid worsening from 1989 to 2013.

China has adopted the 'capital-talent' model thus naturally we expect the same consequence - creation of wealth gap in the nation, although no detailed statistics on household income and household holdings over the past five decades are available. China currently is applying a harsh anti-corruption measure to breakdown illegally created wealth but that is not the same wealth accumulated through the 'capital-talent' model. China has seen an amazing progress of economic development. The speed of economic development is naturally correlated with the amount of capital and talented Human Resources available. China's GDP was less than $100 billion in 1971 to $12.8 trillion in 2017, an increase of 129X signifying a rapid rise. From available data (1952-2017 six and half decades), China's GDP was $30.55B to $113.69B(1952-1972), an increase of 3.72X for two decades, $113.69B to $493.14B(1972-1992), an increase of 4.34X, and $493.14B to $12840.39B(1992-2017), an increase of 26X. These data support the 'capital-talent' model; from 1992 to 2017, China has the fastest growth of capital, educated talents and the impetus of Internet revolution making China the manufacturer of the world. Unfortunately, the higher the speed of economic growth is, the bigger the wealth gap will occur. Big wealth gap will produce social instability in any governance system. Something must be done to reduce the wealth gap, otherwise social unrest will take place. The tax system and welfare program (including minimum wage) practiced in the U.S. can not cure the income inequality and wealth gap problem without destroying people's incentive to take on productive work. Perhaps, one suggestion to redistribute wealth is to encourage wealthy people to make large tax deductible donations to (1) Public infrastructure funds, funds for constructing roads from city to rural regions, airports, train stations, ports, bridges, museums, parks, and public transportation and utilities allowing donors names to be put on them and (2) Innovation funds, funds for supporting science and technology research benefitting the public and the nation. Government can establish these funds with low yields to let wealthy people to invest their wealth but benefit the less wealthy more.

Chapter 21
Trump's Next Move - A Peace Treaty for Korea Peninsula Is Necessary for Real Peace

*****

"Nearly five hours of unprecedented and surreal talks between US President Donald Trump and North Korea's Kim Jong Un culminated on Tuesday (June 12th in Singapore) with fulsome declarations of a new friendship but just vague pledge of nuclear disarmament.", reported by Kevin Liptak on CNN website in an article entitled, 'Trump's North Korean gamble ends with 'special bond' with Kim'. Despite of being a historical event where the two leaders extended their handshake giving the world-wide news reporters an opportunity to capture an image of openly friendly gesture, the real accomplishment of the meeting did not go beyond what Kim had said in April nor added any substance over Trump's praise of Kim being a talented young man. Now the Korea Peninsula issue is in the shadow; the world is preoccupied by the trade wars, President Trump has just put it in high-gear.

But the peace in Korea Peninsula is a very serious matter; it is not only a concern of the Korean people but also on the minds of Chinese and Japanese, neighbors of Koreans, for decades. The essence of the problem is not limited to denuclearization by North Korea (NK) or to stopping military exercises and pulling out troops by the U.S. The core issue is whether or not there will be a real peace treaty signed by the two Koreas (NK & SK) and the U.S. witnessed by their neighboring nations, China, Japan and Russia. For the Korea Peninsula region, the ultimate goal is to have a genuine peace treaty. Of course, the essence of a peace treaty will require denuclearization, removal of foreign troops and final reunification of two Koreas or at least a friendly coexistence of two Koreas under a peace treaty. The history of West and East Germany and the present day united Germany surely serves as a good lesson and model for the Korea Peninsula problem.

Why isn't a peace treaty signed in 1954 when the Korean War was halted by the leaders then, Kim Il Sung, NK, Syngman Rhee, SK and Dwight Eisenhower, the U.S.? At that time, there was no nuclear threat issue. The military strength of the U.S. was overwhelming. It was almost certain that the U.S. could get a peace treaty between the two Koreas if she wanted to. For over six decades, NK has consistently proposed peace agreement to replace the armistice agreement wishing to end the abnormal situation - military tension – to a normal relation - Peace. D. shin, an academician, in his article, North Korea's Perspectives in Its Argument for A Peace Treaty, published in Asian Affairs, 48:3, 510-528, online on September 14, 2017 (https://doi.org/10.1080/03068374.2017.1361244), argued to support the above NK position by "making a detailed examination of North Korean texts to fully understand its perspective, rather than a reliance on conjecture about its intentions and policy objectives".

Many experts argue that the NK proposal for a peace treaty has always been a strategic deception. Shin's study on the NK's proposed languages on peace treaty and various statements over the years was to find what the definition of peace in NK's perspective is and to justify putting peace treaty on the negotiation table to resolve the Korea Peninsula issue. In the past, I have discussed that it is necessary to accept the idea of reunification of the two Koreas and to achieve a true peace treaty in order to resolve the Korea Peninsula problem. I am glad to see that Shin's findings are consistent with my thought.

It is worthwhile to summarize Shin's conclusions below in a few concise statements to appreciate NK's perspective on the peace issue, perhaps helpful in solving the NK dilemma:

1. Peace means ending of the armistice status - the current situation of military tension in Korea Peninsula and isolation of NK from the world -, both are abnormal.

2. The Armistice Agreement does (did) not define the 'final peace'. Reunification is the ultimate goal.

3. Armistice is the anti-thesis of peace. The current armistice did not reflect or honor the agreement. ("For example, the commander in chief of the United Nations Command (UNC) was a signatory of the Armistice Agreement and the UNC was dissolved by the 30th Session of the UN General Assembly held in 1975 but the Armistice Agreement did not reflect this changed reality. In addition, NK claimed that the US violated the Armistice Agreement by appointing a SK general as a senior member of the Military Armistice Commission (MAC) in 1991and by withdrawing the Neutral Nations Supervisory Commission (NNSC).")

4. The assignment of the U.S. military and shipments of large quantity of military equipment to SK by the U.S. are obstacles to peace. (NK realizes the nuclear weapon she developed is a major obstacle to peace.)

NK essentially wants to have a peace guarantee and certain peace mechanisms leading to peace. Peace treaty is the necessary step to reach a genuine peace with reunification or a friendly coexistence of two Koreas as the final goal.

Though the NK and SK governments have not focused on the term 'reunification' frequently due to political consideration but the people of Korea do equate that to the ultimate peace. International problems are often solved by intelligent world leaders; skidding back to the 1954 Geneva conference on Korea may elucidate this point.

Recently, I had the fortune to have met a giant journalist, Mr. Seymour Topping, former NY Times Managing Editor and Administrator of Pulitzer Prizes, and had begun to read his books. In one of his books published in 1971, coauthored with Tillman Durdin and James Reston, The New York Times Report from Red China, I came across many interesting chapters reporting about China, political observations, China's transformation, Nixon's historical China visit, as well as interview with Premier Chou En-Lai. One particular chapter contributed by Audrey Ronning (Mrs. Seymour Topping, a photojournalist and Prose Award Winner, whom I had the honor to be acquainted with), entitled, Premier Reminisces with an 'Old Friend', had a passage very relevant to our discussion here. Premier Chou En-Lai met with Chester Ronning, Audrey's father, Charge' d'affairs of the Canadian Embassy and their conversation turned to the 1954 Geneva Conference on Korea, where Mr. Chou headed the Chinese delegation and Mr. Ronning was the acting head of the Canadian delegation.

Chou was known to push for the peace treaty for the Korean Peninsula. In Audrey Ronning's chapter, she wrote: "It was recalled how Mr. Chou had opposed the permanent closing of the conference when it became deadlocked. Instead, he proposed that it be adjourned sine die, to be recalled when the time seemed more appropriate to replace the Korean armistice of July, 1953, with a peace treaty." ""if we had accepted your proposal at the Korean conference," Mr. Ronning said, "we could have had a peace treaty."" This passage strokes me hard, indeed, Mr. Chou was a great statesman and he could see clear and far. In 1954, Gen. Walter Bedell Smith, head of the U.S. delegate at the Geneva conference and President Dwight Eisenhower were too much influenced by the US military to see the political value of a peace treaty versus an armistice. If a proper peace treaty was established in 1954, history would have been rewritten, no nuclear threat from Korea today.

Sixty four years later, the Korea Peninsula problem falls on the lap of President Trump, a self-claimed non-politician and expert on negotiation. Having a summit meeting with NK leader Kim Jung-En was Trump's bold move but following through to achieve a genuine peace in Korea Peninsula benefitting the world requires Mr. Trump to think and act like a great statesman. We Americans hope that President Trump will reflect on the history and absorb the wisdom of many great leaders before him and make a genuine peace deal for Korea Peninsula.

Chapter 22
Can Taiwan CEO's Simple Logic Proposal Solve the Cross-Strait Confrontation?

*****

Robert HC Tsao, former CEO of United Microelectronics Corporation, a pioneer of information technology in Taiwan, has recently released a video on YouTube making a simple and logical proposal to solve the cross-strait confrontation problem, known as 'unification issue', one perspective or as 'Taiwan Independence' issue, another perspective. There are numerous interpretations or opinions spanning across the two perspectives presenting a very confusing or muddled political discourse in Taiwan resulting in a chaotic political scene. Even though, the Taiwan issue had its origin as a Chinese domestic issue, the evolvement of 'Taiwan problem' since WW II has become an international problem with the U.S. having a deterministic influence and many other nations having a diplomatic revelation such as accepting one China policy and which China to recognize? Mr. Tsao's video presented a clear discussion of the 'Taiwan Problem' and offered a simple proposal to solve the problem with consideration of the political positions of the two parties, DDP and KMT, and the party platform of the Republican and Democrat parties of the U.S. on the Taiwan issue. Mr. Tsao's effort is plausible and his 'impartial' proposal deserves attention not only from the Chinese from both sides of the Taiwan Strait but also from Americans and Chinese Americans in the U.S. Mr. Tsao's video is made in Mandarin, thus this article is written in English to broaden its audience and to engage additional discussions on different perspectives on the Taiwan issue inside and outside of Taiwan.

Mr. Tsao based his proposal and arguments on the following points:
1. KMT has always advocated reunification but lack of feasible method thus adopted a fuzzy and useless policy of "not to reunify, not to be independent and not to resort on military action". On the other hand, DPP has passed its platform regarding Taiwan's future: Taiwan is a de-facto self governed society with a functioning government, any change of Taiwan's status must be determined by all Taiwan citizens through referendum ballot. Based on the above, it is illogical to have a citizens' referendum on Taiwan Independence but it is logical to have a citizens' referendum on unification issue to determine how and when unification is feasible.

2. On the other side, Mainland has passed an anti-separation law. In its Article 16 regarding Taiwan: the government shall use peaceful means to achieve reunification, fulfilling the benefits of the citizens on both sides of the Taiwan Strait and after reunification Taiwan can maintain self-governance.

3. From the position of the U.S., the 2016 Republican Party Convention has passed the following resolution: Any question concerning Taiwan's future must be determined by peaceful means and through dialogue obtaining all Taiwan citizens' agreement. Whereas, the 2012 Democrat party Convention adopted the following resolution: The U.S. continue to adhere to one China policy and the Taiwan Relation Act, all disputes should be resolved with peaceful means with all citizens' agreement and their maximum benefit.

Based on the above, Mr. Tsao argued logically, using citizens referendum with no time limit to determine the acceptance of reunification under what appropriate conditions is a feasible approach to resolve the Taiwan issue. Only a minor modification on Taiwan's referendum Law is required to facilitate such referendum. Both Mainland and Taiwan governments would be encouraged to apply peaceful means and to develop appropriate conditions to fulfill reunification.

Mr. Tsao's proposal, although sounds logical, possibly meeting approvals of many people, but it faces challenges from the following oppositions:

A. A minority of people in Taiwan is not only resisting reunification under any condition but also practicing an anti-China ideology. This minority faction has grown from Lee Deng-Hui's era and has influenced Taiwan's two major parties creating an illogical and chaotic political atmosphere converting a domestic reunification issue to a hostile rebellion movement. So long as the Taiwan citizens are mesmerized by an illogical 'hatred' driven political movement, the reunification referendum proposal cannot be implemented.

B. Judging the positions of the Republican and Democrat parties, one observes that although both parties advocate peaceful means (dialogue and referendum) to settle Taiwan issue, the two parties have never genuinely promoted reunification. In fact, the Republican Party dropped the 'One China Policy' term in its party resolution in 2016 and the current US Republican Administration is doing the opposite against 'reunification'. The US diplomatic plays and sales of military gears to Taiwan including offering submarine development assistance all indicated that the U.S. is changing her China and Taiwan policy revealing somewhat devious motive and hypocritical elements.

Mainland China's concern on Taiwan's using referendum to settle Taiwan issue is directly related to the above points. The core concern is that a small fraction of people in Taiwan may hijack the will of 23 million Taiwan citizens which in turn may rob away the desire of 1.4 billion Chinese citizens of a chance to achieve reunification. At this point, it is not whether or not the conditions for reunification are ripe; Mainland China has continuously offered benefits to Taiwan and Taiwan citizens, but the current Taiwan Administration is following a divisive and anti-China recipe to resist reunification. Knowing that Taiwan media and even the U.S. media to some extent can be manipulated; referendum balloting can hardly be trusted. Numerous international referendum events serve as proof of that - all international interferences in national referendum are for foreign benefits and not domestic benefits.

Recently, I have joined a US-China Forum organized fact-finding trip traveling through both Taiwan and Mainland China on the 'reunification versus independence' issue. From my observations, Taiwan problem has become a cancer (constant worries and many rush diagnoses and treatment proposals), the current chemo-treatment (political actions, election, referendum, etc) is destroying more internal organs than killing the cancer cells. The cancel cells are in the brain clouding clear thinking and muddying judgement and logic). Perhaps some herb medicine (education on Chinese history and media reform to quash fake news) is needed to cure the cancer. We hope and pray that the herb medicine is not too late and too slow to save Taiwan from parish, a highly probable scenario due to the possibility of "Taiwan Issue' triggering a war in Asia.

Chapter 23
Trading Never Should End up with A Trade War

*****

Trading is a human trait ever since humans formed societies from the Stone Age, through the agricultural era then to the industrialization centuries. Human civilization advanced by creating and embracing technologies which ever more enhanced the necessities of trading. Trading is a bilateral act consummated by negotiation under a mutually agreed trading system involving transportation and distribution logistics and financing and payment mechanisms. When negotiation is abandoned, history showed us, trading war begins harming human societies to a pain level that a military war may occur. The two past world wars were clear evidence of that. Today, our world is witnessing a serious trading war launched by President Trump of the U.S. Why does a self proclaimed great negotiator want to abandon negotiation and initiate a trade war? This is a puzzling question we need to find an answer.

For the benefit of doubt, since the trade war is just launched, we may speculate that Trump's trade war is really a part of his negotiation tactics. Then why does Trump have to resort to trade war to adjust trading pattern and to correct trading results? Trump's tariff on aluminum and steel not only punishes China but also impacts Canada, India, Mexico, and Several EU countries. The 25% tariff on 34 billion Chinese goods has triggered China's retaliating reaction but Trump has added 10% tariff on $200 billion Chinese goods which are still being tabulated by the Commerce Department. This type of rash behavior can hardly be seen as the action of a rational government practicing a deliberated thought process to develop trade policies. Of course, no one has enough information nor any psychic power to read into President Trump's mind to know the answers to the why questions. As a citizen one has the right to analyze the trade issue at hand based on common sense and voice one's opinion whether the government's current trade policy hurts the U.S. or not.

President Trump seems to feel that the U.S. has been taken advantage of by the world for too long in trading ("allowed by the previous administrations") that it is difficult for the U.S.(for him as President) to correct the ills without taking extreme measures; in his view, the extreme measure can include denying all previous trade agreements and starting from fresh using trade war as a tool to pressure the trading partners since the U.S. has a large market. However, trade agreements and trade practices were accepted willingly by trading partners through negotiations. It is hard to believe that the American people involved in the past trade negotiations were all dummies who would give away the store for not getting anything in return. Looking back we see that the U.S. has always held a strong trading position with her abundant agricultural products and energy resources, despite of an oil cartel and many countries desire to have self sufficiency in food supply. The U.S. conscientiously lets her low-tech labor intensive manufacturing industry disappear and deliberately maintains her hi-tech capital intensive industries to flourish and lead the world. The U.S. also created and excelled in a sophisticated financial industry attracting capitals to the U.S. either for investing in her risky hi-tech development or for financing American debts.

There is nothing wrong with the above strategy except one must realize that every developing country in the world is trying to move up in the technology ladder to take advantage of productivity gain from technology rather than being satisfied with maintaining low-tech industries to produce cheap goods for the developed nations. The above U.S. strategy has been working for decades in favor of the U.S. so long as the advancement and innovations in her own hi-tech industries can keep ahead of the competitive followers. When competitors caught up then the U.S. may lose. For example, the American auto-industry used to dominate the world until competitors crushed them. American airplane industry can export one plane worth more than million pairs of shoes or pants imported if no competitor is behind. With smart marketing and trademark protection, some vast amount of low-tech products imported into the US market is creating huge profits for American companies. For example, a pair of Nike sneakers is typically sold at prices of multiple times than their import value making a huge profit for Nike and its stock holders but no benefit for American workers who lost their Nike jobs. The no brand imports, of course, do contribute to trade imbalance, but their low prices (say shoes and pants) actually benefit lower income Americans who can only afford the cheap imports.

The issue of trade imbalance between the U.S. and China, therefore, is not as simple as the import and export figures indicate nor as "American jobs stolen by China" as retorted by Trump in his campaign. Labor intensive industries face the challenge of labor cost thus they migrate from developed countries to developing countries as a natural economic movement. Any government protection scheme including tariffs can only slow down their migration a bit but eventually fails. This phenomenon existed for many decades and the only sensible solution is to create new industries based on hi-technology components to maintain a competitive edge or gain higher productivity. However, hi-tech industries may create new jobs but they may also eliminate existing jobs especially labor intensive ones. Apparently, China has learned from others' experiences, she is launching a technology and innovation drive ("China Manufacturing 2025") to upgrade their industries to higher value chain but with a focus on achieving a net job increase not job loss. This is nothing new; Germany has her German Industry 4.0. In U.S., the government neglected the manufacturing industry for years in favor of financial industry resulting in today's dilemma: The U.S. highly depends on manufacturing imports and financial product exports. The imports are more physical necessity products and the exports depend more on a debt ridden society (like the U.S. highly depended on debt refinancing to get by).

So Trump's attempt to use trade war to stop China Manufacturing 2025 and force her to open up financial markets is not a logical policy; not only China will not accept it, it also does not necessarily help the U.S. The sensible solution is to accelerate technology innovation and sell more (rather than restrict) high-tech sales to China. China recognizes the value of her market size, capable of attracting technology companies to come to China to make and sell hi-tach products. Technologies are protected by patents but patents are just a piece of paper without markets to accept their applications. The U.S. should exploit the huge market in China to sell her technology products to make profit and sustain her technology development to maintain her leadership position. For example, GM makes 10 million cars; 4 million are manufactured and sold in China. The question is whether GM is plowing back its profit to develop advanced technology to maintain a technology lead or simply to distribute its profit as dividends. Tesla with its technology lead in electric vehicle is setting up manufacturing factory and research and development center in China. Obviously, Tesla is valuing China's market thus ignoring President Trump's pledge to keep manufacturing in the U.S.

The above discussion is just common sense analysis not deep economic theory, but it is sufficient to tell us that Trump's trade war policy does not solve the US trade problem nor help her industry revitalization. The U.S. needs to understand China's market value and the scope of China's 2025 manufacturing industry upgrade. The U.S. should come up with her industry policy to leverage her lead in many technologies and to take advantage of China's market to accelerate manufacturing of technology products, develop and sell products for Chinese markets and sustain her lead in technologies.

Chapter 24
Reciprocal Thinking on US-China Relations: Technology and Trade (I)

*****

Abstract

Regarding US-China relation, there are different views from citizens versus government's perspective. Recently, the US-China relation has tensed up especially with the threat of an all out trade war despite of economists' warning of a mutually devastating outcome. It is time to conduct a Reciprocal Thinking Process (RTP) to understand the issues from both sides' point of view. In this article such an exercise is made and presented as two parts. The fact of life is that every country is pursuing technology development to move up the ladder knowing that such a process always brings endless competition. One has no choice but to face it to succeed or retreat to failure. Perhaps through a RTP, one can find win-win solution to pursue a complimentary path with one's opponent.

Two folksy thoughts on US-China relation existed for decades but now being questioned as the two great nations took a sharp turn in their current relation towards a cliff facing a deadly fall. In the U.S., folks used to believe that their nation is so great, far more advanced than China; the US way of life will induce Chinese people to follow their footsteps to convert China to become more like the U.S. in ways similar to most Atlantic nations and some Asian countries like Japan and South Korea. In China, on the other hand, folks used to believe that their nation has been so weak, far weaker than the U.S.; they must work hard to become a middle income nation and keep focusing on economic development like many other developed nations did to become as rich as Americans. These folksy beliefs however were somewhat countered by a different 'official', 'elite' or 'think tank driven' notion. In the U.S., the notion is that a communist system is a dictator system which will never change unless the leader is toppled or the regime is changed, hence a communist country will always be an enemy of the U.S. This notion is repeated in every presidential election year with Russia and China being the targets. In China, the official notion is that the U.S. will always behave like an imperial nation trying to dominate the world, putting American national interest far above everyone else's. The American government will ask you to do what they say but not to do what they do.

Therefore, the US-China relations had never gotten more than a lukewarm mutual recognized relationship. China tried seriously to improve relationship but cautiously concerned with the US China policy treating Taiwan more as a US military outpost than a province of China making Taiwan as a thorn on China's sea fare side. The citizens of two nations interacted fairly well with exchange students, inter-race marriages and gradual understanding of the cultural differences. However, the interactions of citizens have little effect on the governments' foreign policies both in China and in the U.S. with their media ignoring their citizens' opinion in different ways. Therefore, the official US-China relation remain to be lukewarm but it didn't get any worse for decades until now. China was very cautious (low-key) in her nation building process and the U.S. was pre-occupied by many other international issues until she had recognized that China's economy had surpassed Japan to be the number two in the world in merely two decades. Surprised and envious about China's rapid rise may have stimulated the government's strong reaction.

For three or four decades, the US-China relation has indeed been seesawing up and down when encountered with international affairs but never broken. But today, the headline news in the U.S. about the US-China relation tends to paint a hostile story - China is a threat. China is rising too fast using unfair practices. China is the culprit causing the US domestic ills by stealing her manufacturing jobs. Thus, the U.S. is launching a trade war, specifically against China and her developmental plan – China manufacture 2025, to prevent China catching up with the U.S. China, on the other hand, claims that she deserves to have their Chinese dream, rising peacefully. She is contributing to the world economy and prosperity by working diligently since joining the World Trade Organization (WTO). China claims that she will never kneel to imperialism like a century ago (forced to sign unfair trade treaties under the naval gun power of the imperialists) and she will rigorously defend her sovereignty and hard earned achievement by retaliating against any tariff war or any war. Therefore, the U.S. and China appear now pushing each other towards a dangerous cliff. Histories have taught us world wars had been started under such a sentiment. Citizens of two countries cannot help be concerned that the U.S. and China may break out an all out trade war hurting each other even possibly a military war leading to mutual destruction.

War can be started by emotional flare but it also can be avoided by cool logic thinking. It is time for the U.S. and China to do just that. The best way to obtain a fair and logical analysis is to conduct a 'reciprocal thinking process' (RTP). Of course, this RTP should not just be applied on the military confrontation where the thought process is primarily focused on willing a military war. The RTP must be applied on a higher strategic level where the objective is to understand the thinking of the other side, why the two nations develop tension and how the tension may be reduced to avoid war, even possibly finding win-win solutions to improve the two nations' relation and to obtain mutual benefits. Put in a folksy description: We must put ourselves in each other's shoes and wear each other's hats to think, walk and act so to feel how each may appreciate how the tension is generated and how it may be reduced. In the following, we will try to conduct a RTP on the US-China relation in technology and trade.

The U.S. claimed her independence from British colonial control by revolution. She became a great nation through 'acquisitions' more or less justified by imperialistic behavior prevalent during the colonial era (America 1492-1820 World 1492-1945 Decolonization 1945-1999). To some degree, the U.S. has refrained from being an aggressive colonial power like U.K, France, Germany, Spain, Portugal, Japan and other nations. The U.S. did acquire territories through border conflict or acquisition but she ultimately maintained peaceful relations with her two major neighbors, Canada and Mexico. Thus, the American citizens were taught not to think their country as an imperial nation but a country welcoming immigrants against colonialism. The U.S. is rich with resources and blessed with huge amount of farm land allowing them to become a big agriculture exporting nation. The U.S. is a big nation with relatively a small population; hence their agricultural products meet more than her own needs. With technological advances, the surplus is huge. The US government uses subsidy to regulate agriculture production, to maintain prices of farm goods to allow farmers to make a good profit. That policy is for the interest of the U.S. not for the needy countries or world food supply. The U.S. led the allies to fight WW II and was the only country spared with war damage on her continent other than the surprise attack of Pearl Harbor by the Japanese military. The WW II victory had propelled the U.S. as the de facto world leader strong militarily and in most areas of technology. Her persistent fight against the expansion of communism not only collapsed the Soviet Union but further secured her position as the strongest nation leading the world. It is understandable that the U.S. treasures and desires to preserve her leadership position.

Chapter 25
Reciprocal Thinking on US-China Relations: Technology and Trade (II)

*****

Abstract

Regarding US-China relation, there are different views from citizens versus government's perspective. Recently, the US-China relation has tensed up especially with the threat of an all out trade war despite of economists' warning of a mutually devastating outcome. It is time to conduct a Reciprocal Thinking Process (RTP) to understand the issues from both sides' point of view. In this article such an exercise is made and presented as two parts. The fact of life is that every country is pursuing technology development to move up the ladder knowing that such a process always brings endless competition. One has no choice but to face it to succeed or retreat to failure. Perhaps through a RTP, one can find win-win solution to pursue a complimentary path with one's opponent.

Now look at it from the other side. The world has seen famine and starvation for centuries. The populated nations with limited farmland like China, India, Japan, etc. must have sufficient agricultural products to feed their citizens. Their policies can only fall on two choices, one to work hard to produce their products to trade for food and other resources lacking; and the alternative is to develop their own agricultural products to feed themselves. The former case depends on a fair stable functioning trading system free of price manipulation and trade barriers. The latter approach is hard to achieve but necessary if the trading route is not reliable. The U.S. has always been in an envious position regarding agricultural industry. Why today many nations, including China and Japan, work extremely hard to develop their own agricultural industry, even limiting importing the abundant US agricultural products? This is an RTP question to be pondered. Did the U.S. do something wrong in her policies? Why do the other countries feel insecure to rely on US agricultural supply? Now with trade war looming, a serious RTP should be made on these questions immediately to avoid a trade war or a military war triggered by food supply.

As countries develop, they move up in the technology ladder. The U.S. has been leading in many technologies and certainly understand the phenomena of obsolesces created by technology advances. Come with technology advances, there is productivity gain but unfortunately often incurring loss in manual jobs. That is the fact of life; every developing country is pursuing that route knowingly. It is the government and industry leaders' responsibility to manage the development process. A technologically advanced country must be prepared to maintain her advancement and accept other countries catching up in some technologies. This will happen within an industry and selectively industry by industry; ultimately the process will make some industries disappear in hi-tech nations. If a high-tech nation cannot create new jobs and new industries to replace the lost ones, there will be a serious social problem. Again this is a fact of life and one cannot blame other countries for losing an industry or its jobs. The hi-tech nation must accept this outcome and try to fix this problem with innovation. Keep developing hi-tech products and selling to low tech countries is the logical way of keeping the hi-tech industry growing. Restricting hi-tech export and forcing other countries not to pursue technological advances do not seem to be logical nor fair policies. One must apply the RTP and figure out complimentary technology development since no country can monopolize all technologies either due to limitation on natural resources (such as oil or rare earth metal) or lack of educated or trained talents. As reflected in the stock market, hi-tech and innovative companies drive the economy. That is the fundamental reason that nearly every nation wants to move up in the technology ladder if possible. It is no surprise that China and most developing countries are pursuing technology development and innovation.To help their progress, they use their markets as a leverage to obtain technology. The U.S. considers that an unfair practice from a technology leader's perspective. But let's apply RTP on technology and market holders. Technology is protected by patents. Presumably patents can enable hi-tech product manufacturing but hi-tech products need markets. Without market, product is useless then patents become worthless. Therefore, countries with markets can use market value to bargain and gain technology value. History tells us corporations sometimes buy and bury patents to protect their existing products and their market share. This corporate practice may prevent competitive products to surface for a while but eventually the corporations will get beaten by the startups unless they strive in innovations continuously. The startups must find their market place to grow. This process has no national borders in today's world. Technology companies must find market place to make profits as long and as fast as they can before competition arrives. To deal with competition, one must keep inventing and innovating to stay competitive or move on to a newer and higher technology territory. Countries are just like collection of corporations; they should not thwart other country's competitiveness which is the impetus for technological advances. Therefore, technology leading countries have no choice but work in the same way like hard working startups to compete and to keep moving up in the technology ladder.

China has been growing fast in the past several decades. They have cleverly recognized the value of her market size. Perhaps learned through her sad experience in late 19th and early 20th century when the Western powers forced her to open her markets under naval guns. Japan is a living case for striving in technology acquisition and eventually developing her own technology in certain key areas. If Japan can succeed, why can't China succeed since China has far more natural resources and human talents than Japan does? It is understandable that China is not only protective of her markets but is also strategically leveraging her markets for gaining technology advances. For example, in the area of high-speed railway arena, Japan's fast bullet train was leading the world competing with France. Now decades later, China has surpassed them to be the leader of high-speed rail. China has the need for high speed public transport because of her large population and vast land area. The government made conscientious decision to develop the technology to serve her own market. Now they can export that technology. The U.S. with just as big land mass also has a need for high speed public transportation, but why isn't she developing her high-speed rail systems? Some blame the US auto-industry which pushes for high-ways and automobiles than for rails and trains. The question is what should the U.S.do to correct mistakes of public transportation policy and stay competitive?

The electric cars, buses and trains are the next wave of new technology. It is never too late to do a RTP to figure out a sensible approach. The American electric car company, Tesla, elects to build a huge 500,000 vehicle manufacturing factory in Shanghai, China to address the need of a strong Chinese electric car market, will they succeed like IPHONE becoming a dominating technology product making vast amount of profit? IPHONE faces competition from Huawei and Xiaomi and Tesla probably will have a strong competitor as well. But so what, while one is leading in technology, it can open markets and make profit, the important thing is to plow back the profit for new technology development rather than just paying back to shareholders or greedy investors. In fact, conducting a RTP will yield simple conclusions: technologies bring progress to civilization but inevitably always bring competition as well. One must accept competition as a fact of life. Face it to succeed or retreat to failure.

Chapter 26
Outlook of US-China Trade Relations under WTO

*****

World Trade Organization (WTO) is an international institution. Although it is not an agency of the U.N., it has a strong relation with the U.N. WTO is an intergovernmental organization concerned with international trade regulation. It was established on January 1, 1995 under the GATT Marrakesh Agreement, signed by 123 nations on April 15, 1994. GATT (General Agreement on Tariffs and Trade) was established after WW II in 1948 after economists recommended the establishment of three international institutions to manage, promote and regulate world economy, namely the International Money Fund (IMF, concerning with fiscal and monetary issues), the World Bank (WB, concerning with financial and structural issues) and the International Trade Organization (ITO, for international trade and economic cooperation). The three organizations were proposed to be part of the United Nations system. The ITO was to be a UN specialized agency to address not only trade barriers but other issues indirectly related to trade, including employment, investment, restrictive business practices, and commodity agreements. However, the ITO treaty was not approved by the U.S. and a few other nation members thus never became a reality. Hence, GATT had to transform into an international organization to deal with international trade. Reviewing GATT's history, one can see its complex growth just from the statistics of its 'meeting rounds' - starting year, number of members and length of meeting in months: (4/47, 23, 7; 4/49, 34, 5; 9/50, 34, 8; 1/56, 22, 5; 5/60. 45, 11; 5/64, 48, 37; 9/73, 102, 74; 9/86, 123, 87; 11/2001, 159, still going on). Membership grew to 159 with meeting became continuous nearly every month.

It was at the end of Uruguay round (1986-1994), the Marrakesh Agreement was signed to establish WTO (commenced on 1-1-1995). The standards of GATT on trade in goods were updated and additional 60 agreements added into the WTO agreement, falling under six categories: 1. General WTO member agreement, 2. Goods and investments, 3. Services, 4. Intellectual properties, 5. Dispute settlements and 6. Review of government trade policies (TPRM). In fact, WTO just published its TPRM on China on July 13, 2018.

The report contains 38 summary points mostly with positive comments, meaning making improvements and adhering to WTO regulations. China is moving more to consumption based economy, reducing merchandise trade in percentage of GDP with growing services, improving in processing imports, one third of imports through one window taking 16.7 hours in 2017 down from 22 hours in 2016 and only 1.1 hour for processing exports in 2017, amazing efficiency. China has opened more free trade zones and allowed more foreign investment especially encouraging oil exploration. China's State involvement in economy remains (which contributed to China's success but also drew criticism from the U.S.) and China still maintains a price control list on commodities and services (that impact national economy and people's livelihood) which was updated with items such as explosive materials, tobacco, drugs and construction projects removed. Over all, the WTO has a positive effect on China in managing her economic development and contribution to the world economy.

The last WTO review on the U.S. was in 2016, the 2018 report has not been produced yet. The 2016 report pointed out the deteriorating infrastructure and rising income gap as the challenges for the U.S. as well as her concern of anti-dumping, having 269 AD orders as of 6/2016 against China, EU, India, Japan, S. Korea and Taiwan concentrated in the steel industry. The anti-dumping issue is an odd topic in economics. When nations selling goods to another nation at low price (subsidized), the Importer has the freedom to accept or reject the sales. It is hardly a devastating problem, say, compared to a nation monopolizing a certain technology or material or goods and selling at a very high price. One well known example is medicine which many poor countries cannot afford to buy. It will be interesting to see how the WTO 2018 TPRM report will say about the trade war launched by President Trump and what impact it may have on WTO members. The WTO deals with regulation of trade between participating countries by providing a framework for negotiating trade agreements and a dispute resolution process aimed at enforcing participants' adherence to WTO agreements. Most of the issues that the WTO focuses on were derived from previous trade negotiations, from the **Uruguay Round** (1986–1994) to Doha Round (2001 to present). For example, the average tariff levels for GATT participants was 22 percent in 1947, reduced to 15% in 1960's and further reduced to below 5% after the Uruguay Round. The economic historian Douglas Irwin at Dartmouth attributed the prosperity of the world economy, the growth of world trade, over the past half century to the creation of GATT and WTO. Now the U.S. is threatening to pull out of WTO, unilaterally imposing tariffs (25% on steel, 10% on Aluminum imports and 10% on Chinese imports and threatening to apply new tariffs on 500 billion Chinese goods), rejecting existing trade agreements and seeking unilateral preference negotiation. Granted, President Trump might have a point that the

US economy and her trade relations with the world were the result of previous US Administrations, however, any change of policy must be well thought out and debated. The current US action seems to be random and impulsive, certainly disturbing to the world economy and the stability WTO was created to maintain.

China first gained observer status in GATT in1986, working towards joining that organization. China hoped to be a WTO founding member but her attempt was thwarted by the U.S., European countries, and Japan. When China later joined the WTO, she had to agree to considerably harsher conditions than other developing countries. She was required to reform various tariff policies, including tariff reductions, open markets and industrial policies. China also had to deal with transparency and intellectual property issues. These changes were difficult steps for China as they were conflicting with her prior economic strategy. Accession required China to engage in global competition according to rules that she did not make. China's admission was a collective decision symbolizing a clear commitment towards **multilateralism**. After China joined WTO, her service sector was considerably liberalized and foreign investment in previously prohibited areas was allowed; restrictions on retail, wholesale and distribution ended. Banking, financial services, insurance and telecommunications were also opened up gradually to foreign investment. China's economic growth is definitely helped by her membership in WTO, but it was her decades of hard work contributed to her success and benefitted herself as well as other WTO members.

The issue of deteriorating US-China trade relations is not the problem of WTO nor caused by it. The US-China trade imbalance can be summarized in one phrase, 'mismatch of economic development policy', no one especially WTO should be blamed for it. The U.S. has been favoring service sector, particularly the financial service sector, over manufacturing. Her technological lead is also heavily applied to the financial sector. Thus, domestically, the U.S. suffered job loss in manufacturing which could not be made up numerically by the thriving financial industry. This economic trend also contributed to widened income gap and less goods export. On the other hand, China has been focused on manufacturing thriving in an export oriented economy. China is slow perhaps planned so purposely in pumping her service sector growth, particularly in financial services. Therefore China was not a ripe environment to receive financial services from the U.S. This mismatch of economic development policies between the two great nations created a trade imbalance solvable only by policy adjustment. As China is moving more into consumption based economy and a more service demanding country, she will import more services including the financial services. China's strategy to upgrade her manufacturing (China Manufacture 2025) will need more technology imports from the advanced nations like the U.S. The above two areas are both strong suits of the U.S. Looking forward, the mismatch will be disappearing. The US-China trade relations will ensure a more balanced trade. This can be achieved under the sound WTO umbrella.

Chapter 27
Does Trump have a Strategy to Run the U.S.? Yes, But…

*****

Donald Trump was an unusual Presidential candidate. His campaign style was unusual, combative, rude, impromptu and rash in presentation. His tweets were also unusual but he was successful in getting millions of followers and creating a new political fad, now adopted and imitated by many politicians. He was not eloquent in speeches with his limited vocabulary, but he was persistent in his claims, attacks and promises even without backup data or being challenged by the media. His ability to occupy the media limelight by attacking media was another unusual political phenomenon never occurred before. He was able to cast almost all his opposing and negative media reports into one disposal - 'fake news'- amazingly, it worked.

Donald Trump surprised the media and the nation by winning the 45th US Presidency. He surrounded him with new faces in cabinet and White House appointments leaning towards right wing, hawkish and supportive to his 'America First' political slogan. Not everyone adjusted well in his new Administration. Trump was not shy in blaming his subordinates for blunders or crises whether they were created by them or him. One thing has become clear is that Trump is determined to deliver his campaign promises as his way of proving his worth to the people who elected him. On the issues raised during his presidential campaign, such as immigration, military revamping, job creation, trade imbalance, infrastructure as well as general economy, he has been focused on fulfilling his promises in his term.

Taking the immigration, he was serious about building a wall along the US-Mexico border. He was also harsh in dealing with illegal immigrants demanding deportation even mercilessly causing separation of children from their parents. He is pressuring Mexico to pay for the wall by saying "one way or the other Mexico will pay for the wall". Trump's immigration policy is stopping the illegal from consuming the US social welfare dollars and building a wall to stop inflow of illegal immigrants and drug smuggling into the U.S. draining the US economy - conceptually nothing wrong. President Trump's desire to expand the military was a core promise during his presidential campaign. However, his proposed $54B increase in military budget raised concerns on federal budget cuts on non-military spending. He encouraged updating US Navy and Air Force military power but demanded more frugal budgets on weapon development from military suppliers - a balance sheet approach. Under Trump Administration, the U.S. sold more military gadgets than his predecessors enriching the military industry complex, good for winning more campaign donations and votes but little to do with long term national defense or world security.

President Trump had proposed gigantic tax cuts to induce American corporations to move their manufacturing facilities back to home to create jobs, but no coherent policy is announced to make that happen. Trump's solution on job creation is also bottom line thinking. He hopes to induce corporations to bring headquarters and factories back to the U.S. simply by cutting taxes but not tackling the skill obsolescence problem - a fundamental education issue. He decided to initiate a trade war to reduce trade imbalances with US trading partners without a clear road map to hit homerun. Thus we see Harley Davison announcing moving part of its manufacturing to Europe citing the impact of 25% tariff on steel imports. Tesla, valuing potential China market for electric cars, is making plans to establish a huge manufacturing factory capable of making 500,000 electric cars per year in Shanghai free trade zone. Trump wants to levy tariff on imports, a simple balance sheet approach, to balance trade with no careful analysis of the impact to the entire national and global economy.

Trump claims; "for too long, US lawmakers have invested in infrastructure inefficiently", ignoring critical needs, and resulting in deterioration. Therefore, the United States has fallen behind other countries. Trump wants to give Americans the working, modern infrastructure they deserve, but his plan of creating a $1.5 Trillion program for infrastructure repair and upgrade hinges on leveraging $200B federal dollars for five to one State and local government funding – simply a transfer of burden. The infrastructure burden has been shifting to the State and local governments for decades, however, most local governments on deficit budgets are unable to upgrade the infrastructure. So shifting the burden off the federal balance sheet is too simplistic a wish for solving the deteriorating national infrastructure. Without understanding what resources are needed, what magnitude of the budget is required, what priorities must be set up in a coordinated national plan executed in a timely fashion, can local governments fix the infrastructure problem – It seems impossible.

After the recovery from the housing-loan bubble in 2008, the U.S. general economy has slowly recovered and been stable with stock market showing a healthy pulse showing the second longest bull market cycle. However, all these can burst like a balloon again, if Trump's trade war would bring down the US

GDP by half or one percent point like some economists warned. In the main stream media, the anti-Trump sentiment is running feverishly high, although Trump seems to be able to hold his core supporters together sustaining his approval rating. What troubles the public including his supporters is that he has not laid out a clear blue print to make America Great other than repeating his 'America First' campaign slogan and 'money-driven agenda'.

The trillion dollar question is whether Trump has a strategy and a secret plan for governing the U.S. domestic issues and directing the foreign affairs. The media does not believe he does thus constantly bashing him in a bad light. But in all fairness, based on his track record in office for the past nineteen months, I will say that President Trump had been very active in taking actions and initiatives. Analyzing what he has done so far, I am willing to say that Trump does have a strategy. His strategy is a 'money-driven agenda' to bring money to the U.S. treasury. He wants others to pay for the US spending, demanding NATO and other US allies (Japan, South Korea, etc.) to increase their defense budget, selling more arms worldwide and squeezing defense contractors, all based on a businessman's simple balance sheet mentality with little security analysis. In Trump's business mind, a positive cash flow and bottom line on the balance sheet represents success. More money and better fiscal state means better can the U.S. manage her national and international affairs – nothing wrong with that concept.

However, this kind of money-driven balance sheet approach to deal with the U.S. domestic and international issues is very much like using an abacus to solve a complex economic problem which can hardly be characterized by a differential equation. We expect that the Trump 'money' strategy will run into more problems than providing solutions in the long run. Take the trade policy or tariff war alone, many analysts have questioned its wisdom; some call it a poker player's bluff that the U.S. can't afford the consequence. The U.S. cannot solve the trade issue by bluffing. God has dealt the U.S. very rich resources. The heart of US economic problem is productivity, work ethics, and effective education and economic development policies. The trade imbalance was a result of trades made between willing partners. Trump's tariff threat may get trading partners to negotiate faster, but the Trump Administration must have a deal in mind with every trade partner and must be prepared with a viable alternative if a deal goes sour.

Trump's deal with EU President Jean-Claude Juncker made on 7-25-2018 is a reasonable tactic to calm US soybean farmers' protest. But asking China to give up her 'made in China 2025 plan' and deny her market value to attract capital and technology investment seems to be a no deal and unfair proposal.

Based on the tariffs already enacted by Trump Administration (and the total impact by escalated retaliation), the consequence may be a reduction of long-run US GDP by 0.06% (0.47%), wages 0.04% (0.33%) and full-time jobs 48,585 (364,786). (Erica York and Kyle Pomerleau, Tracking the Economic Impact of U.S. Tariffs and Retaliation Actions, Tax Foundation 6-22-2018 updated 7-20-2018) A Wharton Budget Model even predicted a reduction of GDP 0.9% and wages 1.1% by 2027. Trump must realize a 'money-driven' strategy is not adequate, more in-depth analysis with fair assumptions must be made to support a government policy.

Chapter 28
Legal and Illegal interference in Elections

*****

The U.S. has been a promoter and defender of democracy treating it as an ideology rather than a decision making method for establishing government, electing officials, legislating laws and deciding policies and public affairs both domestic and international. Since electing public officials is the most important element in running a government, it became the most prominent element of democracy. Thus national elections draw national and international attention. When attention is elevated to action then interference may occur. If action is protected or sanctioned by law then the interference is legal otherwise it is illegal. Most foreign direct interferences on elections are illegal even in the form of advertisement or donations supporting or opposing any candidate in an election. On the other the hand, often interference is done indirectly through a legal front such as an action group or registered lobbying organization or a citizen or retired official.

Paul Craig Roberts in his website (democracynow.com 7-27-2018) quoted Noam Chomsky saying Russians were not interfering our elections but Israel definitely is - "whatever the Russians may have done barely counts or weighs in the balance as compared to what another state does, openly, brazenly and with enormous support. Israeli intervention in U.S. elections vastly overwhelms anything the Russians may have done, I mean, even to the point where the Prime Minister of Israel, Netanyahu, goes directly to Congress, without even informing the President, and speaks to the Congress, with overwhelming applause, to try to undermine the President's policies—(that was what happened with Obama and Netanyahu in 2015). Did Putin come to give an address to the joint sessions of Congress trying to—calling on them to reverse U.S. policy, without even informing the President?"

Robert's article caught my attention thus triggered my thoughts as expressed in the opening paragraph. Israel's Prime Minister, Netanyahu, presumably was invited by the Congress, thus his action should be considered as a legal interference in the U.S. policies and/or elections. However, strictly speaking, if the Congress had not unanimously voted to invite him, his speech or action on US elections or policies would not be 'kosher'; the opposing legislators and citizens of the U.S. certainly have the right to protest and render such speech

---

and action as foreign interference. So regarding elections, foreign countries should refrain from direct interference other than making public opinions as individual observers through public media. Any non-public or secretive action from a foreign entity trying to influence another country's election should be considered as illegal interference. The U.S. certainly has the right to investigate the "Russia-gate" if she suspects foreign interference occurred.

Chomsky's comment deserves further analysis from 'fairness' or 'seriousness' point of view when one considers what is a legal standard practice and what is a double standard. Governments undertake secretive actions in international arena is almost a standard practice but it is not an international legal practice even when it is endorsed by the home country. The secretive interference of the U.S. in Russia's elections or policies or vice versa may be a de-facto 'standard practice' but they are not legal based on international or domestic laws. When a country is crying foul about another country's interference actions but is practicing interference on other countries, she is then having a hypocritical double standard. Examining the history of the international affairs, there is no shortage of U.S. and Russia interference in other countries' domestic policies and elections (Middle East exhibits ample examples), perhaps mostly done secretively but some openly clearly of "unfair" and 'double standard practice'.

The Taiwan issue in the U.S. - China relation is the perfect example for discussing the legality of 'interference' and 'foreign interference' issue. The U.S. recognizes China as a sovereign nation and acknowledges that Taiwan is a part of China; so do the U.N and 175 countries. Therefore, China regards Taiwan as a domestic issue unsettled from a Chinese civil war between KMT and CCP, two political parties emerged during China's revolution in the late 19th and early 20th century. KMT retreated to Taiwan in 1949 and evolved into a multi-party government. (Although there are nominally close to 300 parties in Taiwan, the New DPP is the only party ever replaced the KMT Administration in 2000 by Chen Shui-bian and then 2016 by Tsai Ing-wen). On the other hand, the CCP remains the dominant party in control of Mainland China since 1949 under China's Constitution permitting multiple political parties to exist and form a united front as well as allowing different governmental systems to administer special regions in China. Thus China regards Hong Kong and Macaw as special administrative regions and Taiwan as a province or special region subject to reconciliation. Therefore, the elections in Hong Kong or Taiwan are considered domestic elections in China.

The above factual situation raises an interesting question on whether any country or the CCP government can interfere in the elections held in Hong Kong or Taiwan? Basically, no other country should interfere in the elections in Hong Kong or Taiwan, not the previous colonial ruler, the Great Britain (controlled Hong Kong over one hundred years), nor Japan (ruled Taiwan as a colony for fifty years) and certainly not other countries including the U.S. except China which under her Constitution and international recognition has the 'legal' right to monitor the elections in her special regions and provinces. Regardless how The legal right would be interpreted according to the local laws and China's Constitution, we can first simply and clearly state that the U.S., U.K. and Japan definitely have no right to interfere in Hong Kong or Taiwan's elections. As for the domestic interpretation of election laws in Taiwan and Hong Kong, the Mainland China's position is a cautious one. On the one hand she is respecting as much freedom and independence of the local voting population under local laws as possible barring treasonous activities such as premeditating separation (an interesting case of Catalonia in Spain is a good reference) and on the other hand she is upholding sovereignty rights over the regions under Chinese Constitution.

Unfortunately, as stated above States do practice illegal interference in foreign land's elections. Since it was returned to China in 1997, Hong Kong had held several elections already, but foreign interferences persist albeit they are getting less and less influential. However, foreign interference is a die-hard activity mainly because governments can hide behind diplomatic immunity and practice double standard fooling their own citizens. The 'Russia investigation' could be a blessing in disguise for American citizens to understand the election interference issue and see through double standards. When it comes to Taiwan, it is amazing such a double standard was so vivid and yet escaped the scrutiny of American citizens.

When the U.S. established diplomatic relation with Mainland China and cut off legal ties with Taiwan, the U.S. passed a Taiwan Relation Act as a foreign policy statement with high moral overture that the U.S. expects Taiwan to be peacefully united with Mainland China and the U.S. values a long held friendly relation with the people in Taiwan. However, this act and subsequent laws such as the Taiwan Travel Act, etc., are passed and interpreted less as a moral statement but a tool for practicing interference (to the point that the Taiwan election candidate must come to the U.S. to get her blessing) and applying double standard (such as the U.S. can interfere in Taiwan's election but China cannot lobby the U.S. Congress to stop legislating 'Taiwan Relation' laws). The U.S. certainly has the right to legislate any law by her Congress but should Americans condone a double standard? Should they cry foul about Russia interference, permit Israel interference, legislate laws interfering foreign land's political affairs and yet forbid lobbying actions from foreign entities? Where is the justice and moral standard? How can the U.S. be the model for the world?!

Chapter 29
How Can One Fix Cheating in the Global Trading System?

*****

Jake Werner wrote a teasing article, entitled, China Is Cheating at a Rigged Game - The Trade War Is a Sign of a Global System Gone Badly Wrong, in Foreign Policy, Argument section, on August 8, 2018. The Day 8-8 is recognized as Father's Day in Mainland China and Taiwan because 8-8 is pronounced as Ba-Ba in Chinese similar to Pa-Pa in many other languages. Werner may have given some logical arguments that the global system has gone wrong but he certainly has not given any hint of how to fix it in his article thus leaving readers in a teased mode. He did, however, point out that there is no analysis on what motivates this Chinese policy. He also stated that the aligned anti-China entities interpreting it (Chinese policy) as 'cheat' action actually creates an image which is badly resembling the 'anti-Chinese racism' started in the U.S. in 19th century lasted quite a long time in US history. What Werner really achieved in his article with such a title was making readers questioning how was a game rigged and how was the global system gone wrong? Werner did not provide any answers rather he cast a doubt in his title statements.

The global system should be an evolving system supported by all members who voluntarily participated in the system. Any rules governing the system should be developed over time with modifications and improvements introduced by participating members. Certainly large countries with big economies may have more influence on the rules governing the system, but the system must be democratically evolved and managed honoring the principles that all members adhere to with the objective to facilitate trading among members while each will act to provide and protect the interests of its people within the confines of the system rules. So the global system governing trade and economic development can be metaphorically compared to the Father's Day Celebration, a celebration to honor the fathers who provide and protect his family interests regardless whether the celebration is held on the third Sunday in June as declared by President Johnson of the U.S. in 1966 or on March 19th as originally celebrated in Europe since Middle Ages or on August 8th as the Chinese do. The Father's Day Celebration (trade) can be conducted on different days with different styles but with the same objective to honor the Father's deed (protecting his family). The trading game is played by every country with its own trading policy and the global system is maintained collectively by all participating members on a voluntary basis. Every member should adjust its own trading policy to play the game and every member should work together to manage the global system.

The 'cheat' word defines a trading action violating fair trade rules without people recognizing it. In global trade, deals are made and accepted voluntarily with due deliberation and negotiation with little chance for 'cheat' to occur between two trading partners at any time, never mind over many years. Every country, in fact every trading entity be it a global corporation or a public company or a private enterprise, enters into a deal voluntarily and signs treaties or contracts willingly. In each deal, there is gain or loss interpreted differently by different parties but the fact is each trade takes two or more willing parties to consummate. If any party felt it was cheated by another party, it certainly would not trade with that party again or changing its trading policy. Of course, a trading partner may make mistakes and feel cheated and if that happens over many years over many deals, then the trading partner must have a bad trading policy or an incompetent government. In 19th and early 20th century, China was cheated by her foreign trading partners because her government was corrupt and weak and the foreign countries used gun power to force unfair trade treaties onto her even forcing her to cede trading ports to them and forcing her accept opium knowing opium destroys her citizens. Today, we live under the United Nation and we have World Trade Organization to prevent unfair trade. Hopefully, trading will never be forced with military power.

The U.S. is the largest economy in the world. By and large, she has greater influence shaping the global system, in fact to favor her as a trading nation. If she felt she was cheated then it could only be caused by her bad economic and trade policies. No one could use gun power to force her into an unwilling trade. So the issue is to analyze what did the U.S. do wrong not just blame the global system gone wrong?! Every country wants to develop economically, elevate her technologically and leverage her market for achieving the above goals and bring up her citizens income. Large country has large market thus has more leveraging power to achieve their goals. When China leverages her market for buying high technology content products with technology infusion, the seller has two choices, one is to refuse to sell or two is to sell with an adequate profit which may be big enough to recover the seller's investment in intellectual properties. American pharmaceutical industry has been successful in doing that both domestically and internationally. Selling hi-tech products running the risk of being copied was one of the 'cheat' issue. History showed all developed countries had copied and been copied by other countries. The international patent law becomes a part of the global system. It worked well protecting developed countries but it is also a fair game for hard working countries to catch up. Germany and Japan caught up with the U.K. and the U.S. becoming the developed countries. Now China is catching up with highest patent growth in the world about to surpass the U.S. in annual patent grants. Countries own patents naturally will honor patent laws. A global system cannot be fair if it prevents a hard working country to become a developed country. Developed countries should not form a club to exclude developing countries or prevent the developing from becoming developed.

With the above analysis and Werner's arguments, it is clear to conclude that the globe system may not be perfect but it is not broken nor gone wrong. The fix for the U.S. trade problem lies in her policies, how to pump the nation's productivity (education reform, for example, the STEM emphasis), to formulate strategic industry development (for example, emphasizing infrastructure over military development), to urge citizens to save more and to put savings into investment to stimulate technology and economical growth (for example, spending habits and life style moderation) and to reduce debt and over dependency on foreign investments which can turn around leaving the U.S. and going to another country say, China and India, overnight. The current Trade War does not appear as a good long term policy to fix the U.S. trade problems but it may just trigger investors to realize that the U.S. is not dealing with fundamental problems just putting bandages to stop bleeding. I echo with Werner (which may not be made explicit), we should stop anti-Chinese rhetoric or discriminating against Chinese. We should focus on finding fixes. China has her share of problems but she is smartly focusing on fixing the problems rather than scheming to win the trade war. It is obvious from her reactionary and defensive moves dealing with the US initiated trade war while maintaining her nation building objectives.

Chapter 30
The future of Empire State and the United States

*****

New York State is called the Empire State for many reasons. New York State has other nicknames such as Excelsior State. Empire State was adopted in 19th century generally referring to its wealth and resources as a big state in the United States. Some attributed the name to the remark George Washington made while viewing the map of New York prior to the battle of New York in the independence war, "New York is the seat of an empire." The 102 story of Empire State Building in the Big Apple, New York City, built in 1931 as the world's tallest building at that time, remains as the famous icon of the City and State of New York. Nearly all tourists came to New York would visit the Empire State Building, ascending to the top to take a panoramic view of the Manhattan Island. The first King Kong movie made with the Empire State Building in 1933 had captured the hearts of many millions of movie fans not only for loving the actress Fay Wray and King Kong but also for appreciating the Empire State Building's architecture. The name Empire State is now on every license plate of vehicles registered in New York.

New York State is now the third largest state in the union. Interestingly, the Encyclopedia Britannica had kindly described New York in a paragraph which will lead to my discussion on the title subject, "Until the 1960s, New York was the country's leading state in nearly all population, cultural, and economic indexes. Its displacement by California beginning in the middle of that decade was caused by the enormous growth rate that has persisted on the West Coast rather than by a large decline in New York itself. Texas overtook New York as the second most populous state in 2000. Still, New York remains one of the most populous states in the country, and its gross economic product exceeds those of all but a handful of countries throughout the world." Unfortunately, an updated assessment of the New York State in many New Yorkers' view is that the state, especially New York City, although remains the centre of much of the country's economy and finance, as exhibited by the power of Wall Street, as well as the driver of America in art and culture, as displayed through Broadway and media and entertainment industries influencing the national political and social lives, however, the state and the city have been divided in political philosophy as liberal against conservative, down State suppressing upstate and rural population opposing city folks among its nearly 20 million people over land of 140, 000 square kilometers.

The upstate of New York has been on decline economically for decades. The manufacturing jobs have dwindled post World War II from 2.2 million to less than 300,000 in 2008. From 2010 - 2016 while manufacturing jobs grew nationally 6.5 % from a decline, New York on the contrary further lost 3% or 14,000 jobs despite of decreased taxes on manufacturing industries, he lowest level in decades. When Volkswagen invested $1B for auto manufacturing it selected Tennessee State for lower labor cost and free of labor union. Manufacturing site selection focuses on labor cost, market access, friendly business environment; New York is just not competitive comparing to other states. Many manufacturers had been scared away after they had examined the financial state of the prospective New York municipalities. New York's financial center status is no longer a significant attraction to manufacturers. Of course, the lack of growth (turning to paper economy) and high taxes are driving residents and retirees leaving the state and forcing the 1.2 million degree-credit students in New York's 270 colleges seeking jobs in other states.

The prognosis of the future of New York State is not great. Politically, the State is deeply divided with a frustrated Republican Party forever unable to gain control of the full government and the legislature. The Assembly is essentially controlled by the Democrats in New York City whereas the Upstate counties barely contribute to maintaining one vote margin in the Senate. The long decline of New York State manufacturing since 1945 has a close correlation with the politics in the State. One notices that out of 44 previous US Presidents, New York has more than its fair share of producing six. However, one further notices that the six from Martin Van Buren (8th), Millard Fillmore (13th), Chester A. Arthur (21st), Grover Cleveland (24th), Theodore Roosevelt (26th) to Franklin D. Roosevelt (32nd, 1933-1945)) were all serving prior to WW II. This is probably not a coincidence judging the economic performance of New York post WW II.

The 2016 presidential election was an unusual one having twenty three candidates (17R and 6D), including three contenders from New York, Hillary Clinton (D), George Pataki (R) and Donald Trump (R). Pataki dropped out early leaving Clinton and Trump eventually becoming the final candidates. Donald Trump finally won the presidency after a vigorously contested primary and a bitter campaign against well funded Hillary. However, Trump could hardly claim that he was representing the State of New York. He did not serve any public office in New York other than being a real estate tycoon; he did not even get a fair support from the New York State Republican Party machinery. Thus his victory had little to do with the economic performance of New York, in other words, unlike Franklin Roosevelt who served as the Governor of New York prior to becoming the US President nor like Ronald Regan who served as the Governor of California before becoming the US Commander-in-Chief, both won their home state support.

Now the future of the U.S. is in the hands of a New Yorker, Donald Trump. Perhaps, it is a good thing that Trump is not minted out of Albany or New York politics, since the poor score card of New York economy has to be blamed on the politicians in Albany and New York City (poverty rate 19.5% in 2016, high rent problem and sheltering homeless 60,000 per night) and their recent scandalous corruptions and long impotence in revitalizing New York. Whether or not Trump can make America strong again with his "America First" campaign pledge perhaps depends on how fast and well he can learn on the job. He has given lots of campaign promises and has taken many actions on his own initiatives. His bold tax cuts and unwavering positions on trade issues and immigration problems have all yielded early or temporary results that the frustrated Americans find refreshing; hence, the US economy shows a tick-up and the stock market gives him approval and vital support with watchful eyes.

If Trump were able to learn on the job and steer the country onto the right path smoothly into a second term by getting our trading partners to agree on a new set of trade agreements benefitting the U.S. economy, negotiating and stabilizing a number of international or global security problems (such as North Korea and Iran) and energizing our domestic programs to create jobs and improve our national infrastructure, the future of the U.S. would be bright. Then, what about 2024? Even though New York State performed poorly since 1945 and showed no sign of revitalization, the New York State is not short of ambitious politicians inspiring for the U.S. Presidency. Clinton might make a comeback and the current Governor Andrew Cuomo already showed his interest for 2024 even 2020. Cuomo is an Albany product used to seeing (or managing) the miserable New York State economy. Cuomo issued an unwelcome welcome statement when Trump visited New York supporting mid-term election candidates. Cuomo even made the statement, "America was never so great.", a foolish statement to counter Trump's America First to make America great slogan. Sadly, despite his track record, Cuomo is expected to win his reelection. Hence, I see no good future in New York State. As for the future of the U.S., we must pray for Trump's fast learning and self-correcting skills. But with so many enemies against him and he keeps making more, the future is at best uncertain. If another authentic New Yorker politician becomes the 46th US President, I may say our future is beyond praying. What the US future would be like? Your guess is as good as mine!

Chapter 31
An Objective Advice for US and China Leaders

*****

Two recent opinion articles, one entitled, Some Friendly Advice for China's Leaders, published in Wall Street Journal on 8-22-2018 by Maurice Greenberg, founding chairman and CEO of AIG and current Chief of C. V. Starr & Co having insurance business in China and another in-depth strategic essay, entitled, From Engagement to Rivalry: Tools to compete with China, appeared on Texas National Security Review 8-21-2018 by Peter Mattis, a former CIA Counterintelligence Analyst, currently Editor of China Brief and a fellow of Jamestown Foundation, have compelled me to write this piece to respond to the cited papers above. Greenberg recounts history of US-China engagement since 1900 giving credits to the U.S. helping China throughout her miserable period of nearly being colonized by Europeans and the savage invasion by the Japanese. His advice to the Chinese leaders is to level the playing field by reassessing the terms of bilateral trade and making them more fair and equitable without specific suggestions to Chinese leaders other than urging them to recognize the critical importance of maintaining a constructive and open relationship. Greenberg looked at the trade issues with a narrow lens and offered a somewhat oversimplified interpretation of the trade issues.

Mattis's article on the other hand is a thorough analysis of the US-China Relations, particularly focused on a review of the American China policy beyond the trade issues. Mattis regarded the past 'engagement' policy as a failure and attributed the failure to misunderstanding of the Chinese Communist Party and wishful thinking of changing the CCP or expecting China to be liberalized. Thus Mattis called for a new examination of the China policy and a different approach to analyze and "order the China knowledge" to develop a workable China Policy.

Although Mattis's suggestion is plausible but he is essentially biased against the 'engagement' approach and favoring the 'competition' approach treating China as a strategic enemy calling for adopting a set of right tools (targeting the Chinese Communist Party and capture the individual wealth deposited in the U.S., a familiar tactics used against terrorists) to deal with China. This bias is perhaps coming from Mettis's CIA background, I submit though if a fair and logical examination of China's historical behavior and recent assertive diplomatic actions would not necessarily yield his conclusion that the 'engagement' policy was wrong and a hostile 'competition' policy will be right.

Looking from high on the US-China Relations over the past century and far into the next several decades, one can discover a number of logic conclusions on why the US-China Relations fell to a new low in recent years with an uncertainty for the future. The first logical conclusion is that the U.S. has always placed her national security strategy as the top priority in formulating her foreign policy and conducting her foreign relationship including trade relation. At the same time, the U.S. does not regard other nations', case here, China's national security strategy of any importance in formulating her China policy. On the other hand, China having keen respect to the U.S. as the world's superpower observes and analyzes the U.S. diplomatic behavior carefully and wishes to learn and follow suit as China is developing up as a sovereign big nation. When China was rising from a weak developing country, the above mismatch of security strategy consideration did not amount to any significant concern simply, therefore tolerated.

When China maintained a steady economic growth with near double-digit annual advance, the U.S. certainly had noticed it. If one observed the transformation taking place in China and how rapidly China had embraced capitalism, the 'engaging China' and 'bringing China into the global economy' policy actually succeeded not failed. Treating China as a trade partner helped the US foreign policy to contain and eventually to cause the Soviet Union collapsed making the U.S. the only

superpower in the world. However, as the U.S. maintained her superior military strength, her national economy took a transformation favoring financial and service industries over basic manufacturing and industrial sectors. On the contrary, China focused on manufacturing and continued her rapid growth to become the second biggest economy of the world and the greatest manufacturer in volume. So in a fair analysis, the 'engagement' China policy did succeed in bringing China to the open world and securing the U.S. superpower position. The real issue is what does the U.S. have to do to deal with the inevitable competition element which always comes with a big rising economy. It happened with the European allies and it happened with Japan both created big trade imbalances with the U.S..

The U.S. essentially obtained concessions from EU and Japan as they had been US allies relying on the U.S. for national security protection. The trade imbalance issue with China is far less complicated than the competition perceived by the U.S. The U.S. never treated China as an ally, on the contrary, more like an adversary, thus never offered her security protection. The U.S. from her national security point of view targets China as a threat despite of China's denial; China solemnly advocates her peaceful rise and from her national security point of view she regards the U.S. Pivot to Asia policy posing military threat to China. Therefore, concession of trade deals cannot resolve this trade war launched out of misunderstanding of national security considerations. China is a single large country with 1.4 billion hard working people, very different from EU, a collection of smaller countries and also different from Japan a natural resource limited aging nation by US design relying on US protection for national security. Of course, the U.S. has a right to negotiate and try to reduce the trade imbalance; however, she must take a fair and honest approach to solve this trade conflict without compounding the trade issue with twisted national security consideration and misunderstanding. Just imagine, if the U.S. and China would have a national security alignment treaty, the trade issue could easily be settled over a negotiation table.

Blaming is not a fair approach in solving conflicts. China did not and cannot steal American jobs. As an MIT professor said, no one can build and dominate any industry by stealing. You need skilled talents and hard working people to build a successful industry. China's desire to elevate her technology by charting a 'China Manufacturing 2025' is a legitimate competitive economic development plan. The U.S. must have a legitimate counter measure to deal with competition. China has become the number one patent producer and the largest producer of STEM graduates. It is obvious that the U.S. must accept and work with China for mutual benefits. The U.S. still leads in many areas of high-technology. Sanctioning hi-tech export only destroy hi-tech industry's future. Mattis is taunting a 'competition' policy to replace 'engagement' Policy, but in all fairness, he did not dwell in the fundamental question - What is the definition of national securities for the U.S. and China? The leaders of the U.S. and China need to understand this question and reach an agreement. Then the U.S. can develop an 'engagement and competition' China Policy and China can develop an 'engagement and competition' US policy both under a fair and mutually acceptable definition of national security strategy.

Chapter 32
Authoritative Administration and Ineffective Government Must Change

*****

At a time that foreign policies decisions and international diplomacy are reduced to a 'tweet' level concerning the citizens, media and international community, it is refreshing to read a long but very well written scholarly essay, The Unconstrained Presidency - Checks and Balances Long Eroded Before Trump, written by James Goldgeier and Elizabeth N. Saunders and published in Foreign Affairs 2018 September/October Issue. I recommend that every federal legislator and 'Presidential Aspirators' as well as all political science students read this article. Professors Goldgeier (American University) and Saunders (Georgetown University) both with former experience at George Washington University are political Science scholars, thorough bred so to speak, Goldgeier educated from Harvard (BA, Government) and UC Berkeley (MA, PhD, Political Science) and Saunders educated from Harvard (BS, Physics), University Of Cambridge (Master of Philosophy, International Relations) and Yale (PhD, Political Science).

Their scholarly essay may have used a title influenced by current Trump phenomenon (viewed by his supporters) or Trump soap opera (watched by his opponents), but its content started with a rigorous historical review on foreign affairs and foreign policy decisions lending support to their thesis - the U.S. Presidential power is over inflated with no proper checks and balances from Congress as well as from career foreign policy experts in the executive branch. The career foreign policy experts are forced to yield to the power of White House staffs who are appointed at the pleasure of the President. The fact that the National Security Council (NSC) in the White House (WH) grew from 50 staff (under GWH Bush), to 100 (Clinton), 200 (GW Bush) and 400 (under Obama) showed that the NSC had moved beyond its role of coordinating policies to dominating the foreign policy making. Under Trump Administration, The former appointed Secretary of State (Tillerson) cooperated with the WH to reduce the size of the State Department, leaving undersecretary and assistant secretary vacant and the current appointed secretary (Pompeo) withdrew from his role of negotiating with North Korea under the direction of 'tweet'. If these acts were to boost the power of the Presidency, they indeed succeeded. Unfortunately, as described by Goldgeier and Saunders, the

Congress had been bogged down by extreme bipartisan behavior and by election concerns of individual elected representative wielding no power to check the Presidency in case of misuse of his power.

The U.S. was the pillar and defender of democracy and yet judging from the foreign policy decision making and US international diplomacy, the U.S. had not shown a sterling example of democratic governance especially since the end of Cold War or 1990's. The U.S. Presidents were able to make unilateral decisions circumventing international institutions as well as the U.S. Congress' checks and supervision. Goldgeier and Saunders attributed this problem to Congressional delegates spreading their interest in breadth by sitting on too many committees rather than building expertise in depth. I rather consider it as a fundamental deficiency in the short tenured representative system in our democracy. It is very difficult for legislators to build any sort of expertise if they have to spend bulk of their time worrying about their own political campaigns and re-elections. Just look at our election system, every two year, a Congressman has to be re-elected, a Senator every six years and the President every four years, This system gives so much unnecessary turbulence to our government with no apparent benefit of getting talents to serve for the executive or legislative offices. Is there any remedy to this problem? Should we think about a solution? I do think so.

Just imagine an alternative slightly modified system that the above elected officials are all given eight years of tenure but providing an effective monitoring measure, lowering the threshold of their being fired and impeachment and installing an effective evaluation and approval mechanism. First, an eight year tenure maintaining a staggered term (for example, for the legislative branch, one quarter subject to reelection every two years, called quarter-term election) will give our government more stability. Second, a mere simple majority vote should be sufficient to expel a Congressman or a Senator if his or her conduct is violating the law or ethics rules. This will encourage legislators to mind their personal conduct and improve their collegial cooperation. Third, from district voters' point of view, a reasonable monitoring process for voters to express satisfaction or dissatisfaction each year is needed. It can be simply done by printing an approval box in every election ballot in their district elections, local official elections, state elections, school district elections even fire-chief election ballots, to collect cumulative and continuous approval ratings (via electronic tallies collected on local voting ballots, published through media). This puts pressure on elected representatives to focus on their job performance instead of campaigns. An eight-year tenure system will give our government much needed continuity and effective operation and prevents frequent turnovers as well as many money influenced elections with less qualified or dedicated candidates. The continuous and cumulative monitoring by approval rating can be used to trigger an election to remove an ineffective elected official and select a new choice. The normal 8-year vs 2,4,6-year term for elected officials reduces greatly the costly campaign time and le the elected officials concentrate more on their duty and job performance.

We are living in a digital world and citizens lives are governed by data, so should government officials and especially elected officials. Our President needs checks and balances from the Congress and our Congress representatives need checks and balances from the voters. It is time for us to modernize our election system so that elected officials will be respected and treated as a professional, a career public servant, with a career path to achieve significant accomplishments serving the public not just to hang on to the office. Our law makers should be given long enough tenure to do a good job and their tenures must be monitored by their constituents on a continuous and cumulative basis; with today's technology, this system can be implemented with inexpensive voting machines. Even if it requires resources, it is a good cause to invest money for the sake of democracy. This is a conceptual change deserving political scientist to pay attention to. The digital technologists will sure ascertain that the above suggested system is doable with today's high speed and low cost data processing system. I am afraid though the resistance will come from the existing Congress, just like online learning was initially opposed by classroom professors; now it has become not only a viable teaching and learning system but benefitting millions of learners. Citizens do not have a simple way to make this change simply because the existing political threshold for making a change is too high. I urge the progressive thinking citizens with the help of political scientists to help educating everyone to realize such a change!

Chapter 33
What Is Happening with North Korea De-nuclearization?

*****

Foreign affairs are more like weather news nowadays, the foreign affairs happening today are reported quite accurately with little surprises by multiple parties but predictions of what will happen in the future longer than a few days are anybody's guess, at best speculative. No matter how many political analysts from any party (country) are writing about the issues involved in the foreign affair, the development of the affair is rarely predictable. The more serious (often more complex) is the affair, the less one can predict its evolvement. The North Korea (NK) nuclear threat is one of those foreign affairs which has become totally unpredictable in its outcome even though the issue was on the world stage over decades. Along with status review and analysis, there are usually plenty of proposals for dealing with the issue, however, in the case of NK nuclear threat, the proposals for solutions have been swinging between hard-line applying maximum military and economic sanction pressure to soft-line exploring diplomatic dialogue leading to the negotiation table, both with the same goal of achieving de-nuclearization on the Korea Peninsula.

Trump as a non-conventional President, perhaps free from U.S. legacy policy, baggage of NK 'strategies' from previous administrations and personal indoctrination of classified information on NK, took a bold and fresh approach to tackle the NK issue on his own initiative outside of the State Department and Pentagon guidance. As remarked by Christopher R. Hill in his recent article, The U.S. Needs a New North Korea Strategy, in Foreign Affairs Snapshot, September 5, 2018: "After Singapore's Failure (meaning Trump's meeting with Kim in Singapore), It is time to Change Course." Christopher R. Hill is a Professor of the Practice in Diplomacy at the University of Denver. He is a four-time ambassador, also served as Assistant Secretary of State for East Asian and Pacific Affairs from 2005 to 2009, during which he was head of the U.S. delegation to nuclear talks with North Korea. Therefore his statement of "Singapore's failure" is a weighty conclusion, even though Trump's Administration may not be so readily admitting failure.

Hill's conclusion is based on the factual development of a series of events, from mutual angry threats between the U.S. and NK, to NK and SK warming up their relation through dialogue, meeting and 2017 Winter Olympics, then to

Trump and Kim's agreement to a summit in Singapore (a Nobel Peace Prize worthy effort and music to many in Hill's words) and finally returning to today's NK rhetoric calling the U.S. deceitful after the bi-lateral negotiation effort yielding no fruitful result. The main thrust of Hill's essay is calling for multi-lateral negotiation stressing the importance of having SK, Japan and China all participating, especially advising that working with China has far more advantage than working against China. This proposal of changing strategy is nothing new, since China has always understood the essence of multi-lateral negotiation in NK case and pushed all parties including Russia to work together for achieving de-nuclearization in Korea Peninsula.

Citing China unable to endure U.S. leading in solving China's neighbor NK's nuclear issue as the reason, Hill claims that the U.S. should engage China in a multilateral negotiation. This is somewhat outdated consideration. China cares about 'face' so does the U.S. in the diplomatic world, but the two giants are both mature nations capable of making rational decisions. China not only is the only country that understands NK (and her generations of leaders) better than anyone else but is also far more serious than any country in viewing the NK issue as a long-term regional security problem. Studying the history since Korean War, I would rather conclude that China's national security view embraces and bears the East Asia regional security in mind simply because she is surrounded by a number of nations including NK, SK, Russia and Japan. On the other hand, the concern of the U.S. with respect to NK nuclear threat is more of her somewhat selfishly defined national security from nuclear attack point of view than from East Asia regional security. The U.S. Defense Secretary, General James Mattis, has put it plainly that the presence of the U.S. military in SK will shorten the time for responding to a NK nuclear attack to seven seconds from 15 minutes by the detection system stationed in Alaska. Defending SK to have a second Korea War is hardly expected.

Ever since the 34th US President, Ike Eisenhower, to 37th President Richard Nixon to 40th President Ronald Reagan, all have believed that a full engagement with China will be beneficial to the U.S. with a view of "a better China is better for the U.S. and better for the world". Even today in Trump's Administration, Treasury Secretary Mnuchin and other officials in the State Department still hold this view. Many nations in the world in Africa, Europe and South America also believe in this notion. The opposite view of "China Threat" can only be interpreted as a fear that China will become a world dominating power shaking the leadership position of the U.S. and her close military allies. As the third world desires to progress further in economic development and more countries are advancing economically, they look for leadership in economic development not in military strength. Since WW II, the U.S. has been a super power in military and in the size of economy. The rise of

China, because of her large hard working population and determination of implementing strategy for economic development, should not surprise anyone for her growth to be the second largest economy in the world. Hill is right that working with China is far better a strategy than working against China in solving the NK nuclear threat. I would extend that conclusion to a broader context concerning other issues, especially in global trade.

As US-NK bilateral negotiation falters, what is the option for the U.S.? Returning to applying maximum pressure both militarily and economically through a UN-wide sanction is not a sure strategy since we came that way. The crux of the matter is that NK wants to have a genuine peace treaty and the U.S. wants to have a real verifiable de-nuclearization in NK. The past tentative agreements broke down were basically because one side or the other violated the agreement. So the issue is how can we ensure a negotiated agreement will hold. Here multi-lateral participation and a multiparty agreement can offer more accountability to participants than a bi-lateral agreement. If all six parties, the U.S., China, NK, SK, Russia and Japan, can really hash out a plan and timetable for military withdrawal and de-nuclearization truly with regional security in mind under an umbrella of regional peace treaty, a genuine nuclear free and peaceful Korea Peninsula may eventually be realized. A recent letter from Kim to Trump suggested a second summit and implied that NK desired to complete de-nuclerization within Trump's term by 2020 and the absence of ballistic missiles at the NK 70th national anniversary parade are good gestures from NK for moving forward, however, for achieving real progress, a serious multilateral negotiation at the highest level will likely be more fruitful than a bilateral summit.

Chapter 34
The Nature of American, Chinese and African Debt

*****

Debt would be a bad thing if it could not be managed properly. In modern economic theory, capital is the necessary fuel for keeping the economy churning and debt or loan is the necessary oil for lubricating the economic engine. Managing debt is a challenge on either a personal or a national level. The traditional philosophy particularly in the Orient preaches debt-free and savings, whereas in the modern world, the developed or developing countries have been accustomed to a credit system encouraging borrowing thus making debt management a vital skill, on both personal and national levels. Personal debt is often expressed in absolute dollars whereas national (Government) debt tends to be expressed in terms of percentage of national Gross Domestic Product (GDP), the U.S. (105.4%), China (47.6%), and Africa (9.95-125.3% for its 51 countries). The top ten in-debt nations are Japan (253%), Greece, Lebanon, Italy, Portugal, Cape Verde, Congo, Singapore, Bhutan, and the U.S. (105.4%), in terms of percentages of GDP. The economic health of a nation is judged on its ability of managing debt and assets to guarantee payback of debt in time.

The American debt (105.4% of GDP-$19,391B, 2017) is equivalent to $20.438 trillion dollars. However, the U.S. is the wealthiest country valued at $93.560T, about 4.5 times of her debt. By straight math, the national debt of the U.S. is less than 22% of her assets, far below a bankruptcy level. The population of the U.S. is 324.5 million (2017). Thus every American shares $62,991 national debt. It is this figure that worries the American citizens and the international debt market. From debt management point of view, it is illogical to expect each American citizen to bear and pay off $63K, so the government must manage it by selling the Treasury bills to extend the loans or getting the cash to pay off maturing debt and refinancing new debt. So long as the debt is not reaching close to the National assets; this refinancing scheme of pushing debt down the road is a workable scheme. Of course, this scheme requires other nations or individuals or corporations to buy the Treasury bills to support refinancing. Most trading partners of the U.S. with a trade surplus hold US Treasury bills, T-bonds or notes. China used to hold over three trillion dollars of Treasury securities one time, now maintaining at 1.2 trillion (6/2018, Japan now holds about 1 trillion).

Loans or debts always carry interest, the more debt a nation owes, the more interest its government must pay each year. This interest burden is eating a big chunk of the U.S. budget or tax revenue. For fiscal year 2016, the interest payment was about $271B, 6.8% of total federal expenditure (474.5B for 2017). The debt interest payment has risen up 27% over the past decade, luckily at a low interest rate. As of June 2017, about 28% of the American debt (19.39T) is owed to Social Security (~$5.45B). Generally an internal (inter-government) debt is not as serious as foreign debt; however, the Social Security Program is a 'pay benefits as you collect taxes' program with surplus put in a trust fund and invested in Treasury securities. Starting 2018, Social Security payouts will begin to draw its trust fund reserve, which means, its earned interest is no longer sufficient to pay for all the benefits. The Social Security trust fund may be depleted by 2034 (sixteen years away), thus it faces two issues, one, the government must implement a tax scheme to build up its reserve to avoid bankruptcy and two, its investment in Treasury securities must be secure. Understanding the above debt discussion, we realize that the U.S. is not healthy financially. If no one buys the U.S. Treasury bills, the U.S. government and its Social Security Program will be in trouble. The trade war U.S. initiated may temporarily add cash to the Treasury but it won't solve the American debt problem unless fundamental fiscal policy, industrial revitalization and life-style moderation are introduced to reduce the heavy American debt.

China's debt according to IMF is at 47.6% of her GDP ($12015B 2017), $5719B, much less than the US debt. However, many economists caution that China's total debt is much more than the 'government debt' indicated. Some claim China's debt size is over 300% of her GDP due to her stimulus measures after the recent global financial crisis and her loose credit practice fueling her economic growth. This dire warning has been quieted down simply because the Chinese Central Bank has taken measures to stabilize credit market and keep her economy humming at a healthy 6-7% growth rate. The Chinese debt mountain is protected behind 'Great Wall' avoiding foreign capital manipulation. Western economists do acknowledge that China is able to avert financial/debt crisis but insisting her debt problem remaining a serious burden to her economy.

China has stepped up on the world stage becoming a significant creditor nation, lending money to other nations to fund their infrastructure and economic development, recently through her Belt Road Initiative (BRI). Some economists regard the above Chinese loans as a problem, citing examples: lending Venezuela $60B and Argentina tens of billions, both country facing economic problems. Argentina has applied to the IMF for a bailout. They also cite China loans being of questionable value, for example, China built a high-speed railroad line in Kenya currently operating at 20% of break-even level. Similarly, China has built a high-speed railroad in Laos and a new port for Sri Lanka with generous low interest loan terms (for Laos) and a 99-year port lease as payback(with Sri Lanka). Some economists regard these loans as problematic and compare them to the bad experience of Latin American debt crisis in the 1980's. However, we must point out that although the debt structures are similar, China's loans are based on a very different motive, a true win-win and long-term mutual-benefit basis. It is true China needs money to deleverage credits for her local banks to dissolve Chinese corporation debts, but China's government foreign debt is low. It is true that a rise in borrowing or credits without significant economic gains potentially will crush the Chinese corporations but they seem to perform well.

This may be why that the U.S. launches a 'trade-plus' war against China, intended to disrupt the current 'red manufacturing chain' (will hurt Chinese corporations but also US corporations), to sabotage China's BRI (will impact world economy) and to stop China's 2025 Manufacture Plan (may backfire to accelerating it) hoping ultimately crushing Chinese corporations and their industrial base. Whether the US 'trade-plus' strategy will hurt China badly or not is hard to predict but the trade tariff does not solve the U.S. own debt problem in the long run. Some economists even predict that the collapse of China's economy would be a big blow to corporate America. China's debt problem is very different from the US debt problem. China seems to be able to manage her debt problem and regulate her credit structure if no external intervention. Hence, China is carefully handling the strategic issues triggered by the U.S. 'trade-plus' war, such as industry upgrade, the role of RMB as a global currency, etc.

Africa has over 50 nations, their national debt ranges from 9.95% to 125.3% of their GDPs. The larger economy tend to have larger debt, for instance, South Africa and Egypt, which have a debt of 52.7% (0f GDP), $47.9B (2017) and 103%, $94B respectively. Most other countries are developing nations with smaller economy (< $100B) and smaller debt (<< $100B). Some African countries are among the world's poorest nations, like Uganda and Democratic Republic of Congo, needing capital investments for economic development but sometimes unable to repay their debt. If the country produces oil or other mineral resources, the debt refinancing may be sustainable; otherwise, it may have to get relief from IMF. The above discussed loans made by China to African countries certainly carry financial risk; however, it is a worthwhile risk since a developed Africa will elevate the world economy. The infrastructure investment in Africa may not yield an immediate return but the agricultural and energy investment do give back return quickly. China's investment in Africa sometimes being criticized as projects robbing Africa's natural resources or causing corruption in governments and businesses or falling into China's debt trap, but judging from the recent 3rd Forum on China-Africa Cooperation (FOCAC, 9-3-2018 in Beijing) attended by 53 African States, the African countries not only welcome China's investment in Africa but also enthusiastically anticipate closer China-Africa ties in support of China's BRI program. Many news reports on China's restructuring and extension of loans in Africa do suggest that China is not backing off from her Africa policy despite of some Chinese economists worrying whether China will be a sucker in Africa getting no return for her investments.

Chapter 35
Americans Should Really Understand the Taiwan Issue

*****

American people are proud citizens better versed in American history (The American Revolution and Independence (1776) and her own democratization process: The States grant white male land owners voting rights in 1789, free black male lose right to vote in some States 1792-1838, property qualification dropped for white men 1792-1856, women allowed to vote from 1920, all native Americans granted right to vote, 1924, Chinese immigrants granted the right to citizenship and voting right, 1943, adults 18-21 granted right to vote, 1972) than in foreign relations and global conflicts. The reason may be that there were never wars or foreign invasions occurred on the continent of the United States. Americans went to foreign wars generally out of patriotism, serving the country and the military and supporting the government's foreign policy, interpreted under national security consideration. The engagement of the U.S. in global conflicts prior to WW II and WW I were limited and constrained, it became full scale during WW II making the U.S. the strongest nation in the world as a result. Post WW II, when the spread of Communism flamed to threaten the capitalistic established nations and societies in the first half of the twenties century, the U.S. raised the flag to resist Communism and led the world to fight any Communist country. The American citizens generally accepted that doctrine whole-heartedly but rarely had learned the deep issues involved in the global conflicts, for example, the Korean War (6/27/1950 – 1/31/1955), the Vietnam War (2/28/1961 – 5/7/1975) and the Gulf War (8/2/1990 – present).

Korean War was an anti-Communist war but it evolved into a global conflict of nuclear threat not so much as a threat of Communism. It was obvious, Communist country fared poorly in economical development. The North Koreans finally realized that no suppression could hide the fact that South Koreans live with nearly 20+ times higher per capital GDP than their northern brothers. Now the South Korea and the North Korea are seeking a peaceful settlement, would the American government encourage that or reignite another Korean War to remove the nuclear threat? Wouldn't it make more sense to work with NK, SK and all their geopolitical neighbors together to resolve the nuclear issue by peaceful dialogue?!

Vietnam War was another bitter war; many Americans lost their lives for it, again under the flag of anti-Communism. The U.S. sort of inherited the Indochina regional unrest like a hot potato created by colonialism and the Japanese invasion. The U.S. picked her support and created South Vietnam waving the flags of democracy and anti-Communism but in the end giving in to nationalism that the local people wanted their way of life because of their history, culture and their will of self-governance with no foreign interference. After the war, North Vietnam and South Vietnam are united; perhaps still having conflicts with her neighbors, but Vietnam is striving in her own way of focusing on economic development. Ironically, the U.S. is now considering enticing Vietnam to become one of her strategic partners for her anti-China Policy. Does that make sense?

The U.S. has given up her national draft policy, that is, every eligible citizen (18-25) must serve in the military to meet the call of duty in case of war. As the Vietnam War drew to a close in 1973, the Selective Service announced the cease of draft calls after Richard Nixon, a conservative Republican, won the Presidential election over Senator George McGovern of S. Dakota, a Democrat and outspoken opponent of war. The present voluntary army system means that the military service has become a professional career which will respond to any duty of war called upon by the Pentagon under the Commander of Chief, the President.

We all knew how George W. Bush started the Iraq war with false information. Subsequently, there are debates of withdrawal from the Middle East from Bush through Obama and now to Trump. But the Gulf War debate had never reached the level like the Vietnam War debate. The simple reason is the draft system. It has become apparent; the President of the U.S. and the Congress must be prudent in managing global conflict and especially careful in initiating any war **and** the American citizens must raise their understanding of global conflicts so that the citizens can impose their understanding and will onto the elected officials to conduct foreign policies and make sensible war decisions. Citizens must realize that the career military system would not offer the nation a debate process about a war (where the entire nation participates) like a draft system would (since every family has a stake in it).

Recently, the U.S. confronted the "China Competition" by initiating a trade war to reduce trade imbalance. This measure itself can be understood by American citizens (to apply pressure to our trade partners to make them to trade fairly, to open up their markets and to stimulate American industry and corporations to focus on US economy). However, what is not understood by

American people is the ever growing anti-China attitude based on national security argument, same arguments similar to previous ones which led to Korean War, Vietnam War and Middle East Wars. In those wars, the American citizens were led to war with no deep understanding of why and whether or not the war was justified. The recent development of US-China Conflict seems to have more issues than the trade imbalance. One issue showing possibility of war is the Taiwan issue. The Taiwan issue was a seven decade old Chinese domestic conflict elevated to the global stage because of geopolitical conflict in Asia, recently heightened by the US Pivot to Asia Strategy. Similar to Korea and Vietnam, the Chinese domestic division was triggered by Communism, thus the U.S. was involved (supporting Taiwan and opposing the Mainland). The involvement of the U.S. should have been ceased when President Nixon signed the Shanghai Communiqué (1972) confirming Taiwan is a part of China and later reinforced by President Carter by formally recognizing PRC as the sole legal entity representing China and severed the official diplomatic relation with Taiwan (1979).

The American people should really understand the Taiwan issue to avoid another mistake of creating a war in Asia involving American military for no benefit. China regards Taiwan as a domestic issue, hoping to resolve it peacefully. The American people should try to understand the issue from Taiwan, China and the U.S. perspective. One article published in World Journal (9/5/2018), by Su Qi, a former Secretary of Taiwan's National Security Council, offers such a perspective. On the crucial issue, whether Mainland China would use military force to unite Taiwan and whether the U.S. would interfere with military force, Su states: Based on historical facts, China has not engaged in any military conflict after the Cold War; her wars were taking place only at peripheral regions of her national border, over sovereignty issue, nothing to do with Communism. He further points out that China's war management generally goes through three clear phases, a warning period, then surprise attack and quick ending and withdrawal, meaning a rational behavior.

Su reemphasizes that whether (or not) the Taiwan Strait would break out into a military conflict depends on the behavior of the Taiwan government. Whether a conflict will escalate into a war would depend on the U.S. and whether the war would become serious would depend on China's decision. At the moment, Taiwan's current administration is marching onto an anti-China path mimicking the U.S. despite of Mainland China's friendly gesture and generous offering in trade and benefits to Taiwan. The U.S. currently seems to be using the Taiwan issue to antagonize China by passing the Taiwan Travel Act, dedicating a big building for the American Institute in Taiwan (US Representative in Taiwan) and encouraging Taiwan to buy more US arms and develop submarines, all challenging the redline of the Mainland China raising probability of war. As American citizens, we must ask: Why do we want to trigger a war in Taiwan Strait? What will we gain? What did we learn from the Korean and Vietnam wars? Should we seriously rethink of our present and changing China Policy?!

Chapter 36
Should and How Can the West Contain
China's Global Aspiration? (I)

*****

The Chappaqua Library Foreign Policy Discussion Group sent out an announcement that on October 16, there will be a Skype linked seminar, entitled, China's Challenge - How Can/Should the West contain China's Global Aspiration, to be facilitated by Tyler Beebe, a Chappaqua, New York resident. The speaker will be Dennis Wilder, the managing director for the Initiative for U.S.- China Dialogue on Global Issues at Georgetown University and an assistant professor of Asian studies. Wilder has served as the National Security Council's Director for China and as the NSC Special Assistant to the President for East Asian Affairs. He is also a former CIA Deputy Assistant Director for East Asia and the Pacific. The topic is an interesting and important one, but the title suggested that the speaker came with a background to discuss 'how can the West contain China's global aspiration' first before the more logical consideration of whether or not 'should the West contain China's global aspiration'. Judging from the speaker's resume, I am not surprised that he is more versed on the "how can" methodology under the strategy that the West "should" contain China rather as an academic scholar who studies: What is global aspiration? Should any country have global aspiration? Can any country define its own global aspiration? Should any country or a collected group (for instance, The West, a rather old fashioned imprecise term used by Wilder's speech title compared to G7, G8 or G20) contain another country's global aspiration?

I certainly will attend Mr. Wilder's talk but I feel obligated to remind him of the above logical thinking. As the US-China relation has reached to a multi-lateral intersection, the China issue is more of the U.S.'s Challenge to ponder on the "should" question before the "how can" question and less as a China's challenge to worry about "the West". China seems to have come a long way, steadfastly, to pursue a simple goal to raise her citizens' livelihood into middle class by economic development and to engage herself in the world body to earn her respect and dignity by rejuvenating the glorious Chinese culture and heritage which was nearly destroyed by 'the West' and 'the Communism' in the 19th and most part of the 20th centuries. Yes, we do need to understand

China's global aspiration, but more importantly we need to understand both the U.S. and China's global aspiration and why and where is there a clash?!

First of all, we should not have a bias to discuss the China issue. Thus, I am less interested in "how can" (a relatively easier question) than in the question of "Should" (a harder question to answer) the West contain China's global aspiration. As modern seminars sometimes do beg for questions from the prospective audience in advance for the speaker, I decide to write about the above seminar topic in a logical sequence in this column before attending the seminar, more as thought provoking questions and a preparation for me to join the coming discussion seminar.

The logical thinking about this serious topic must be 'Should the West contain China's global aspirations?' first; then second, 'How can the West contain China's global aspirations?' Since WW II, the world has gone through many transformations, abolishing colonialism, rising of super powers and communism, collapse of the Soviet Union, revision of communism to embracing capitalism, striving developing countries in the third world, numerous regional wars and enduring global financial crises. Now the international community is a complex and sophisticated one. It is no surprise that China, as the most populated nation, is struggling with her development and searching her own formula for sustainable economical and political stability and growth. So, the "should" question must be asked by Americans, Europeans, Russians, Asians, Australians and Africans all with their own perspectives since the rise of China has impacted every one in the world.

However, since the U.S. is a superpower, self-charged with world leadership and global aspiration (American version), it is more important for us to focus on Americans' view (of course including Chappaqua citizens) on the "should" question. First, I ask myself, am I qualified to answer that question? Based on what? On Justice? Should any country other than the U.S. have global aspiration? Does global aspiration mean challenging the U.S.? Challenging the world leadership of the U.S.? Challenging militarily by force? (No, no one is strong enough to challenge the U.S.) Challenging economically? May be so, however the U.S. is still one of the richest nations on Earth. The U.S. spent a defense budget over $700 B versus China $150 B, thus still maintaining her super military power status in the world. But the U.S. can't stop N Korea, a small country, to develop nuclear missiles, what makes us sure that the U.S. can stop China to continue her military development, especially when the U.S. adopts a hostile containment policy to agitate and induce China to compete in military strength. What would this arms race lead to? The end result is not going to be a happy ending! Hence, we need to rethink the 'should' question.

Many hate-China people want to justify a containment policy towards China by stressing that economically the U.S. is threatened by China! Let's take s historical view, not too long ago, when China was the number one economy in the world in 18th century, she did not threaten any country, did she? It was the West brought colonialism to the world, invaded China, inflicted more than one century of misery to China. The U.S. played a minor part in the West aggression to squash China and later helped China fighting the Japanese in early part of 20th century. Post WW II, colonialism was abolished and the U.S. emerged as the strongest nation both militarily and economically. China came out of ashes, experimented miserably with communism, later embraced capitalism gingerly while transforming or reforming with socialistic principles. It took four decades for China to rise economically to be the second largest economy in the world. With 1.3 billion people working harder than the rest of the world, should we be surprised that China rises again? Should China be allowed to have her global aspiration? What is global aspiration? Do the U.S. and China have the same definition of global aspiration? Will human society forever be cursed by the ancient Greek Thucydides Trap? Is the U.S. a role model of global aspiration? Is maintaining superiority of military strength, having military bases everywhere in the world, settling international affairs unilaterally or simply earning world respect on the world stage the definition of global aspiration? Do we understand China's global aspiration? Is there a hidden agenda behind raising the vast Chinese population into middle class, such as mimicking the U.S. or threatening the world leadership of the U.S.? Shouldn't we understand these questions before addressing the 'should' question. (to be continued in Part II)

Chapter 37
Should and How Can the West Contain China's Global Aspiration? (II)

*****

Should we Americans let China have global aspiration is a weighty question, I am afraid that I have not seen enough think tank work to first clarify what is global aspiration? Do we have a double standard under hypocrisy: I can have it but you can't or I did it but no one else should do it. Should the U.S. contain China simply because China would someday become the number one economy in the world? Why China cannot use her wealth to aid Africa, Latin America, etc. to have more 'say' on the world stage? Was it because that we Americans cannot face competition? Some blame China to have succeeded in her economical development by unfair practice, but in my opinion, it is a little too late and too naïve at this point. Reviewing history, one notes that there was no shortage of luring technologies (through copying and/or using market share to obtain technology) by one country from the other. Just tracking the recent few centuries one can see that Japan and the West have absorbed technologies from China; more recently the U.S. from the UK and Europe; then Japan and EU countries from the U.S.; S. Korea and China from Japan and the U.S. and now China is worrying other countries may copy her technologies. The fact that China applies and is granted the highest number of patents each year is a direct proof that when you don't have technologies you must get them to survive and when you have them you worry about losing them. Is there a cure for this cycle, unfortunately, the only solution is to keep developing new technologies to stay ahead. That is what the U.S. must do and what China wants to do as well.

As stated earlier, the 'how can' question, is a lot easier to answer. Yes, if the West were united (like the eight nations united to invade China in 1800's) and determined, perhaps, they could contain China's rise or might slow her down. However, two things have changed, first, China is no longer a weak nation like the Qing Dynasty and second, the West has less reason to gang up together to contain China for their own good. The West now need China more than any other country (even the U.S.) to sustain their economy and world stability; especially, the West's anti-Russia legacy strategy has driven Russia to be closer to China, a complete reversal of the global politics from one and half century ago. UK is now exiting EU and EU is struggling economically with some countries facing bankruptcy. What is the motivation for France or Germany and other EU small nations to engage an all-out containment strategy against China? The current US–led policy of containing Russia built over seven decades is falling apart as the energy not gun power dictates the stability of a country. The use and effectiveness of NATO is being questioned. (The U.S. seems no longer willing to foot most of the NATO cost) Why should UK and EU unite together with the U.S. to counter Russia (which holds the energy supply to EU) and stop the rise of China (which is supporting the global economy) just to keep the U.S. in world leadership? The current U.S. Administration's self-centered America First Policy cast more doubt on the wisdom of an anti-China policy. After all, China's aspiration of building one Belt and One Road (Belt and Road initiative, BRI) seems to be a peaceful win-win program for all participants. The number of nation participants in BRI especially the Asian Infrastructure and Investment Bank (AIIB) is a testimony to the fact that not many nations are motivated to join an anti-China camp.

It is rather unfortunate that the current U.S. Administration is driving an anti-China strategy based on outdated arguments (anti-communism rhetoric), ignoring the changing reality (world transformation) and pacifying a real need of self-examination (what did the U.S. do wrong?). The decline of the U.S. influence on the world stage is not caused by the rise of China. The decline of US influence was gradual and China's rise was rapid, perhaps in contrast, some would use China as the scapegoat. In all honesty, the fundamental reason is that the U.S. does not accept and face the reality. The U.S. loses industry by industry mainly due to her own failed policies. The U.S. favors financial industry over manufacturing, such as textile, steel, aluminum, auto, etc, etc created her economical problems which can hardly be blamed on others. In fact, many other countries following the U.S. economic model suffer the same consequences. Even China herself faces debt financing problems (quantitative easing for example) similar to the U.S. Actually, managing nations just like managing a corporation, the U.S. must focus on the competitiveness issue, not walking away from the global market but engaging it and finding complimentary products and services for the world. China must maintain her competitiveness as well; the U.S. must view China as a vibrant partner to develop win-win collaboration rather than view China as a scapegoat for her failures. In the end, a crippled China does not mean a healthier U.S. One thing that does make the present world different from the past is the advances in technology. The manufacturing processes become more complicated subject to material and skill dependencies often available from other countries. Therefore, division of labor becomes necessary practice which encourages international cooperation to produce the most cost effective products.

Out of G8, China is the only country that has risen without applying invasion or practicing colonialism to other countries. China built the Great Wall to keep out invaders that is a deep rooted philosophy in the minds of Chinese. Making an assumption that China is going to dominate the world with bad consequences (comparing to what the U.S. has done as the world leader) is an unfair and unproven notion. The West invited China into WTO after years of rejection but China persevered and thrived as a WTO member. Many countries benefitted from WTO and some still struggling but there is no proof that under WTO rules it is a zero-sum economic game. In a nuclear world, using military power to settle disputes especially among big nations with nuclear power is not an option. Clearly, nations must work with international bodies to resolve issues. Hence, 'should the West contain China's global aspiration' is not really the question to address, the real question is how can we strengthen the world bodies, the U.N., WTO, or the like to allow all countries to compete under the same rules with their own global aspirations. This must be done under the framework of global democracy. The West has created the United Nations and embraced democracy for its operating principles. Democracy has its value and deficiencies but it is a peaceful means to settle things. All nations have no choice but to work with the existing system and try to improve it while they can. Therefore, it is fair to say that no one should contain another country's global aspiration unless the aspiration is proven to be harmful to the world.

Chapter 38
Anti-China Trade Wars in 19th and 21st Century
- Silk Tea Opium and Toaster Dryer Weapons

*****

Since the U.S. launched a trade war against China, a lot of discussions about trade wars and its negative impact, on both sides, leading to potential inflation, shortage of goods and decreased quality of life, have appeared. Yet, the present US Administration seems to believe that, it can dictate the consequence of the trade war ignoring the historical lessons and China's resilience. This attitude seems to prevail among the White House leadership. China as the largest country in population has suffered from trade wars for 100+ years with bitter memory. Hence, China is extremely conscientious about trade frictions, not only eager to avoid trade conflict but also mentally and physically prepared for trade wars. Observing the past six months since President Trump initiated a tariff on aluminum and steel imports followed by two waves of tariffs on $250B of Chinese imports; China has taken cautious and calculated counter-measures to respond to the trade war and vowed to fight it to the end and never to give in. In this article, we first review the last trade wars China endured during the 19th century (launched by the British eventually evolved to include the eight nations including the U.S. and Japan, ganging together against a militarily weak China), then we discuss the present anti-China trade war initiated by the U.S. (hoping to gain allies to jointly punish China). We hope that, by studying the history, we can draw lessons from the past trade wars so we may make wise decisions to avoid future trade wars that may lead to the collapse of world economy and possibly the downfall of a nation.

Silk Road was a symbol representing trade between China and the West anf the mid-East. Silk routes were established during the Han Dynasty of China (130 BCE -1453CE) by its strong emperors such as Han Wu Di. The silk routes linked the commerce regions of the ancient world between Asia and Europe. The West is familiar with the European explorer Marco Polo (1254-1324 CE), who traveled along these routes and described them in his famous work but this network of roads were actually coined as silk routes by the German geographer and traveler, Ferdinand von Richthofen, in 1877 CE, ('Seidenstrasse' or 'Seidenstrassen'). Polo and later von Richthofen categorized the goods transported back and forth on the Silk Road including horses, camels, animal products, fruits, gold and silver, …armors and slaves (from West to East) and silk, tea, dyes, gems, china, spices, rice, bronze and gold artifacts, medicine, perfumes, ivory, paper and gunpowder (East to West).

China was the world's largest economy from 17th and 18th century up to the 1820s while the British Empire has become the world's greatest military power with colonies all over the world. The trade imbalance between England and China grew simply because China's tea, silk and porcelain etc were in high demand in the West. Pressured by this trade imbalance and burdened by her big military expense, England resorted to opium trade backed up by her military power. History taught us that China resisted the opium trade but lost to England in two Opium Wars (1839-1842 and 1856-1860) resulted in some of the world's worst unequal treaties which not only required China to pay huge sum of war reparation but also forced China into opening free trade ports to England, waiving tariffs and leasing the Hong Kong Island to England for 99 years. Opium is addictive which can destroy one's ability to live a normal life, thus, an opium trade is a sin. Following the Opium Wars, the West powers all descended in China seeking the same unfair treaties from China. During the 19th century, colonialism coupled with militarism were at the peak, even the small Japan, had embraced such doctrines and became an imperialist nation setting her eyes on conquering China. The first major Sino-Japan war began in 1894 resulted in another unequal treaty, paying Japan war reparation equal to six times of Japan's annual national budget, ceding the Taiwan island to Japan for fifty years and permitting Japan to encroach the Korea Peninsula and territories in North East China. China was a sad victim of trade wars during 19th century. The trade wars not only destroyed her economy but devastated her as a sovereign nation way into the 20th century.

Fortunately, the ambitions of imperialistic Japan and Germany were finally checked as they were defeated in WWII. Colonialism and imperialism were denounced allowing many former colonies to gain independence and pursue economic development. China was briefly united after WW II but divided as the civil war wounds broke again eventually resulting in a split of Mainland and Taiwan allied with the Soviet Union and the United States respectively. Cold War formed almost immediately between the U.S. (NATO allies) and the Soviet Union (WARSAW allies) right after WW II. Mainland China and Taiwan caught in between. Mainland China experimented with communism with poor result then gingerly embraced capitalism under the dominating party (CCP) producing a fast economic growth. Taiwan experimented with democracy and gained prosperity during the Korean War and the Vietnam War in Asia. The economic success of Mainland and Taiwan should be credited more to the Chinese people's strong work ethics rather than the political system or the U.S. financial aid to Taiwan or Mainland China's admission to the world trade organization (WTO). China has maintained a double digit economic growth over several decades; hence, her becoming the world's second largest economy should surprise no one.

Today, China sells household goods like toaster and dryers to the world and maintains a significant trade surplus with the U.S., in fact with most of her trading partners. This trade imbalance is now a pressure to the U.S. because she has run a national budget deficit since 1970's except briefly during 1998-2001. The U.S. has built a huge national debt (> $19 trillion surpassing her GDP) which is held by her trading partners, China being the biggest holder. When the U.S. launches a trade war against China today, it reminds the Chinese and us of the vicious trade wars British launched in 19th century. England was the strongest nation in the world then but burdened by a large military expenditure and suffered with a trade deficit and a stagnant GDP. The British Empire chose to use her military power to solve her trade imbalance by enforcing opium trade onto China. Today, the U.S. is in a similar situation having to maintain a huge military force outreached worldwide under a deficit national budget. The US trade imbalance and huge national debt are probably worse than those of the British Empire's two century ago. The real difference is that the U.S. has weapons with hi-tech which the British Empire did not have. So the U.S. appears to use weapons (instead of opium) to solve her trade imbalance. The recent approval of sales to Taiwan $37 billion worth of weaponry is a suspicious motive. If the intention is to stir up a war between Mainland China and Taiwan then the weapon sale is more evil than selling opium.

Of course, China is very different now than in 19th century. China is modernized with a solid industrial base and a large patriotic population willing and ready to fight trade wars. The bitter trade war experience in the past has imprinted on the minds of Chinese people and given them the will and right to build a strong nation. Therefore, naturally China will continue her nation building, reacting forcefully when threatened or pressured by a foreign power. The more pressure the U.S. applies to China with whatever means, the more will China resist for survival. If the U.S. is concerned with 'the China Manufacture 2025' development plan, pressuring her to stop is just the wrong strategy. China has always stressed her desire for a peaceful rise but vowed to fight the U.S. initiated trade war to the end. China emphasizes win-win collaboration and seeks cooperation with the U.S. If the U.S. accepts that and maintains her self-confidence as a strong nation (better endowed with natural resources and well advanced in technologies than China), a planned collaborative US-China relation is the obvious winner, beneficial to both countries economically, politically and helpful in keeping world peace and prosperity. A premeditated war plan will likely destroy both and the world!

Chapter 39
Culture War - 20:80 Strategy to Control the World

*****

Media serve(s) a vital function in human society no matter what political system it is functioning under. Journalists, including everyone contributing to the media, perform a noble duty to report truth and maintain justice for mankind. However, today's media industry and some media professionals are corrupted and become a tool of the ruling elites whether they control a single party or multiple party political system or government. The controlling elites possess wealth and power far more than the mass. Around the world, say 193 member countries in the United Nation, they strive for economic development, but unfortunately, all face a common problem - the huge wealth gap in society. Putting it simply, the 20:80 phenomenon occurs because that twenty percent or less of the population posses 80 percent or more of the wealth, thus creating a 20:80 division in the society where the 20% elites are the ruling class. Fortunately, this 20:80 phenomenon has become more observable and understandable by the masses both in capitalist or socialist societies begging for changes.

The Mainstream Media are generally controlled by the elites (20%), however, with advancement of internet technology, Organic Media appealing to the mass (80%) has sprouted. One often can find publications in the Organic Media dealing with an important topic normally discussed in the Mainstream Media but appeared to reach the 'innocent' masses. I found one such publication integrating the news in the mainstream, presenting with in-depth analysis and aiming to sound an alarm about the 20:80 problem and a concern about the future of human society, namely the aspiration of young people for their future. This article, written anonymously in Chinese and entitled, "范冰冰事件暴露出美国对华计划，令人胆战心惊！"， has appeared in Xila.com and other websites. The tax evasion by the famous actress Fan Bingbing, is a current news widely reported but this article links the news to a big topic, Culture War, a strategy of the elites to control the world. The article specifically refers to Zbigniew Brzezinski, a political strategist who, served as the national security advice under President Carter, had written books about how to maintain the leadership position of the U.S. through a non-military strategy which I would characterize it as 'Culture War' or in his words: How to Win in World Competition. In this column, I shall use the above Organic media article to extend the discussion on the big topic which it alluded to - from culture war to the future of mankind.

First, the background of the above article can be summarized briefly as: 1. Tax evasion of Fan Bingbing (hundreds of million dollars) is the result of greed prevailing in the movie industry, originated from Hollywood, hiding income with devious means to avoid taxes. 2. Hollywood is the key component of the 'Soft Power' of the U.S. to influence and control the world consistent with Brzezenski's thesis of winning competition. 3. Specific means of providing the masses with A. Entertainment that dissipates people's energy (examples, sex, games, gossip talk shows etc.) and B. Media Games that satisfy people's mental void (examples, soup opera, talent shows, idol worship, etc.). The article highlights Brzezinski's books such as America World (2008) and Grand Chess Board (1997) and placing Brzezinski's 'winning competition' as an evil strategy. These arguments are probably more substantiated by facts observable today on media power than supported by his intent long before writing his books. However, the above two flags raised by the Organic Media attributing "tittytainment" as the weapon of 'soft power' and 'culture war' initiated by the media industry do have their own merits; the media industry has been globalized and its world-wide influence and financial control certainly belong to the 20% elites of the world.

The masses of the world do seem to lose interest in serious thinking in political ideology and life aspirations giving in to trivia entertainment. Gossip news filled the media and Internet amplified them. Young people are lost substituting media stars as their life advisor rather than studying learned philosophers. To these points, the article presented the following observations: 1. People lost thinking ability, 2. Rigid new classes formed by 20:80 and attributed to the 'soft power' and 'culture war'. Money is used to buy and generate elites (recruiting and scholarship to elite students). American values and brainwash are delivered through media. Providing financial support to opposition even enemy's enemy to topple a government. Buy and corrupt government and military power to achieve regime change. Again, these charges can be substantiated with facts despite the control of mainstream media, however, the prevention of the above or reversing the tide is possible.

For a culture war, there can be a culture defense even a culture revival. When there is an invasive 'soft power', there can be a defensive 'soft power' even a counter soft power. China seems to be seriously concerned with the above issues initiating policies to deal with the 'soft power invasion'. Long before Fan Bingbing's case being a hot news item, one can see that China has exerted as much counter effort to deal with the 'West soft power invasion'. China allocated significant funds to support the Chinese culture media productions from movies, culture shows on traditional Chinese poetry, arts and music. China sponsored a global television network to cover the neglected news from Africa, Asia and Latin America. China especially focuses on motivational media production highlighting not only heroes of the past but also the great achievers of the modern time, scientists, inventors and engineers who have contributed to the advances of modern China in fields of architecture, bridge building, dams for generating electricity, high-speed rails, jumbo planes and various technological advances from satellite positioning, space shuttle and exploration, agricultural to Chinese and western medical sciences.

The above Organic Media article most likely will not get as many eyeballs as the Fan Bingbing's gossip news. As a person dedicated his retirement life to media work, I hope to do my best to reach out to the masses in the world with facts and truth.

Chapter 40
Real Threat to the U.S. and China
~Possible Peaceful Solution (I)

*****

Abstract

The China Threat or the US Threat to each other and to the world is false. The real threat is that mankind is facing the shortage of energy and resources to sustain economic development for the purpose of having better living condition and advancing civilization. Through an energy consumption analysis, one can see that adopting a 'Competition Model' between the U.S. and China will not eliminate the 'real threat' to the two nations and the world but lead to war and mutual destruction. Only adopting a 'Collaboration Model' and stopping mutual interference of each country's political system can achieve long-term objectives to sustain each nation's economic development and world peace and prosperity.

History showed us that human societies compete for Earth resources, land, water, minerals, agriculture produce and industrial products for survival then for higher standard of living motivated by human aspiration for civilization and economic welfare, ultimately measurable by food, material and energy consumption. Nations form, civilizations advance and countries compete for their people's welfare (in varied degree since no government can completely satisfy its people's desire) by securing Earth resources, producing goods, trading with others and maintaining economic growth and improving standard of living. Nations do not always have to compete; collaboration can yield win-win benefits; notably medical research has led to elimination of human diseases and immigration policies have led to talent migration and many successes in mining, farming to technology development. Unfortunately, competition was prevailing in the past 100 years, the developed countries advanced faster than the less-developed countries thus creating a large wealth/productivity gap between nations, especially in technology applications exhibited by the standard of living and GDP.

Today, the world population is about 7.3 billion; huge wealth gap exists between and within nations. All 195 countries (193 UN members) on Earth want to develop economically. China (1.4 billion people), has made exceptional progress in that endeavor in the past 30-40 years lifting several hundreds of millions of people above the poverty line and making her the number two economy in the world. China's success has become an envy of the world. Many countries want to emulate China's success but sadly some countries tout a China Threat Theory using speculative arguments partly ideological and partly historical stories such as the Thucydides Trap. As the world leader, the U.S. has helped and claimed the credit for opening to China and contributing to her growth but began to contemplate the China Threat Theory. This shift of position, from engagement/collaboration to threat/competition will impact the future of China and the U.S. as well as the entire world. This is a serious issue; we must understand 'what is the real threat to the U.S. and to the world'? Is there a peaceful solution to the real threat? What will be our future under a competition versus a collaboration model?

We have gone through a Cold War, but it did not change the world for the better. Shifting the China policy and reviving a new Cold War does not make sense at all because China is not a real threat to the U.S. or to the world. The **real threat** is that the world is resources limited and almost depleted which will thwart the economic development of the world, including the U.S., China and every country on Earth. Global trade is not a zero-sum game. Businesses will adjust their strategy depending on the market shift and market needs. The world market grows as population grows as people desiring for better-living. Economic growth should not be a zero-sum game if the Earth resources were not limited. Unfortunately, Earth is resource limited, thus a 'competition model' is vulnerable and destructive whereas a 'collaboration model' is the plausible alternative.

Human societies require many resources which can be categorized broadly as food (including land and water to grow food), materials (including minerals and production materials and technologies) and energy (including oil, gas, coal, nuclear and renewable). In the food category, the world has been able to produce sufficient food to feed the Earth's population if nations collaborate and trade with a 'charitable mind'. Barring natural disasters such as quakes, floods and tsunamis or poor government policies and management, there will be no food shortage. Although Earth does not have infinite mineral supply but with technology improving discovery, production, material recovery and recycling plus innovative design, manufacturing, and ingenious applications, the material supply is not a threat. Even in the case of 'rare earth' minerals, a collaborative approach rather than a competitive manner can satisfy the world demand for generations.

The energy category is the most important element in sustaining human civilization and its advances. In fact, the energy consumption level, with heating and cooling needs in regions near the poles and the equator adjusted, is a good indicator for the standard of living. The ultimate need in energy is electricity, except some old appliances burning oil, gas or coal for transport, heating and cooking. Scientists have already shown that the above three energy sources are being depleted fast. On top of that, they contribute to pollution and climate change that are harmful to human. The renewable energies are also limited because of the limited land, water, sunlight and wind cycle. The nuclear energy is expensive and requires careful control, management and waste disposal to avoid devastating accidents. To explore high efficiency and high power nuclear energy such as fusion energy (man-made sun), it requires collaborations among world scientists and researchers to achieve breakthroughs.

The technical indicator most useful for illustrating human society's energy dependency (civilization, GDP etc) is the per capita electric power usage (KWHr per person). Most appliances, facilities and utilities humans use all require electricity, and it is more desirable to convert other forms of energy (heat from burning substance to hydraulic, geothermal or wind power) to electricity for the end application for efficiency and convenience. It is desirable to develop electric cars to replace gasoline cars for pollution reduction and energy conservation. Of course, electric power comes from other forms of limited energy sources, thus human electricity consumption is ultimately limited unless breakthroughs such as fusion energy becomes a reality.

The world electric power consumption is about 22 trillion KWHr per year (2014 CIA data). Divided by 7.3 billion people (2014 data), it means that 2700 KWHr/person/yr. However, the world electric power usage is not even and fair among nations reflecting their economic status. For example, the U.S. uses about 4 trillion KWHr/yr amounts to ~12 KWHr/person/yr (2015-2016 CIA data) and China uses about 6.4 trillion KWHr/yr amounts to only 4.4 KWHr/person/yr (2017 NEA data), less than 40% of the US per capita usage. In comparison, India uses 1.1KWHr/p/yr, Japan uses 7.5KWHr/p/yr (2016 CIA data) and African nations use very small amount of electricity, all reflecting the nation's per capita GDP and its people's the standard of living. The real threat is that the limited energy sources on Earth cannot support the growth of world energy demand.

As nations develop, raising their people's standard of living, human society needs to find new energy, otherwise, the zero-sum formula (energy) will dictate. As populated developing nations such as China and India develop their economy, they have to take more share of the world energy supply. This is the real threat to the U.S., the biggest per capita electricity user next to Germany, and China, the most populated nation, because their combined usage of electric power is about 50% of the world supply. Apparently, China is aware of this problem and is conscientiously seeking solutions. China has allocated huge budget to develop energy sources, notably several large hydraulic power stations on their rivers, Yangtze, Yellow and Qinghai Rivers. China makes a great effort in renewable energies as the largest producer and user of solar panels and perhaps also wind turbines. China explores geothermal energy and the frozen methane under Deep Ocean. China is also educating their citizens on conservation through life style curtailing waste, tightening pollution control and limiting carbon emission. China is a keen supporter of the Paris Climate Control Agreement.

Chapter 41
Real Threat to the U.S. and China
~Possible Peaceful Solution (II)

*****

Abstract

The China Threat or the US Threat to each other and to the world is false. The real threat is that mankind is facing the shortage of energy and resources to sustain economic development for the purpose of having better living condition and advancing civilization. Through an energy consumption analysis, one can see that adopting a 'Competition Model' between the U.S. and China will not eliminate the 'real threat' to the two nations and the world but lead to war and mutual destruction. Only adopting a 'Collaboration Model' and stopping mutual interference of each country's political system can achieve long-term objectives to sustain each nation's economic development and world peace and prosperity.

The energy shortage is a threat to China but is just as real to the U.S. even though the U.S. is blessed with large deposits of fossil energy and gases. These resources eventually will be depleted and worst their usage will hasten the deterioration of the Earth environment and climate change. The U.S. energy policies had been practicing pro-conservation and seeking renewable energies, but recently, there are signs of change - a dangerous one - to thwart other nations' economic growth (and need of energy) based on the zero-sum logic – This is essentially a Competition Strategy. The U.S. wants to slow down China's growth in order to sustain her competitive advantage and her demand of energy. But this logic is false, it is not just China, but Brazil, Russia, India and the rest of the world are all developing and demanding more energy. The U.S. cannot constantly thwart the development of every other nation, to maintain her own growth. This is not only unethical but also impractical, since 300 million Americans cannot dictate 7 billion people's fate. Even the U.S. is the superpower; it is not possible to sustain the 'Competition Model' through economical, military or any other power against the rising nations. The competition model leads only to a result of mutual destruction. The BRICS is one group which has formed an alliance to protect their economic growth challenging the U.S. if necessary. The U.S. cannot afford to and should not take on the rest of the world to compete for limited Earth resources.

The competition model is vulnerable but there is a peaceful solution, perhaps the only workable one, that is, the 'Collaboration model'. Science and technology breakthroughs have slowed down after one century of rapid development. The U.S. had achieved the leader position in science and technologies. Atomic theory, Quantum Mechanics and Relativity have brought us great advances in physics, material sciences and various technologies but we are reaching the limits. For example, one of the greatest inventions, solid state integrated circuits, is now miniaturized to 3 nano-meter (angstrom) level, meaning not far to shrink. In order to get more inventions and innovations, scientists, engineers and researches must collaborate and work hard to find breakthroughs and solve the toughest tasks. The U.S. was the leader in inventions in 20th century represented by patents rewarded to US government and corporations but now others have caught up. China is now receiving the greatest number of patents with her technological advances visibly in infrastructure construction (bridge and tunnel technology), manufacturing processes (automation and robotics), transportation (high-speed rail and electric vehicles), agricultural (conversion of desert to farm land, salt water rice field), energy (storage, ultra high voltage transmission and fusion experiments), and even in space technology (satellites, Beidou geo-positioning and space shuttle and space station) China made these achievements despite of decades of technology sanctions from the West. To squeeze the last mile productivity or to explore new energy, for instance to make man-made sun with fusion and to explore outer-space for new discoveries and resources, it is obvious that collaboration is the best bet to yield positive results, especially between the U.S. and China.

The U.S. had shared the low and middle level technologies with the world by exporting and domestically reducing her manufacturing base in low and mid-tech industries. The U.S. favored hi-tech industries and finance engineering and systems for her economical growth. However, the 2008 financial crisis and the stagnant economic growth followed in recent decade showed that the U.S. must change her policies. In view of the above analysis, one can see clearly that the U.S. must abandon the zero-sum competition model and adopt a collaborative model to pursue win-win projects in various fields, especially in energy. For example, the U.S. can offer her abundant energy resources to obtain favorable collaboration with other countries. Instead of making military provocation in South China Sea over navigation around small islands, it is far more productive to collaborate with China to explore the deep sea frozen methane energy in that region to alleviate the world energy shortage threat. Similarly, working with China in electric cars, energy storage, fusion energy and space exploration may yield solutions to solve the resource limitation problems on Earth. Mankind has come a long way in making progress in civilization. It is time for great nations to lead the Earth to think as one community to deal with the real threat to humans rather than to compete in an ancient style such as Thucydides behavior.

China's constitution defines China as a socialist unitary state under the people's democratic dictatorship. It defines China's political system as an alliance of the working classes, all workers and peasants. The constitution does not mention The Chinese Communist Party of China (CCP) as the ruling party in China. CCP claims to represent the working classes and wants to remain in power forever. (Which political party on Earth does not want to remain in power for as long as it can? The answer is none.) Only the working class can take away the power from the ruling party through a constitution provided political process, in China's case, the People's Congress, or the alternative by revolution. Thus, the CCP places people's welfare as the top priority and very much mindful of any people's dissatisfaction that may lead to a revolt. True, revolution is not easy but a ruling government's constant concern of people's dissatisfaction is an effective accountability measure. China seems to have adopted a reform process to ensure that the ruling party is placing people's welfare and maintaining national unity as the highest priority and have enacted measures to prevent and punish corruption. China has not showed any real aggressive expansion towards other countries other than defending her historical sovereignty. China's military spending and defense effort are mainly reactionary to external threats and provocation. Judging China's current policies, one cannot deny that the CCP is fulfilling the above national objectives effectively. The U.S., for her own interests, has worked with many democratic and dictator governments in the past 70 years; it seems that a stable Chinese government led by CCP would be a preferred government for the U.S. to collaborate with.

Some think tanks in the U.S. including a few current Administrative officials seem to believe the U.S. can adopt the 'Competition Model' and make the U.S. great again. The above analysis tells us though such a view is short-sighted; a 'Competition Model' will eventually lead to war and mutual destruction. Only the 'collaboration model', on the other hand, can be a peaceful solution to solve the real threat to both countries and the world. If the U.S. and China can collaborate to face the challenges and threats together, there is a good chance that the two nations can not only sustain their own economic development but also lead the entire world to better living condition. For the 'collaboration model' to work, interference of the other nation's political system must stop. Only under stable political systems, collaboration on long-term objectives can be achieved. As Trump and Xi may meet again in the future, let's hope that the U.S. and China will move towards collaboration rather than confrontation!

Chapter 42
The CPTPP Can Be an Effective Trade Agreement for the Entire Asia Pacific Region

*****

CPTPP is an acronym representing 'the Comprehensive and Progressive Agreement for Trans-Pacific Partnership', also known as TPP-11, a trade agreement between eleven nations after the U.S. pulled out. The original Trans-Pacific Partnership (TPP) was involving twelve nations including Australia, Brunei, Canada, Chile, Japan, Malaysia, Mexico, New Zealand, Peru, Singapore, the U.S. and Vietnam. Oddly, the TPP excluded China, the biggest trading partner in the Pacific. The original TPP grew out of a trade agreement between Brunei, Chile, New Zealand and Singapore, known as P4, initiated by Brunei and signed in 2005. In 2008, it attracted the eight additional nations under the New name TPP.

The U.S. under the Obama Administration with its Secretary of State, Hillary Clinton, was supportive of the TPP, although there were arguments that TPP was not beneficial to the U.S. The twelve nations signed the agreement on 2/4/2016 allowing two years for each member nation to ratify the agreement; the effective date was set to be December 30, 2018, 60 days after 50% of members ratified it. One of the motivation factors in reaching this agreement was that the TPP might have a geopolitical effect of reducing the members' dependence on Chinese trade. On this point, it is debatable whether the 'China dependency' is a good or bad thing from global trade perspective. The TPP issue had become a debate item in the US 2016 Presidential Election. Presidential candidate Trump had, since April, 2015, expressed opposition to TPP claiming that it would be unfair to the U.S. causing more unemployment and trade deficit. Candidate Hillary Clinton also took an about-face opposing TPP during her campaign. Thus, when Trump won the election, only days after taking office, he issued an executive order to pull out of the TPP.

The legally verified text of the Comprehensive and Progressive Agreement for Trans-Pacific Partnership (CPTPP) was released on February 21, 2018. The text of the agreement contains 30 chapters, numerous side letters between specific member nations and annexes to the chapters. Since the Pull-out of the U.S. many chapters and languages pertaining to the U.S. are no longer valid.

Even excluding the U.S. and China, the economies included in the CPTPP are significant, amount to 13.5 percent of the world GDP – worth a total of $10 trillion. Of course, the main purpose of CPTPP is concerned with reducing costs for doing trades and businesses, but more importantly, it includes commitments to safeguard and enforce high labor and environmental standards across the Asia-Pacific region preserving Member Nation's right to regulate for legitimate public policies and creating new opportunities for international trade and generating jobs leading to a better standard of living for Member Nations.

The CPTPP inherited many of the elements that were negotiated as part of the Trans-Pacific Partnership (TPP), but following the pull-out of the United States, the remaining participants had to agree and suspend 22 items from the TPP, particularly in the areas of investment, intellectual property and pharmaceuticals. One of the concerns in global trade is the threat of the effective operation of World Trade Organization (WTO) rules, including its dispute resolution mechanism. With the two largest economies, the U.S. and China excluded from the CPTPP and currently (they) engaged in a trade war and legal proceedings concerning WTO rule compliance and interpretations, the real effectiveness of CPTPP could be limited. Of course, the more members joining the CPTPP, the more effective the CPTPP agreement would become. Therefore, it is desirable that the current CPTPP members recruit the U.S., China, and other significant economies in the Asia-Pacific region, namely, South Korea, Hong Kong and Taiwan into CPTPP and broaden its scope and effectiveness.

Trade agreement could not be totally disconnected from international politics and nationalism but if it was overwhelmed by political conflicts, it would lose its significance. Japan should be given credit for laboring and transforming TPP to CPTPP, while the U.S. was moving towards protectionism in an opposite direction of reaching global trade agreement. This change of US behavior is exhibited in the new USMCA orchestrated by the U.S. replacing the old NAFTA with Mexico and Canada as well as in the trade war initiated by her against China. From lowering tariff and protectionism point of view, the CPTPP may be considered as the 'Gold Standard'. The Twenty-two TPP provisions suspended were more of the interest of the United States rather than that of other negotiating partners. One of the most contested provisions advocated by the U.S. was increasing the abilities of companies to sue national governments over strict government regulations on oil and gas developments. Another issue, the extension of author's copyright to life plus seventy years, different from the standards in other countries but insisted by the U.S., was substantially reduced in the CPTPP language. The original chapter on state-owned enterprises (SOEs) is unchanged, requiring signatories to share information about SOEs with each other, an obvious intent of preventing state intervention in markets. CPTPP also includes the most detailed standards for protecting intellectual property of any trade agreement, from protections against intellectual property theft to corporations operating abroad.

Six nations, Mexico, Japan, Singapore, Australia, New Zealand and Canada, have already ratified CPTPP, thus, it will become effective December 30, 2018. Looking into the future, there may be new members wishing to join in. The U.K. has already expressed interest in joining CPTPP after her Brexit in March 2019. The Trump Administration had kept the door open by saying that she may join if the agreement is renegotiated. Further on 4/12/2018, Trump even ordered his staff to look into the rejoining Issue. As mentioned above, South Korea, Hong Kong Taiwan and China should be invited into CPTPP, ideally with China and the U.S. joining as full members at the same time. It seems that the CPTPP 11-members may have an opportunity to transform their 'Gold Standard' to a 'Diamond Standard' by making extra efforts to persuade the above members to join CPTPP.

South Korea and the U.S. had just concluded a bilateral trade agreement. If the U.S. could be persuaded to join CPTPP, South Korea would likely to follow. On the other hand, if China was persuaded to join, Hong Kong would be a sure in. Taiwan is in fact the most vulnerable economy being excluded from the CPTPP and yet Taiwan may be the only obstacle for Hong Kong and Mainland China to join CPTPP out of a political dilemma created by a post WW II political division of Mainland China and Taiwan followed after Japan's surrender and returning Taiwan to China. Mainland and Taiwan each claimed to be a part of China and yet politically divided in the world arena for no good reason. Accepting one China with two separate political systems is advocated by Mainland, practiced by Hong Kong and Macao but resisted by Taiwan out of insecurity. Taiwan seems to have an excellent opportunity to use the CPTPP as the test case to evaluate whether Taiwan can function under 'the one China two political systems', in fact three or four political systems if including Hong Kong and Macao in CPTPP. Taiwan's economy is very much dependent on the Mainland market and so do many other CPTPP member nations. Collaborating with Mainland China and inviting her to join the CPTPP makes logical sense. When Taiwan and every country finally realize that by putting aside the political confrontation with Mainland China aside, all the significant economies in the AP region can work under a renegotiated CPTPP for everyone's benefit. Then the CPTPP can become a 'diamond standard' trade agreement for the entire Asia Pacific region. Therefore, it makes perfect sense for the present CPTPP or TPP-11 members to work hard towards getting China and the U.S. into the CPTPP along with the two Koreas, Hong Kong, Macao and Taiwan.

Chapter 43
To Resolve the Economic Competition
between the U.S. and China

*****

Henry Paulson, the 74th Secretary of Treasury and former CEO of Goldman Sachs, spoke at the Bloomberg's New Economic Forum held on November 6-7, 2018 in Singapore. His Opening Remarks were entitled, Cross Road from a Healthy Strategic Competition Will Tip into a Full-Blown Cold War. Paulson's astute observations on the economy and trade issues stressing the U.S. and China include the following: 1. Common interests did not yield common actions (N. Korea), 2. Disagreements on maritime rights created tension (South China Sea), 3. Opposed views on international governance (security issue), and 4. Dialogue yielded poor results (trade war has no winner) and 5. Views towards each other are diverging (hostile rhetoric).

He summarized the sentiments of the U.S. as: I. China's 17 years in WTO still made her closed to competition, II. China requires joint venture and ownership on foreign investment and III. WTO must be reformed or modernized. The current situation is leading the two economies to decouple. The two political parties in the U.S. agree that China's rise is at the US expense hurting American workers. Some US corporations accept the current situation by maximizing profit but jeopardizing future competitiveness. In contrast, Chinese firms can freely operate in other countries but not reciprocal. Chinese government (CCP) has strong command on all businesses, requiring private businesses to support State goal and foreign technology to become Chinese technology (indigenization process), which with its success is extending to OBOR or BRI, a central issue and a source of tension in US-China relations.

China's sentiments can be summarized as follows: I. Chinese investments in the U.S. for job creation with no security risks are turned down by the U.S. government, II. Forty years of integration of two economies should mitigate security competition but it did not happen and III. Technology is critical for business success and is blurring the line between economic competitiveness and national security. China's desire of technology collaboration (import and joint development) gets ignored by the U.S. and regarded as a strategic challenge thus treating China as a peer competitor with adversary policies. Unnecessary security competitiveness is bleeding into economics and businesses creating risks such as broken supply chain damaging goods, hindered investment reducing capital flow, suffocating global innovation stopping technology and people exchange and integration, all creating an economic iron curtain.

Paulson warns that decoupling or divorce between the U.S. and China is not easy because others will have a say. No country in Asia can afford to neither divorce China nor want to. No country in the world will divorce the fastest growing economy. Yet the U.S. is pursuing de-integration to protect her economy and security. Instead of a calibrated de-integration, focusing on sensitive and critical areas, the U.S. is flirting with a comprehensive de-integration attempting to disrupt all aspects of China's internal growth and external economic relations. The bad trade policies of the U.S., for example the USMCA allowing the U.S. to veto her partner's effort to open China's markets through their own trade initiatives and the U.S. pulling out of PTT leaving 16 countries to form CPTPP, will drive companies and countries away from her. The U.S. in attempts to battle with allies and partners to alter Chinese behaviors may actually cause US self-isolation.

Paulson's recommendations and suggestions offered no fresh ideas other than responding to the prevailing rhetoric rooted in the difference of political philosophies persisted in the two nations. Paulson recommended: 1. foreign firms allowed to compete with Chinese firms on a level playing field, 2. Chinese firms run as commercial firms not as an agent of the State, allowing market to influence decisions, and responding to market and not government signals, and 3. protecting innovation and ending forced technology transfer, cyber theft and not using China's own standards to limit competition unfairly. His suggestions to China are: 1. Do no harm (PLA Navy in the South China Sea), 2. Work constructively with the U.S. and her allies, especially on securities (e.g. N. Korea), 3. Bold to open, and 4. Honor IP protection. For the U.S.: 1. Dial down rhetoric, 2. Enlist partners to foster understanding with China, 3. Negotiate with China with clear objectives (investment agreement), and 4. Invest in America (military, economy, education, science and technology), open to the world and investment in alliances (Asia and EU). The above words ignored the causality principle of political philosophy driving economic development. The U.S. is founded on capitalism and free enterprise system with socialism adopted only as remedies for fixing her social problems. Thus private companies are encouraged to grow in a free enterprise mode allowing maximizing, retaining and distributing corporate profits to their limited shareholders and handful executives. China on the other hand is founded on socialism with a constitution placing all her people as the owner of the nation and all its assets. China did embrace capitalism in her economic reform but by no means giving up socialism. Therefore, China's State Owned Enterprises (SOEs) are owned by China's citizens with profits shared by the citizens not just a few stockholders and CEOs like the US corporations.

It is very important to respect and accept each nation's political philosophy to understand her economic development plan and policies. To lessen the economic competition between the U.S. and China we must incorporate the above understanding. Asking China to abolish the SOEs when China is able to keep a high economic growth rate and elevate millions of people out of poverty per year is unreasonable. The wealth gap is a critical issue in any society and it is an acute problem in the U.S. China was poor but fair across the board before; she opened to experiment with capitalism. Now she is witnessing the phenomenon of wealth gap, partly due to corruption and partly due to capitalism. China is addressing corruption with heavy handed crack down but she must find a safe ground between growing GDP employing capitalism and free enterprise system and preventing the worsening wealth gap problem so apparent in the capitalistic world.

Free enterprises grow faster and make more returns than SOEs, but profits go to a few share holders. The Western conglomerates complain about State government's interference in protecting its local industry but never complained when they were monopolizing an industry and market by having control in IP property (patents), industry standards and capital flow. All the criticisms on misdeeds such as industry espionage, copying technologies, trading markets for technology, etc can be found practiced by many countries before they became developed and long before China arrived on the stage of world economy. Of course, the misdeeds are misdeeds but they are not the essential issues in the U.S.-China economic competition. In fact, China is now the highest recipient of patents and leaders of many key technologies; thus China is already facing the unleveled playing fields in other rising economies. The issue is how to find win-win collaboration to lessen the inevitable competition.

The political philosophies behind economic development plans must be understood and respected. The international institutions, such as WTO, do need to be reformed from time to time to accept the changing political philosophy and economies. Such changes in big economies like the U.S. and China must be seriously studied in order to provide inputs for reform. Instead of suing each other in WTO, it is more productive to engage in a study to adopt most optimal economic development rules accommodating different political philosophies.

To deal with economic competition between the U.S. and China, the two great nations must abandon their legacy rhetoric (and WTO litigation) to engage in a dialogue to understand each other's political philosophy and changing economy. Only by accepting each nation's freedom to adopt a political philosophy and a workable economic development plan, compromises may be found.

We can use Singapore to emphasize the importance of political philosophy. Lee Kuan Yao was a brilliant leader; he led his party to create a prosperous economy. Then the people voted for his party to stay in power making Lee appearing like a dictator. But it is his political philosophy and economic development plan derived thereby that has made Singapore a prosperous nation, nothing to do with democracy. This example simply tells us to keep an open mind about political philosophy especially when it worked and created a prosperous economy for a nation. I urge the Bloomberg Economic Forum to sponsor a conference theme: Compatible Development Plan and Political Philosophy for Creating A Successful Economy.

Chapter 44
Ancient Silk Road，Evolving OBOR (BRI) and Future Outcome (I)

*****

Abstract

China's Bell and Road Initiative (BRI) program is inspired by the ancient silk road and its successful history, but unfortunately that part of history had not been well appreciated by the West. The BRI in the past five years have shown sufficient progress and significant achievements. They should not be ignored by anyone. The Asia Infrastructure Investment Bank supporting the BRI has grown to 87 member countries and launched numerous construction projects. The BRI offers an opportunity not a threat to world economy. It is time for the few skeptics to do an honest analysis of BRI, and endorse the initiative.

The ancient Silk Road was started so long ago that we may say that it represents a network of trade routes over time connecting the East (China) to the West (mid-East and Europe) from 114 BCE to 1450s CE, referring to both the terrestrial and the maritime routes connecting East Asia, Southeast Asia with West Asia, East Africa and Southern Europe. The term Silk Road was coined by Ferdinand von Richthofen, a German, as *Seidenstraße* and *Seidenstraßen* ("the Silk Road(s)"). Richthofen made seven expeditions to China from 1868 to 1872. The term Silk Route was also used in the 19th century but it did not gain widespread acceptance in academia or in popularity. One should note that the first book entitled *The Silk Road* was published by a Swedish geographer Sven Hedin in 1938. The Silk Road was central to cultural interaction in addition to commerce between the Eurasian regions for many centuries, but at least from 200 BCE, the trade (silk and spice) along the seaway from the East and South China Sea to Indochina was initiated and continued through Tang, Song,Yuan and the Ming Dynasty. The famous Zhenghe expedition in 1405-1433, seven voyages exploring around the world with advanced ships covering Indian Ocean and Pacific Ocean were a testament to the effort of culture and commerce interaction conducted by China through seaway.

The land Silk Road began in the Han dynasty (207 BCE–220 CE) and was expanded in the Central Asia around 114 BCE through the missions and explorations of the well documented Chinese imperial envoy Zhang Qian. The Chinese took great interest in the safety of their trade products and extended the Great Wall of China to ensure the protection of the trade route. Trade on the road played a significant role in the development of the civilizations of China, Korea, Japan, India, Iran, Afghanistan, Europe, the Horn of Africa and Arabia, opening long-distance political and economic relations between the civilizations. Because of the Silk Road, many other goods in addition to Chinese silk were traded; more profoundly, interactions of culture, civilization, religions, philosophies, and exchanges of sciences and technologies, even transmission of diseases (such as plaque) and medicine were spread along and expanded and by the Silk Road. The Chang'an-Tianshan corridor of the Silk Road had been deservedly designated as a World Heritage Site by UNESCO in June 2014.

The significance and impact of the ancient Silk Road although traceable in limited recorded history but it was not well researched and discussed by scholars nor was well presented to the public in comparison to the exploration of China by Europeans (e.g. Famous Marco-polo story). The proposal of One Belt and One Road (OBOR or BRI, Belt and Road Initiative) by the Chinese leader, Xi Jin Ping, in 2013 at Kazakhstan (September) and Indonesia (October) seemed to have not aroused much attention on the ancient Silk Road initially. As the OBOR plan was evolving with expanded modern infrastructure construction, the significance of the ancient Silk Road attracted more recognition of the antiquated road infrastructure on the land route and the limited maritime capability on the sea lane. One can imagine with modernized infrastructure what impact OBOR may bring. (*OBOR was described in an article, Understanding of China's World Development Program, OBOR, in the book, The Changing Giants, The U.S. and China, pp. 186-190, 2017, ISBN 0977159450)

OBOR was a brilliant vision for promoting globalization especially for activating the land locked Central Asia in economic development and its interaction with the rest of the world. With today's advanced communication capability, the announcement of such a grand plan did not immediately catch the world's attention was a surprise, in fact being ignored by the West from America to Australia was unreasonable. The reason OBOR didn't reach every person in every corner on Earth, perhaps, was due partly to a lack of PR work by China, partly to China's not ready to articulate the scope, depth, evolution path and future impact of a germinating idea and perhaps mostly due to the West media unwilling to accept and comprehend such a grand proposal. After the financing bank for supporting Asian infrastructure investment (AIIB) proposal received sufficient support in 2015, the OBOR program got its blood supply thus gaining more self-confidence and kicked off with a new name, Belt and Road Initiative (BRI).

The idea of "Asian Infrastructure Investment Bank" surfaced in the Bo'ao Forum in April 2009. The frustration of getting World Bank to finance Asian infrastructure construction needs triggered the thought to make better use of Chinese foreign currency reserves. The AIIB initiative was officially launched by Chinese President Xi Jin Ping on a state visit to Indonesia in October 2013. Even though the proposal met cold reaction from the U.S. and Japan, but it soon gained global endorsement and at its inauguration in 2015, the AIIB had 17 members subscribed 50.1% of its Authorized $100B Capital Stock. Jin Liqun was elected as its first President of five-year term with the bank opening for business on January 16, 2016. Currently, AIIB has 87 State members including European and Asian powers. (*The AIIB was described in an article, chronological account of the establishment of AIIB and its Significance, in the book, Understanding the US and China, pp 65-69, 2016, ISBN: 0977159442.)

The U.S. has opposed China's BRI plan from its start taking an allegedly-high-moral position that it may fail to stimulate the economic development of the developing countries and the financing organization such as AIIB may not meet the high standards maintained by the existing world financial institutions, even worse accusation was claiming that China purposely set debt traps by make easy money loans and reap bountiful fruits as the debtor countries default. But as time passed by, more countries came on-board BRI, the U.S. had changed her reasoning of opposing China's BRI to a debatable strategy - targeting China as a threatening competitor, destined to dominate the world, thus any program accelerating China's rise should be opposed. This hostile view is self perpetuating with little objective analysis while BRI is gaining momentum and traction. The facts and interpretations reviewed in part II may explain the hostile view and help us to make a fair analysis to reach some conclusions.

Chapter 45
Ancient Silk Road, Evolving OBOR (BRI)
and Future Outcome (II)

*****

Abstract

China's Bell and Road Initiative (BRI) program is inspired by the ancient silk road and its successful history, but unfortunately that part of history had not been well appreciated by the West. The BRI in the past five years have shown sufficient progress and significant achievements. They should not be ignored by anyone. The Asia Infrastructure Investment Bank supporting the BRI has grown to 87 member countries and launched numerous construction projects. The BRI offers an opportunity not a threat to world economy. It is time for the few skeptics to do an honest analysis of BRI, and endorse the initiative.

Independence movement does not happen every day. Catalonia's quest for independence from Spain has its cause but whether or not she will succeed is uncertain. Nevertheless, this is not only a serious matter for Spain but also a current event that has caught the attention of the world. Reports claimed that the referendum on the independence movement in Catalonia received 89% of yes vote, but only 43% of the registered voters turned up to vote, hardly an absolute majority. There were also plenty of citizens opposing independence by parading and protesting. Thus, the President of Catalonia, Carles Puigdement is in a bind. He can't simply announce and declare independence but requests a negotiation meeting with the Spain central government, whereas the Spanish Prime Minister, Marion Rajoy, is taking a hardline position, not giving up independence no negotiation. He even threatens that he will invoke the article 155 of the 1978 Spanish Constitution to replace the defying local Catalonia government - if Catalonia declares independence. The constitution is not specific on what the central government can do, but according to legal scholars and media analysis, sending troops into Catalonia to replace government is not out of the question.

Although Catalonia has its own language, she has been under Spain's royal sovereignty since 12th century. Catalonia is located at the Northeast corner of Spain with a beautiful and famous coastal city, Barcelona, as her capital.

Catalonia is the richest and most industrialized region in Spain and Catalan people are very proud of their history and language with independent minds. So some Catalonians think they are really an independent country. Of course, some Catalonians have other rational thinking considering separation unwise. The independence issue is naturally the making of the politicians and political parties. Since the death of Spain's dictator, Francisco Franco, in 1975, Catalonia had become an autonomous region again and had been ruled by the conservative nationalist party, CIU, for 23 years. Spain has many political parties, the Social Democratic Party, like PSC-PSOE, is one of the largest in Spain. In 2003, CIU was replaced by a coalition of three left-wing parties. The industrialized Catalonia attracted many immigrants from other parts of Spain and elsewhere. The immigrants and lower class speak Spanish but the middle and upper class speak Catalan. So besides the issue of taxation and the corruption of the central government, preserving the Catalan language, but not really a racial issue, is one reason for the Catalan's quest for independence.

Unlike two other autonomous zones in Spain, Catalonia has no independent taxation system; the local government's budget comes from national tax revenue. This is another factor influencing the separation movement. Catalonians pay more taxes than getting back from their central government budget, thus some resentment there. However, Catalonians should understand their constitutional obligation which cannot be simply based on money. Previously, I have discussed a question of California's quest for independence. The U.S. and her every other State will never accept California to become independent. Therefore, no matter how rich California becomes or how many Asians and Mexicans immigrate in, any independence dream is out of the question. Although not the same as California, Catalonia's quest for independence is not optimistic. So Puigdement is hoping for international support, but no major powers in EU come forward. Recently, media reports of Spanish police using batons and rubber bullets in Catalonia to deal with protestors created a bit of international attention and sympathy, but the police was just doing their job. Unless extreme violence is involved, there will not be any external interference. So Puigdement has no choice but asking for negotiation, hopefully getting a tax break or something beneficial to Catalonia.

Of course, one cannot make a definite conclusion on the Catalonia separation matter yet. However, from external observer's view, the conclusion would not be far from the above discussion; the separation issue would be over soon. However, we may extend the Catalonia case to discuss the concept of 'independence' in general. From nationalism and political science viewpoint, independence, especially successful independence movement, succeeds mostly after a successful revolution and the reason for revolution is usually caused by ruling government's oppression, incompetence, and corruption to the point of depriving its citizens' human rights and chance to make a decent living. Independence movement is for survival. Only when people lost freedom, unable to live and become desperate, would they sacrifice their lives to revolt. Only under this circumstance, others, sometimes foreign nations, may lend a helping hand. However, many independence movements are motivated by selfish reasons and they are promoted by political forces, internally or externally. Catalonia's quest for separation is because of money, resentment of paying more money than other poor regions of Spain. Isn't it selfishness? If this would be a justifiable reason, then wouldn't every rich village, town or province ask for independence? Would the world be in peace? So it is hard to justify Catalonia's quest for independence. From preserving Catalan language point of view, everyone under a free and democratic regime has the freedom to speak and learn any language. Seeking independence for the reason of preserving a particular especially minority language is just another selfish idea. If this selfish thinking and behavior were acceptable, then India would have become a dozen nations and the U.S. would be separated into English, Spanish, German, French, Italian even Chinese speaking parts?!After all, Catalan is already one of four official languages in Spain.

From Catalonia's separation movement, we can also see that the separation movement in Taiwan is a selfish idea and behavior. It is certainly not acceptable by people desiring to have a free and democratic society. It is unbelievable that any political party in Taiwan would try to change the language and to remove the deeply rooted, thousands of years, Chinese culture to cultivate the sentiment for separation from Mainland China. How can it succeed? Would the 1.3 billion Chinese allow it? No! Worse than Catalonia, Taiwan will not receive any sympathy from the international community, never mind support. The U.S. and Japan certainly have no justifiable reasons. Decades ago, when the Mainland was a lot poorer than Taiwan and politically less stable than present, the minority political force in Taiwan violated its constitution to promote 'independence', that was pure politically motivated idea based on selfishness. Now, the Mainland China has become the world's second largest economy (which Taiwan derives trade benefits from) and politically China has become confident enough to defend globalization and to launch modern Silk Road programs to help global development. Isn't it childish and stupid for some politicians continuing to promote 'Taiwan Independence'? From external observers' view, it is like pushing Taiwan people off the Chinese high-speed train; they will either get killed or seriously hurt. This is not threatening words; this is observers' reasonable deduction. The people in Taiwan, especially young people, can't afford to be blind or ignorant any longer. They must abandon the selfish and childish idea of separation or independence and look forward to a new world order of global harmony.

Independence is a dead alley for Taiwan, only cross-strait unification will lead to genuine cooperation and a bright future for Taiwan.

Chapter 46
Caravan, Immigration and Lifting World Poverty

*****

The caravan of refugees from Central America via Mexico to the U.S. has created a crisis that needs to be addressed properly and quickly. Refugees felt unsafe to travel in small groups elected to travel in caravan to the U. S. to seek asylum. Of course, Mexico is the necessary pathway for entering the U.S. According to international law, refugees should apply for asylum at the first country they arrived in, thus a huge burden falls on the Mexican government and also an opportunity for Mexicans to interfere in the immigration process. The application process is personnel and time consuming because courts are congested. Mexico and the U.S. are yet to reach an agreeable application process while the U.S. is already facing a big issue of huge amount of illegal immigrants from Mexico.

Another problem in handling the asylum application from the caravan is a troublesome clause in the US anti-trafficking law allowing under-aged (children) refugees (Mexicans and Canadians are excluded in this clause) to stay in the U.S. while waiting for asylum application. From humanitarian viewpoint, the U.S. government is urged to provide a quick solution to the thousands of refugees coming by the caravan. From national security and protection of legal immigration and true asylum considerations, the U.S. government must act prudently with due processes and expenses to deal with the applications processed through Mexico. Like many issues, the nation is divided on the caravan problem with no good fix.

Although the caravan problem is an immigration issue with humanitarian concern, the root cause of the problem is really related to poverty in Central America which affects people's ability to survive and make a decent living. Poverty and ineffectiveness of government have a mutual causality relationship. One generally does not see people from the rich and/or well governed countries emmigrate in mass to other nations. Refugees are directly or indirectly caused by poverty and the economic condition in where they reside. Those who chose to migrate are generally the more energetic citizens daring to make a change rather than tolerating and suffering.

There has been a remarkable progress in reducing poverty over the past decades. According to the most recent estimates by World Bank, in 2015, 10% of the world's population (about 750 million) lived on less than US$1.90 a day, an extreme poverty condition, compared to 11% in 2013. That's down from 44% in 1981 and nearly 36 percent in 1990. In 1990, there were 2 billion people living in extreme poverty and down to 750 million in 2015. This means that ending extreme poverty is optimistic if the number of people living on less than $1.90 a day had fallen by 68 million every two years. (* see discussion below on the effect of birth rate on poverty rate)

The global population in extreme poverty went from 80% in 1820 to 10% in 2015 by the latest estimates. This remarkable achievement was largely, though not exclusively, due to the important historical improvements of living conditions in China. By plotting the extreme poverty rates in the world, with and without China, we can see that the reduction of global poverty has been more substantial (faster rate of reduction) in China from 1980 up to 2005, comparable rate during 2005 to 2010 and then China picked up faster rate of reduction again from 2010 to 2015, certainly reflecting on China's economic growth. Of course, the birth rate in the poverty population will have a detrimental effect on the reduction of poverty rate. China's one child policy certainly is another factor which has helped her reducing her poverty population. If the birth rate were increased 1% in the extreme poverty population, then we would have additional 70+ million babies born into extreme poverty which would more than cancel out the 68 million reduction achieved from 2013 to 2015.

Immigration is definitely not a solution to reduction of extreme poverty rate of the world. It took the U.S. 100 years to have an immigration policy to absorb productive immigrants to the U.S. If the U.S. would open her arms to take in one million immigrants from a poor country, it would take seven and haf centuries or more to absorb the current 750 million extremely poor people. (Roy Beck has given an excellent speech using gum balls to graphically illustrate the pitiful effect of immigration on poverty population) Besides, when immigrants left their countries and entered a better world, they make the world left behind worse off. Because the immigrants tend to be the one who can affect a change if stayed behind. Most Americans are immigrants from other countries, it is fare to post a question to the Americans, has your immigration to America benefitted your homeland significantly beyond sending money back to relatives? The answer is most likely not much. Perhaps, out of feeling bad and selfish about their immigration, Americans are most generous people in making donations to help the world poor.

However, donations are not the solution to world poor either. Humanitarian effort just like accepting immigrants is a noble idea but not an effective way of helping the poor countries. Donating to poor countries, say temporary lifting poor from $1.9 a day to $102 a day say for 30 days by giving food, clothing etc. to the 2 billion poor, would require 30x100x2billion = $6 trillion dollars, 160% of the U.S. annual federal revenue. So, how often can the U.S. afford to make donations?

The true heroes of lifting poverty line are the poor people themselves and those who went to the poor country and worked with the poor to improve their living condition and economic welfare. The poor countries and their people need external help, but it is the sincere help to develop the poor countries' economies. As China has risen up in her economic development, she has gradually increased engagement with world affairs. One of her foreign policies is to help Africans to develop their economy. She invests in agriculture in Africa, sending farm workers to Africa to teach them how to do farming. China also invests in Africa's resources (forest, mineral) exploration and helps them to build basic infrastructure, roads, railroad, electricity, port facility, etc. China's action may not be pure humanitarian or unselfish but they do provide what African countries needed the most. In the end when Africans are lifted from poverty and have imporoved economy, it would benefit Chinese commerce and her efficiently manufactured goods, a win-win position.

The U.S. seems to be walking off her pedestal of humanity and high morality in helping the world poor and moving towards a self-centered international policy. (One recalls an online story: when President Carter asked Chinese Leader Deng Xiao Ping to allow Chinese dissident citizens to emmigrate to the U.S. Deng responded, how many can you take in, one million, five million or more?) Deng apparently understood the root of dissent was mostly because of poverty and the government's ultimate responsibility is to improve citizens' economic welfare. China has certainly been pursuing that strategy successfully.

Because of imbalance of trade and increasing competition in technology development with China, the U.S. turned protective in her dealings with China and the world. However, the U.S. must keep an open and fair mind about China's engagements with the world, from Asia, Africa, Europe to South America. We can not ignore her success and right approach in pursuing win-win projects with developing countries by offering investments and loans to help them to develop their economy. China, still a developing country herself with a large population, perhaps, has a better understanding of what the developing countries really need. It would be a win-win for the U.S and China and the world, if the two great nations could join hand in dealing with world affairs especially the issue of lifting world poverty line.

Chapter 47
Objective Analysis on US-China Trade Relations
After G20/G2

*****

On December 1, 2018, US President Trump and Chinese Leader Xi Jin Ping held a 150-minute dinner meeting at Buenos Aires, Argentina where the 13th G20 took place. The meeting was highly anticipated and hyped in the media to world attention. At the end, the two sides reached an understanding by announcing a 90-day truce stopping the escalating trade war. Both sides will not increase any tariff rate nor add new items onto the current tariff list. Within the 90 days,both sides will negotiate and tro to reach an agreement. The caveat is, if a satisfactory agreement could not be reached, they would be back to the trade war. This transnational conclusion is certainly better than no conclusion. The question is: will they reach a final agreement? Let's make a fair analysis on each side's demands and see whether a satisfactory agreement can be reached in 90 days.

This trade war was initiated by the U.S. China was on the defensive firmly stating that she would rigorously defend her rights. The most important matter to China is her right to maintain her economic development and to continue pursuing the China Manufacture 2025 plan which is designed to elevate her manufacturing and product technologies. The U.S. had made more accusations and demands in asking China to cease or correct her trade practices in addition to objecting to the China's 2025 manufacturer plan. Apparently, the U.S. had realized that it is unfair to forbid anyone to have its own development plan unless the plan contained measures violating international law and damaging to the U.S. economy. Thus the U.S. did not mention 'China manufacturer 2025' but focused on the specific practices that were deemed damaging to the U.S., such as deploying predatory tactics in its tech drive, including stealing trade secrets and forcing American firms to hand over technology in exchange for access to the Chinese market.

According to the White House announcement, Trump agreed to hold off raising tariffs on Jan. 1, 2019 on $200 billion in Chinese goods and China agreed to buy a very substantial amount of agricultural goods, energy, industrial and other products from the United States to reduce the huge trade deficit with China. The media (Times) noted that the White House appeared to be reversing course on its previous threats to tie trade matters to security concerns (like China's construction activities in the South China Sea). Out of humanitarian reasons, China agreed to label fentanyl, the deadly synthetic opium causing the death of tens of thousands of American drug users annually, as a controlled substance (making seller of fantenyl to the U.S. subject to maximum punishment).

The G20 downgraded their outlook for global economic growth next year to 3.5 percent from a previous 3.7 percent citing the trade conflict as well as political uncertainty as the causes. The U.S. stock market has been jittering downward worrying about the outcome of the US-China trade war. Will this 90-day truce bring us an agreement that will stop the trade war for good? Based on the events including rhetoric, actions and counter-actions happened in the past eight months and the above truce statement, one may be cautiously optimistic about the future. First of all, the rise of China and her economic power was not by steeling from anyone, it has its logical reasons. China's focusing on manufacturing and the U.S. transforming her economy from agriculture and manufacturing industries to finance and service industries are all their voluntary choices. The success of China's goal of lifting her significant number of citizens from poverty line to middle income is commendable and can be credited to her government's right economic policies and her people's work ethics.

China started with low level labor intensive manufacturing which most advanced or developed nations were willingly to transfer for profit and/or to get cheap goods in return. Then China, like all market places on earth in the past history, offered her market place for technology products, from low, medium and high tech with the condition that China would benefit with technology infusion while the foreign firms could rip tremendous profits. The Chinese government might have a concerted plan coercing foreign companies to participate, but in reality no one was forced under a gunboat (thinking of the British forcing opium trade to China under her gunboat power). The foreign corporations voluntarily signed their cooperation ventures. Did they make money, sure they did. Did the Chinese learn from the transferred technology, yes they did with more innovation on her own. Hindsight to cry foul seems to be just sour grape attitude. As for invasion of intellectual property, it has been a sad history since industrial revolution. There was no shortage of stealing, copying and cheating on intellectual properties in all developed countries. China is a late comer and she like other developed nations will soon face the same problem as she has now become the biggest annual patent holder surpassing the U.S., Japan and Germany.

China certainly has the right to have her Manufacturer 2025 plan to upgrade her technologies. China has been shutoff from high tech participation when national security threat from China was a joke. But with 24 neighbors, a number of them technologically and militarily powerful, out of necessity she has to develop her own defense technology. She succeeded in nuclear power but she was the only country declaring that she would never use it first against anyone. She developed her space technology, not only the satellites, space shuttles even her own space station despite of being shut out from the world's space-station research club. Yes, China has risen but she has done it with her people's sweat, body and soul. Is China a threat to the world? Looking back in history, it is safe to bet that China might be the least threatening nation among the major powers in the world. Will China bring competition to the world? Yes, more likely to be beneficially and peacefully.

Facing the ill-initiated trade war, China decided to stay firm to defend her rights. With the 90-day truce, China will likely agree to open up more her markets, modify her investment control process, enhance protection of intellectual properties in a gradual pace as she probably would without the trade war. In addition, China will purchase more substantial American products, perhaps slightly at the expense of other countries. But the sanction of selling high-tech products to China is most likely the obstacle for reaching a trade agreement. The US hi-tech sanction policy places China as a competitive enemy directly hindering her strategy of upgrading her industrial technology base to sustain her economic growth. Yet removing such sanction is the most effective means for reducing the US-China trade imbalance.

For example, an advanced hi-tech Jet plane is priced from $100-500 million, three hundred planes can value up to $150 billion. The US-China trade imbalance is only about $3000-4000 billion. Thus with China's enormous purchasing power, reaching a trade balance between the two countries is an achievable goal. What about China will begin to make her own planes? Just like cars we could not stop the Japanese, Koreans, … we just have to move on and upward in this competitive world. So the key is to make Americans competitive like the Germans, Japanese and Chinese. Regarding IP protection, China also has her concern of outflow of her advanced technologies in the areas of high-speed rail, electric vehicle, robotics, renewable energy resources, transport and storage of energy, etc. So the positions of The U.S. and China on IP protection should quickly converge.

Regarding other structural changes related to trade, finance and investment, it would seem to be more productive for the U.S. and China to begin working together on WTO reform (rather than litigation against each other). China is very concerned with the stability and sustainability of her economic growth, so should the U.S. China will not entertain any drastic changes on her working economic system or any new idea without experimentation nor will she (and the rest of the world) give up current WTO easily. The U.S. should have understood China's concerns and issues discussed above. Therefore, in the 90 days of negotiation, we may optimistically say that the U.S. and China can reach a trade agreement barring any gunboat attitude messing up the negotiation.

Chapter 48
Oh! Sabrina Meng, Justice Will Prevail!

*****

Save Sabrina! Demand Justice for Sabrina! Where were the American liberal democratic ladies when Sabrina was arrested and needed their support? Who is Sabrina? Sorry, our mainstream media seem to pick their political position (bias) and down play certain reporting. You might not know Sabrina, but you should know her story (Google Wikipedia) and defend her if you ever cared about human rights, woman's dignity and American justice system. In the following, Dr. Wordman will tell Sabrina's story, a movie-script like story to urge the world to stand behind her.

Sabrina (Ms. Meng Wanzhou) is the CFO of Huawei Corporation, daughter of the founder Ren Zhenfei and his first wife Meng Jun who divorced Ren and married again. Wanzhou adopted her mother's name at age of 16 (born 2-13-1972 in Chengdu). Wanzhou got out of college in 1992 and started her first job at China Construction Bank then joined Huawei next year as a secretary, some said that she started working at the telephone switch board. In 1997, she went for graduate studies at HuaZhong University of Science and Technology clearly feeling the need of technical training for getting ahead in Huawei. She returned to Huawei in 1998 working for the accounting department, then growing with the company, rising through the ranks in the finance area from head of international accounting, CFO of Huawei Hong Kong, Director of Accounting Management Department, then becoming the CFO of Huawei.

Huawei, founded in 1987, is a very unique company not only in China but in the world. The founder believes in sharing profits with every worker but demands loyalty and hard work. The company stocks belong mostly to workers, a collective company in their own description. Founder Ren owns only 1.4% of the company and humbly holds the CEO position. Huawei's current Chairman of the Board since March 2018 is Liang Hua, an engineer, the previous COB is a woman,

Ms Sun Yafang (born 1955), who had a technical bachelor degree from the University of Electronic Sciences and Technology of China (UESTC 1982) and served in the Chinese army. She worked for Huawei since 1989 and became the Chairwoman in 1999 in ten years. Wanzhou is one of her four appointed Vice Chairmen in Huawei's top executive list. Huawei probably can be considered as one of the world's best companies for women employee.

Sabrina was traveling from Hong Kong to South America for conference and was arrested on December 1, 2018, in Vancouver while in transit by the Canadian government, based on a U.S. extradition request which was revealed later being issued on August 22, 2018 by the U.S. District Court of the Eastern District of New York. Sabrina was treated crudely like a criminal and put in jail while not giving specific charges. Later, some organic news reports stated that she was charged with defrauding multiple international institutions concerning money for Huawei but actually for Skycom, a Hong Kong Company controlled by Huawei. Skycom was charged with selling equipments to Iran violating the Iran sanction, based on a 2013 Reuters report. Sabrina was finally granted her release with a bail of CAN$10million on 12-11-2018 with conditions that she will accept electronic surveillance and pay for the guard services preventing her from leaving Vancouver.

As Huawei's CFO, Sabrina probably signs thousands if not more check transactions for Huawei and its subsidiaries in a month. Picking arrest over serving a legal notice for clarification and employing extradition involving Canada can only demonstrate that the U.S. district court has an extremely long arm in handling prosecution without concrete evidence and with no regard to individual rights, multinational corporation's dignity and value of international diplomacy. Sabrina's release was denied when China made serious protests through diplomatic channels to the U.S. and Canada. The Prime Minister of Canada, Justin Trudeau claimed that his government was aware of the extradition request but did not get involved. (Making an arrest is not involvement?) The PM obviously does not remember those righteous speeches made in Canadian Parliament demanding human rights and justice in foreign lands.

White House staff claimed that Trump was not aware of Ms Meng's arrest happening during his meeting with Chinese leader Xi Jinping (12/3-4/2018 at G20 in Argentina) National Security Advisor John Bolton acknowledged advance knowledge of the arrest but chose not to inform President Trump. (How secure the U.S. would be if our NSA could unilaterally decide to hide a US-China matter from the President while he is meeting with the Chinese leader?) Trump however said later he would intervene in Ms Meng's case if it would help get a good deal in the trade war negotiation. (What an honest President not bothering to hide behind hypocrisy!) The Secretary of State, Mike Pompeo also courageously stated that "foreign policy must be taken into consideration in this (Ms Meng's) case, the mission is American First". (Pompeo's remarks draw some criticisms but the sad fact is that CIA tactics seem to be dominating our foreign affairs, even justice matter.) At the end, China made two consequential arrests of two Canadians (one former diplomat and think tank worker, Michael Kovrig, and one business consultant, Michael Spavor) on suspicion of threatening the national security of China; these arrests might have resulted in Ms Meng's release on bail.

Huawei Technologies Co., Ltd. (Huáwéi) is a Chinese multinational telecommunications equipment and consumer electronics company based in Shenzhen, Guangdong, South China. Huawei sells its products and services in more than 170 countries, serving 45 of the 50 largest telecom operators since 2011. Huawei overtook Ericsson in 2012 as the largest telecom-equipment manufacturer in the world and overtook Apple in 2018 as the world second-largest manufacturer of smart-phones, behind Samsung Electronics. Huawei ranks 72nd on the list of the Fortune Global 500. Huawei had over 170,000 employees as of September 2017, about 76,000 of them engaged in R&D on lavishly designed and furnished campuses (some like palaces) distributed as 21 R&D institutes in 16 countries. As of 2017 the company invested US$13.8 billion in R&D, up from US$5 billion in 2013, recently planning to increase its basic research portion from 10 to 20-30%. No wonder Huawei is now the leader in the fifth generation (5G) communication, Internet and smart-phones. The U.S. is advised by the military not to trust Huawei's communication equipment (likelihood of crippling U.S. military communication capabilities during war), hence the U.S.

government has issued orders banning US government buying any Huawei equipment and not permitting Huawei to sell its phones in the U.S., presumably protecting Apple.

Huawei's success is obviously a threat to many corporations such as South Korea's Samsung, the U.S. Apple and many EU and Indian corporations. However, the U.S. is the only country to use national security as the reason to blockade and crush Huawei products. The U.S. rallies Japan, Australia and any ally would join to boycott Huawei products. Huawei is definitely feeling the giant 'protectionism' claw scratching its back. So far, France and Germany have stayed with Huawei citing no evidence showing Huawei's products are unsafe. In fact, testing of telecommunication equipments has a long and reliable history since the days that every country uses the equipments from the U.S. (ATT, GTE, Motorola, and the like), France (Ericsson) and Germany (Siemens). Huawei's equipments must have been thoroughly tested by the U.S. military. Any evidence of backdoor would have been widely publicized unless there is none or they are being used by the U.S. Military relying on foreign parts 100% is a concern in the event of war, however, using high-priced parts made by US military contractors is equally vulnerable.

Sabrina's case brought the world's attention to 5G and exposed the 'long arm' practice of prosecution tramping human rights and the ugly government tactics in global commerce and squash competition in the name of national security. The coming of 5G over 4G means 20G over 100M in download speed and 100Mhz over 20Mhz in communication bandwidth thus lifting current video, e-Commerce and virtual reality to higher level applications such as auto-driving car with faster and sharper GPS, telemedicine bringing surgical hospital to everywhere, and intelligent cities with artificial reality and intelligence making human lives more comfortable. A folksy appreciation of 5G would be downloading a two-hour movie in two seconds or watching the Super Bowl at a ring seat in your home. Sabrina's case revealed so many facts for thoughts but Ms Meng did not deserve harsh treatment or many sleepless nights in jail. We must speak out for Sabrina. Where were you when she needed your support? It is never too late to demand Justice for Sabrina!

Chapter 49
Blame on Liberalism Not on Economy
for the Ending of Democratic Century

*****

At year end, Foreign Affairs presented one of its best of 2018 essays to its readers, The End of the Democratic Century - Autocracy's Global Ascendance, by Yoscha Mounk and Roberto Stefan Foa, which was originally published in Foreign Affairs May/June 2018 Issue. This article made an observation and concluded that the Democratic Century (of 20th Century) has ended. The authors attributed the failure of democracy to the change of economic landscape and the decline of the wealth and share of world economy of the U.S. led West. Mounk and Foa cited political scientists Adam Przeworski and Fernando Limongi that poor democracies often collapse, only rich democracies—those with a GDP per capita above $14,000 in today's terms, are reliably secure. Since the formation of the postwar alliance binding the United States to its allies in Western Europe, no affluent member has experienced a breakdown of democratic rule (government). The authors further emphasized the effect of economy by stating that "absolute levels of wealth may have been just one of many economic features that kept Western democracies stable after World War II. Indeed, the stable democracies of that period also shared three other economic attributes that can plausibly help explain their past success: relative equality, rapidly growing incomes for most citizens, and the fact that authoritarian rivals to democracy were much less wealthy." Overall, the authors strongly latched on the correlation between the success of democracy and its successful economic state and vice versa.

Mounk and Foa then sounded an alarm that the economies of the democratic nations have been declining for the past three decades. Among thirteen countries with per capita GDP above $20,000, two thirds of them are having an authoritarian government. Thus they proclaimed the end of Democratic Century with a bleak chance of reviving. Mounk and Foa further argued that strong economy translated to strong military power and great soft power which could help promoting democracy and maintaining a stable democracy. However, they noted that the re-growth of economy in the West would not be optimistic and the soft power of the non- democratic countries had increased steadily gaining self confidence. Therefore, they concluded with a pessimistic view: "the long century during which Western liberal democracies dominated the globe has ended for good. The only remaining question now is whether democracy will transcend its once firm anchoring in the West, a shift that would create the conditions for a truly global democratic century—or whether democracy will become, at best, the lingering form of government in an economically and demographically declining corner of the world." They further proclaimed: "Hopes that the current set of democratic countries could somehow regain their erstwhile global position were probably vain. The most likely scenario, then, is that democracies will come to look less and less attractive as they cease to be associated with wealth and power and fail to address their own challenges." They are pinning hope on that "authoritarian countries would find principles of liberal democracy appealing once they enjoyed a comparable standard of living..... If China were to do so, it would end the authoritarian resurgence in a single stroke."

I have no objection to Mounk and Foa's principal point that there is a correlation between successful economy and the stability of Democracy, however, I must point out the illogical conclusion they made about the deterioration of economy in the West democratic nations were the cause of the end of democracy century and the rise of economic performance in authoritarian states accelerated the end of democracy century. I shall present my arguments below to show that one must analyze the cause of economic decay in democratic societies in order to understand why democratic governments failed with failing economy. In fact, I shall argue that it is the liberalism that caused the downfall of democratic governments. Liberalism is responsible for the decaying of economy. Decaying economy with no cure exposed the ineffectiveness of a democratic system. Mounk and Foa's essay had treated this serious topic with a surface level observation, thus missing the link between the end of the democratic century and liberalism. In the following, I shall discuss why the liberalism is the real culprit for the end of democratic century. The infusion of conservatism and socialism into liberalism and capitalism may produce sustainable strong economy under either a democratic or authoritarian government.

First, let us clarify a few conceptual terms. Democracy is not necessarily a political ideology. Democracy, employing voting as a method to elect public servants, government structure and/or policy and legal matters, whether through a representative scheme or a direct one person one vote scheme, does not necessarily define political ideology. In fact, voting is being used in different degree nearly in all political systems (governments). The political system (government) and the political philosophy behind the system actually define ideology. An ideology including conservatism, liberalism, capitalism, nationalism, communism or socialism and/or their combination and/or modifications may be adopted and practiced by any government whether it is democratically created (by voting) or not. (a royal Empire with a king or queen or a leader obtained power through his or her people's choice, party's designation or any other mixed methods). The liberal democracy, Mounk and Foa referred to, is the democratic government adopting and practicing liberalism and capitalism, led by the U.S.

If one examines deeper why the economy of the liberal democratic countries had declined in the past three or four decades, one cannot help but notice that the liberalism is responsible for their economic failure. Liberalism encourages individualism, promotes liberal ideas with no fiscal constraint and divides society into many self-centered factions destroying the philosophy of 'majority rule', the most important merit of democracy. Activists representing many factions of special interest groups elect divided and counteractive government branches rendering government ineffective in decision making and inefficient in policy execution. This phenomenon is clearly exhibited by liberal democratic governments' perennial budget deficit, huge national debt, infrastructure construction impedance, bloated welfare burden and poor economic planning, in many cases leading to bankruptcy. So correlating failing economy with failing democracy is like correlating drug addiction with death by overdose, meaningless. Expecting authoritarian countries with successful economy to turn to liberal democracy is like wishing a live person to choose living in a coffin, laughable. Democracy is only effective and desirable when it has a right ideology behind it to uphold the majority rule principle, i.e., the voters must accept proper dosage of conservatism to curtail run-away liberalism and adopt suitable level of socialism to balance class-generating capitalism with unselfish idealism. In a nut shell, adopting the appropriate ideology to make the government effective to produce a good economy for the people is the key issue, not any voting scheme or any specific form of democracy. China is a living example, perhaps, to have placed defining her ideology (finding a Chinese political and economic philosophy and system by combining and tweaking capitalism and socialism) as her main focus to develop and sustain her economic growth. Keeping one party system and applying 'democracy' within that party while fine-tuning her ideology (not exporting her system) seems to have worked for China for the past four decades. Will China turn to liberal democracy after her per capita GDP passes $20,000? It is doubtful, since the Chinese elites seem to have understood how the countries like Greece, Italy, Republic of Congo, Latin America (poverty issue) ..... failed with their liberal democracy.

Chapter 50
Analysis of Xi's New Year Speech to Taiwan and Her Reaction

*****

Chinese leader has been delivering a New Year speech to the people in Taiwan ever since 1980. Xi's 40th Anniversary speech to Taiwan contains a lot of sincere words and rational statements. He emphasized China's unwavering goal of reunification across the strait and offered concrete suggestions for a peaceful reunification. Xi's speech, to every Chinese people, is a speech of compassion, moral and justice and full of Chinese national sentiments. He explained the history of Taiwan as an inseparable part of China. He warns sternly against the external interference about the cross-strait affairs. Xi thoughtfully explained the international situation, the significance of the Chinese cultural revitalization and the resolve of reunification in the hearts of Chinese. He recalled the political changes in the past 70 years and pointed out 'the 1992 Consensus' and 'seeking common ground and tolerating differences' is the only right approach. He also pointed out the mutual benefits achieved since the three links of post, commerce and travel opened across the strait. He said from now on the mainland's Taiwan policy would be more mutual help, mutual win and mutual exploration of development opportunities, offering young people chances to achieve peaceful reunification.

However, as an observer of Taiwan issues, I noticed Taiwan's political changes towards anti-China and pro- independence and the current Tsai Administration's rejection of 'the 1992 Consensus'. The world witnessed China's rise despite of the suppression attempts from the U.S., especially in her military development and industrial accomplishments. It seems that the 'Taiwan Card' which the U.S., Japan and Korea played had become uncoordinated and unsynchronized strategy probably futile but confusing. All of the above make the peaceful reunification very remote and uncertain. So, Xi's speech although contained sincere words and compassion but also delivered an ultimatum. If Taiwan would not stop the independence push, reunification by military force would become the necessary alternative to peaceful reunification.

In Xi's speech, there were five concrete points. We condense them below to facilitate our discussion on Taiwan's response to them:

Pt. 1, work together for national revitalization and to realize peaceful reunification.

Pt. 2, research 'a second political system' for Taiwan (different from that of the Mainland) and enrich the possibility of peaceful reunification.

Pt. 3, insist on One China Principle and protect the future of peaceful reunification.

Pt. 4, deepen cooperation and integration across the strait and build the foundation of peaceful reunification.

Pt. 5, realize heart to heart and soul to soul reunion between people and increase acceptance of peaceful reunification.

Xi called for open-arm interaction with any party, any business and any person for peaceful reunification but did not rule out using force if pro-independence activities would persist. The above points obviously aimed at achieving a peaceful reunification. However, whether the people in Taiwan will understand and accept these points or not really depends on I. how the Taiwanese feel as they are a part of China, II. how strongly they believe that their 'West' value system and liberal democracy will be forever superior, III. how deeply they believe that the U.S., Japan and South Korea will protect Taiwan in case of a military force reunification occurring, and IV. whether the Taiwanese have a Chinese national sentiment and a growing trust in Chinese communist party's grand plan of revitalization and joint development. Unfortunately, The Taiwanese so far are fuzzy and unclear on these issues.

The official response from Taiwan to Xi's speech was rapid as if they had prepared for it. Tsai Ying Wen for the first time delivered a New Year speech and she also made immediate response to Xi's speech. In 2016 during her campaign and after she won the presidential election, she made fuzzy statements regarding cross-strait issue but her actions were clear, avoiding discussion of 'the 1992 Consensus' but gearing up more anti-China and divorcing Chinese activities, following her party's (DPP) strategy of buying time and deepening 'Taiwan Independence' policy. The 2018 local elections turned out a big defeat to DPP. Tsai regrettably resigned her party chairmanship but seemingly leaning more towards the deep-green pro-independence faction. Her response to Xi's speech had revealed her political intention. For the first time, she openly denied 'the 1992 Consensus'. Although her words (four yes and four no conditions) were soft but she elected to take harder approach. Being afraid that Taiwan's political parties, businesses and individuals would respond to Mainland China's call for dialogue and cooperation, she declared that the cross strait issue and interaction is within national government jurisdiction, any dialogue must be between governments, 'endorsed by the Taiwan people'.

In reality, the last local election in GaoXiong and other municipalities had already shown people wanting increased economic activities with Mainland and endorsing 'the 1992 Consensus'; candidates accepted that got elected. But the national government may try to stop the interaction. Tsai and DPP still believe that more Taiwanese are pro-independence; they can be relied on though a risky call. Recently, some DPP members had voiced to replace Tsai for the 2020 election, that may be DPP's plan of buying time to get another term under another Deep-Green pro-independence candidate. I think when Tsai used the words, 'endorsement by the people of Taiwan', she wasn't very sure, but nevertheless, whether or not the people in Taiwan will have the will and guts to over-throw the DPP hold is still doubtful and deserve careful studies.

The former President Ma Ying Jie of Taiwan had also responded to 'the 1992 Consensus' and Xi's speech, that is one China with two different views, to him it means the Republic of China (ROC). This has been Ma's claims all along but without the 'promoting reunification' which Hong Xiu Zhu advocated. Ma as a law student and practitioner like to interpret issues on legal grounds. The U.S. and China relation of course was with ROC, tracing back before WW II (Potsdam Declaration and San Francisco Peace Treaty, although ROC was not a signatory). But KMT party (Ma's party) can no longer represent ROC especially as an opposition party, thus in its contest with DPP, it had become a fuzzy party with no clear 'reunification' policy. In reality, the Constitution of ROC had lost its significance. Taiwan's education and textbook revision had destroyed Taiwan's history for young people. Legislature Yuan can only represent Taiwan, Penghu and King and Ma tiny islands, in no way supporting the Constitution's claim of the entire China. Under the circumstance that most Taiwanese have no strong attachment to their country name, ROC, nor its jurisdiction issue, and most of the international community do not recognize ROC, Taiwan's current political system clinching to ROC for fuzzy interpretation is a fool's game. That is why, Taiwan had been played by others, so called allies and friends, as a chess piece or an ATM card for quick cash. In Xi's speech, he said correctly, today belongs to young people, the young people across the strait must carry the burden to work for national revitalization and for reunification. But do the young people in Taiwan have that inspiration? Can the people in Taiwan correctly assess the chances and consequences of peaceful reunification versus reunification by force?

Xi's speech is also directed to the Chinese in Hong Kong, Macao and overseas, hoping everyone will work for peaceful reunification and development towards a united China. Although internationally most countries understand and support one China and most Chinese, globally and across straits, recognize that the coming era is a challenge for all Chinese for their cultural revitalization and national development, but the cross strait issue is complicated due to external intervention. The current Administration's persistent pro-independence activities and its wishful belief that the U.S., Japan even South Korea will fight militarily for Taiwan's independence is making peaceful reunification much more difficult thus raising the military reunification more eminent.

Xi's 2019 New Year speech deserves all Taiwanese and Chinese people to read and ponder carefully!

Chapter 51
Exciting News about Space Exploration
and Hopeful Collaboration

*****

2018 ended with not so good ending, the U.S. government was partially shut-down due to a stalemate between Congress and the White House over funding for a wall along the southern border for stopping illegal immigrants and drug and human trafficking. The U.S.-China trade war although temporarily halted for 90 days but its uncertainty and the arresting of a Chinese high-tech company executive by Canada at the request of the U.S. have caused stock markets in the U.S. and worldwide tumbling. The concern of the Chinese economy degrading as well as its impact on the U.S. and world economy is casting a cloud over financial markets worrying recession.

Coming 2019 New Year, though the above problems are still hanging, but a string of exciting news happening in the first week of the New Year is uplifting. This is the news report of a space exploration. First, on the New Year's Day, the NASA asteroid-sampling probe (OSIRIS-REx, Origins, Spectral Interpretation, Resource Identification, Security-Regolith Explorer) was reported circling its space-rock target, 1640 foot wide near-Earth asteroid Bennu at 2:43 P.M (EST) on Dec. 31, setting a new record for the smallest body ever orbited by a spacecraft at a smallest orbit, one mile above the rock. Then it followed by executing the orbit-insertion maneuver perfectly, a project planned for years. Since OSIRIS-REx arrived at Bennu since Dec. 3, a detailed physical measurement and mapping had begun before the insertion signaling that maneuvering around a small body with no gravity is a very challenging task.

The OSIRIS-REx mission ($800 million) was launched in September 2016. Its main goal is to help researchers better understand the solar system's early days, and to shed light on the role that carbon-rich asteroids such as Bennu may have played in helping life get started on Earth by delivering water and organic molecules. Much of this information will come from analyses of Bennu material here on Earth with planned harvesting a sizeable sample of asteroid dirt and gravel in mid-2020 parachuting back in the Utah desert in September 2023. The mission should increase scientists' understanding of the resource potential of Bennu-like asteroids and help fine-tune the trajectories researchers had drawn up for potentially dangerous space rocks. This space program is obviously a significant research hopefully contributing to mankind's knowledge and potential use of space resources.

On Jan. 1, 2019, a NASA spacecraft, New Horizon, was reported to have flown by, in the first hour of 2019, over a space object (named Ultima Thule located in an icy Kuiper Belt) farther than any spacecraft has done before, about four billion miles from Earth (one billion miles from Pluto). The scientists cheered upon receiving the signal, which took so long to reach them. The full scope of observations made by New Horizons will take nearly two years to beam back to Earth. The spacecraft provided the first close-up images of Pluto about 3 1/2 years ago when it traveled past the dwarf planet. The objects in this region so far from the Sun are believed to be frozen in time, relics left over from the formation of the solar system. The space objects like Ultima are believed to be the building blocks of planets, thus its study can lead to the understanding of the formation of planets. The surface features of this small world could provide a window to see the composition of the subsurface of Ultima. By counting the number and impactors that have hit Ultima, the number of small objects in the outer solar system may be estimated.

On January 3rd, 2019, another exciting space news brought cheers all over the world as photos of Chang'e 4 lander and rover Yutu2 and their successful soft landing (Jan. 2nd) on the far side of the Moon were reported on televisions and newspapers. China was a late comer in space exploration; she was excluded from the space club by the West. This turned out to be a blessing, since it motivated many Chinese scientists and engineers to dedicate all their brains, energies and lives to space research. Besides China's rapid advances in transport and satellite technologies, China has launched the Chang'e 1 and Chang'e 2 orbiters in 2007 and 2010, respectively, and pulled off a near-side Moon landing with the Chang'e 3 mission in December 2013. Chang'e 4 was originally designed as a backup to Chang'e 3, so they share hardware similarity. China has also launched an eight day around the moon return capsule mission in October 2014, a mission known as Chang'e 5T1. as a test run for the Chang'e 5 sample-return effort, likely to be launched this year. China also has ambitions for crewed lunar missions, but its human-spaceflight program is focused more on Earth orbit in the short term such as launching a space station up and running by her own effort in the early 2020s.

On Jan. 3rd, the rover rolled onto the gray dirt floor of the 115-mile-wide (186 kilometers) Von Kármán Crater, creeping down twin ramps from a previous position atop the stationary lander. Yutu 2, named after a rabbit in the Chinese legendary mythology, and its lander companion will conduct the first in-depth science investigations on the far side of the Moon. The pair carries four science instruments to characterize the surface and near subsurface of the Von Kármán crater which lies within an even larger impact feature, the 1,550-mile-wide (2,500 km) South Pole-Aitken Basin. In addition, the lander also carries a biological experiment: a small tin containing silkworm eggs and the seeds of several plant species, including potatoes. Mission team members aim to study how these organisms may grow and develop in the low-gravity lunar environment.

The lander features the Landing Camera, the Terrain Camera, the Low Frequency Spectrometer, and the Lunar Lander Neutrons and Dosimetry (provided by Germany). The rover has the Panoramic Camera, the Lunar Penetrating Radar, the Visible and Near-Infrared Imaging Spectrometer, and the Advanced Small Analyzer for Neutrals (contributed by Sweden). The lander and Yutu 2 cannot beam their data home to Earth directly from the far side of the Moon which was the reason it avoided human exploration thus far. So in May, 2018, China had launched a relay satellite called Queqiao (a name also taken from the legendary mythology), stationed at a gravitationally stable point beyond the Moon. From its vantage point, Queqiao can keep Yutu 2, the lander and Earth all in sight at the same time. Chang'e 4 is a robotic lunar exploration. The data flow through Queqiao will likely be extensive. China's Chang'e 4 team should be congratulated for the successful landing on the far side of the Moon, a first for humanity and an impressive accomplishment.

The above NASA space explorations are aiming at finding information about how the solar universe had begun and planets had been developed. China's lunar observations on the Moon's far side are aiming at finding why the lunar near and far sides are so different. The experimentations to be performed there will yield valuable information about how plants such as silkworms and potatoes may ever grow on the Moon. It is obvious that collaboration and sharing information between the U.S. and China will yield more progress on space science and applications. For example, Chengdu City in China is seriously exploring the possibility of launching a geostationary satellite with a mirror array to reflect solar light to the city in the night time to eliminate all city street lights. Such an idea would never arise if there were no satellite and space technology. Let's hope the New Year's exciting news will steer the two great nations and other partners to work together for the common good of mankind, rather than pursuing mutually damaging competition such as trade wars and technology sanctions.

Chapter 52
Singles Day (Double 11) Event and the U.S.Trade Export

*****

My readers may wonder why is Dr. Wordman interested in the title topic? Is it important and related to world politics and US-China relations? Singles Day Event did not exist when Dr. Wordman built his first e-Commerce website, **osmart.us** (originally started as **osmart.com** but that name was first used by a department store). OSMART stands for Online Shopping Mart or O! Smart! with a grand vision. (Believe it or not, stores like Macy's etc all placed their sales on **osmart.us**) OSMART was promoted as a 'mega' e-Commerce site in year 2000. Well, OSMART did not fly as it was suffocated by '**dotcom** crash'. However, for sentimental reasons and patent filing purpose, **osmart.us** has been kept as a historical archive website still accessible today. With the above explained, you will understand why Dr. Wordman is interested and somewhat experienced in discussing the title subject. The subject indeed relates to US-China trade war and globalization.

The Singles Day online shopping event, happening on November 11th, (Well known as Double 11 in China) was started and promoted by Alibaba.com ten years ago (2008). Today, Double Eleven clicked in the biggest shopping spree the world had ever seen; shoppers purchased 314 RMB ($45B) goods and services within 24 hours. What drove people to Double 11? Of course it is discount sales. (OSMART was based on that principle) Average discount of 30% or more were offered by merchandisers on that day. Would merchants make profit? Here are some statistics McKinsey published: For Mom and baby stuff, merchants get 18-19% sales on Double 11 versus 6-7% on normal days, that is, at least 300% increase of sales for offering a 33% marked-up 'discount'. For skincare and cosmetics, merchants get 12-15% sales on Double 11 versus 3-5% on normal days for offering a 30% marked-up 'discount', that is, 300-400% increase in sales on one day. You do the math, would you want to miss this kind of opportunity to get sales, brand recognition and customer base? By the way, $45B is about three times of sales of U.S. Black Friday and Cyber Monday combined. Furthermore, 90% of the Double 11 sales happen on mobile devices versus 34% for Cyber Monday.

According to McKinsey (What Singles Day Event Can Tell Us How Retail in China Is Changing, Lombard Bu, Anne Kronschnabl, Kelly Ungerman and Daniel Zipser, December 2018, McKinsey) the Singles Day Event grew 79%,

59%, 44%, 44% and 24% from 2014 to 2018, tapering off this year. (with sales volume 81B,123B, 177B, 254B and 314B RMB) Would you be concerned that this event will die? This year's Singles Day featured at least four other retail platforms or ecosystems of companies, with Alibaba capturing 68 percent of total sales. The 24% growth was compatible with China's retail growth which suggests that Double11 may have to expand more into global markets. It appears that it is going that way. McKinsey reported, for example, online games and interactive shows, including a "See Now, Buy Now" fashion show that let consumers buy items featured on models, helped creating excitement leading up to Singles Day. The actual day kicked off with a four-hour, star-studded gala of performances in Shanghai's Mercedes-Benz Arena, watched by 240 million viewers. Games and coupons cross offered from online and in-store retailers are obviously also helping exciting the massive consumers.

This year for Singles Day, e-commerce giant Alibaba made a concerted push to connect its online operations with its stores throughout China, that is consumers could find the Singles Day promotions and offers offline as well, in 62 Intime department stores, around 100 Hema supermarkets, and 222 Easyhome furniture and home-improvement stores. But it is obvious that to sustain growth and promote further Double 11, Alibaba must move to global markets. Amazingly, a record number of multinational brands (more than 19,000) already participated in Singles Day, resulting in a major spike in sales from imports.

It is important to emphasize that while overall Singles Day sales grew by 24 percent, the growth of products imported into China was much higher, at 63 percent on Tmall. This is a significant data in view of the US-China Trade War demanding an increase of exports from the U.S. to balance the current trade deficit. McKinsey noted the top-selling multinational brands on Tmall, including Spanish beauty company MartiDerm, Japanese diaper brand Moony, Dyson appliances, and the US supplement brand Schiff. Alibaba's Tmall offers access to a large consumer base and a wide range of supporting capabilities, such as data analytics, logistics, and product innovation, potentially capable of facilitating more global sales.

For example, Lazada, approximately 91 percent owned by Alibaba, featured Singles Day in Singapore, Malaysia, Thailand, Indonesia, the Philippines, and Vietnam simultaneously with its initial sales during the first hour of Singles Day growing sevenfold over last year. Shopee, the leading online shopping platform in Southeast Asia and Taiwan, grew its total customer orders on Singles Day by 4.5 times. Why can't the U.S. retailers join the growth? I don't think it is because the U.S. has no merchandise for exporting to China, it is the atmosphere and attitude the government is casting over U.S.-China trade. We hope that the U.S. will reach a trade agreement with China soon, so the U.S. businesses can ramp up more global sales especially to China.

Alibaba has publicly said its long-term goal is to get half of its total sales from overseas. Alibaba already brought Singles Day to the United Kingdom, France, Spain, Poland, Russia, and Turkey through AliExpress, an online site that exports Chinese products to international buyers. In Europe, AliExpress partnered with El Corte Inglés department store to create more than 2,000 click-and-collect pickup locations, including pop-up stores. This year, AliExpress's total sales on Singles Day were up 40 percent. As Alibaba and other Chinese retail platforms continue their expansion abroad, we should expect the U.S. capturing a significant growth in Singles Day sales among Europe, Southeast Asia and other markets.

Singles Day sales growth tapering from 44% to 24% is just a single data point for one year when the U.S. and China are saber rattling threatening each other with a tariff war. The Singles Day event has a solid five year record and is certainly still a behemoth for Chinese retail, thus representing a significant opportunity for the U.S. brands to grow in China. According to McKinsey's assessment, participating in Singles Day is no longer optional but a requirement for any international brand that sees itself with a future in Asia and wants to build brand engagement and craft unique experiences with consumers. I fully agree on this assessment. Therefore, I urge the U.S. commerce organizations immediately conducting a task force to develop a plan to fully engage with Singles Day (Double 11) Event to stimulate the U.S export to China and make it a success. I personally will be glad offer consulting free of charge on Mandarin language and/or business needs to any American businessman who is interested in engaging the Singles Day Event (Double 11).

Chapter 53
Resolving US-China Trade Dispute must focus on collaboration rather than Isolation

*****

The trade war initiated by the U.S. targeting China has lingered a whole year. On January 22nd, 2018, President Trump placed a 30% tariff on foreign solar panels (China, world leading manufacturer) scaling down to 15% after four years. On the same day, 20% tariffs was applied to wash machines for the first 1.2 million units per year. On March 1, 2018, President Trump further imposed tariffs of 25% on steel and 10% on aluminum on a number of countries; some allies selectively waived. On March 22, President Trump directed the US Trade Representative to investigate applying tariffs on $50-60 billion Chinese goods over 1300 categories of imports invoking Section 301 of the 1974 Trade Act, claiming unfair trade practices by China, including theft of U.S. intellectual property. On April 2, 2018. China retaliated by imposing tariffs on 128 products imported from the U.S. Then on April 5, 2018, Trump responded with another round of tariffs on an additional $100 billion of Chinese imports escalating the trade war. On the next day, the World Trade Organization received request from China for consultations on the new U.S. tariffs.

The US-China Trade Talks started in May, 2018, the Vice Premier of the People's Republic of China, Liu He, the top economic adviser to President Xi, visited Washington for further trade talks on May 15th. On May 20, 2018, Chinese officials agreed to "substantially reduce" America's trade deficit with China committing to "significantly increase" its purchases of American goods (Treasury Secretary Steven Mnuchin announced: "We are putting the trade war on hold"). But on May 29, 2018, the White House announced that it would impose a 25% tariff on $50 billion of Chinese goods with "industrially significant technology", to be announced by June 15 (list 1, $34B) with 25% tariff starting on July 6th and remaining $16B (list 2) to start later. Three days later, the White House declared that the U.S. would impose additional 10% tariffs on another $200 billion worth of Chinese imports (list 3) if China retaliated against these U.S. tariffs. List 3 was released on July 11 to be implemented within 60 days. Thus, the U.S. imposed a total of $250B (all three lists). The 10% tariff on $200 billion worth of Chinese goods would begin on September 24, 2018, increasing to 25% by the end of the year. Tariffs on an additional $267 billion worth of imports would be added, if China retaliated. China promptly did retaliate on September 18 with 10% tariffs on $60 billion of US imports. (list 3) Thus, China has promised to impose tariffs on a total $110 billion of U.S. goods, almost its entire imports of American products (list 1, $16B, list 2, $34B and list 3, $60B). However, a recent article in the Wall Street Journal (1-14-2019) reported, despite US-imposed tariffs, China's 2018 trade surplus over the U.S. was $323.32 billion, a record high, which signified that the U.S. economy depended strongly on Chinese imports and US traders increased their orders to beat the tariff increase.

While the trade dispute is in negotiation, other events occurred having influence on the trade talks. First, on April 16, the U.S. concluded the penalty for ZTE, a Chinese corporation, for violating US sanction against Iran. On June 7th, ZTE accepted a deal with the U.S. court to resume business. Second, the CFO (Ms Meng Wanzhou) of Huawei Corporation, a private unlisted Chinese company, was arrested by the Canadian authority upon the request from the U.S. district court in New York based on an extradition agreement between the two countries. These two cases have connection to the US-China dispute is revealed by the trade negotiation. The U.S. is obviously not satisfied by China's pledge to purchase more American goods to reduce trade imbalance but demands China to scrap her "China Manufacture 2025 Plan" a Chinese national strategy to encourage technology innovation and upgrade. **ZTE** is a Chinese multinational telecommunication equipment and systems company headquartered in Shenzhen, Guangdong, China. It is one of China's leading telecom equipment manufacturers with core products of wireless, exchange, access, optical transmission, data telecommunications gears, mobile phones, and telecommunications software. Huawei Technologies is a Chinese multinational conglomerate specializing in telecommunication equipment, consumer electronics and technology-based services and products, also headquartered in Shenzhen. Huawei has deployed its products and services in more than 170 countries, and served 45 of the 50 largest telecom operators since 2011. Huawei overtook Ericsson in 2012 as the largest telecommunication-equipment manufacturer in the world, now the leader in the next generation (5G) mobile and telecommunication technology. The U.S. government has been boycotting Huawei equipment citing national security concern without evidence. Lately, the U.S. has been lobbying her allies to join the boycott.

At the 2018 G20 meeting in Argentina (December 1-2. 2018) President Trump and President Xi met and agreed to a 90 day truce (postponing tariffs to March 1) to "immediately begin negotiations on structural changes with respect to forced technology transfer, intellectual property (IP) protection, non-tariff barriers, cyber intrusions and cyber theft." At this point, it has become so clear that the trade war is not about trade imbalance but about China's rise in technology strength, not only in manufacturing but across the board threatening the U.S. leadership in technology. Trade Representative Robert Lighthizer led the 90 Day negotiation with a condition of raising the 10% tariff on the $200B Chinese goods to 25% on March 2, if negotiation would fail. Although President Xi reiterated China's previous pledges: protecting foreign investments and eliminating laws requiring global auto makers and shipbuilders to work through state-owned partners, affirming a decision to increase imports, lower foreign-ownership limits on manufacturing and expand IP protection, all central issues in Trump's complaints, China has no reason nor obligation to give up her rights in pursuing technology upgrade.

The arguments that China has instituted an array of non-tariff barriers to protect her critical sectors of the Chinese economy and insulate them from international competition may be valid, but it is no different from the U.S. placing some sectors on sanction list preventing them to be exported to China or preventing China to acquire them through investment. Prof. Lee G. Branstetter, of economics and public policy at Carnegie Mellon University, reported (March 22, 2018) that China has misappropriated foreign technology and forced technology transfer as cited by the U.S. as well as the failure of companies in protecting U.S. IP. This report and the U.S. current tactics were a little too late to be useful. Whether China, like many developed nations in their past, practiced inappropriate technology acquisition or not, China is now the world's number one annual patent grantee. China is just as concerned as the U.S. in patent infringement. China's achievement in many technologies supports the above conclusion: I. Space: landing on the far-side of the moon, launch of multi-satellites, the largest radio telescope, quantum satellite, quantum computer, and dark matter probe, II. Transportation: 1st passenger drone, drone crate delivery, trackless virtual rail technology, magnetic floatation transport, solar expressway, 3D printer car, auto-driven car, electric cargo ship, 1st amphibious drone, electric bus fleet (16000) and longest sea bridge, III. Medical: robot doc passing license exam, cloned monkey, 1st lung regeneration therapy, auto dental implant, ultrafast 3D microscope, discovery of revitalization agent from urine, IV. Energy and Environment: largest floating solar power plant, largest waste to energy plant, forest city, 3G AP1000 nuclear reactor, largest air purifier (100 meter tower), intelligent city and V. Commercial and Military: robot bank, battleship mounted rail gun (hypersonic 6720mi/hr), 1st 4K resolution VR headset, deep sea mining vessel (8000 ft), AI Teaching Assistant, satellite big data for agriculture and AI multi-language translator.

China's fast advances in technology certainly pose serious challenge to the U.S., however, this challenge cannot be dealt with complaint, jealousy or restraining/retaliating tactics. Competition is the fundamental driver for technology advances. As human civilization is advancing in an interactive global world, everyone faces common challenges from the environment, its limited resources and possible challenges from outside of Earth planet. Humans must elect to collaborate rather than to exercise a zero-sum game leading to mutual destruction. So the current US-China trade dispute is handled wrongly. China has no reason to stop her innovation progress to yield to the U.S. demand in dominating all technologies. In reality, the U.S. is still leading in many technologies such as semiconductor, super-precision mechanics, material science, aeronautics and jet-engine technology, medical and biological research and development and AI and big data applications. Therefore, it makes sense to collaborate with China exploiting her large population and huge market for American technology applications rather than exercising technology sanction. Technology without application and market will eventually die and be replaced. Only through market applications, a technology can thrive and stimulate new innovations. Hence, during the trade talk, the U.S. should seek for open markets and technology export opportunities from China to establish open and fair platform for technology collaboration, transfer, joint development and market application to obtain mutual benefits. Working with China's huge market, balance of trade and sustained technology innovation should be easily obtainable. Any move to isolate China or from each other is unwise; the best it would accomplish is to slow down technology advances and stall world economy.

Chapter 54
Legal Corruption in the U.S. with Long Legal Arm
(Implication for ZTE and Huawei cases)

****

'Legal Corruption' in this article means corruptions protected by law under a politically correct banner. This type of corruption often involves the legal system in the U.S. with lawyers, legal professionals and judges corrupting the legal system and vice versa. Therefore, legal corruption may be interpreted in a narrower sense as corruptions happening in the legal system, applying law to protect corruption. In either definition, the legal corruption in the U.S. is growing tremendously hurting individual citizens, corporations, foreign nations and the U.S. reputation. This type of corruptions is usually well protected by law and cleverly executed by the legal system from law enforcement to court system involving lawyers, consultants, law enforcement agencies and courts (judges). These people involved in the corruptions generally keep a low profile and hide behind laws.

We may start with a small case to illustrate a 'legal corruption'. First example is the traffic law which has been used by law enforcement and court system to generate revenues for the government, court system and law enforcement benefits. Speed traps are well known in certain areas and certain times being set up mainly to catch out of jurisdiction travelers. The travelers often cannot come to the local courts to defend their cases thus willingly paying a fine which can be an unreasonable amount. Many citizens had this type of experience which might be blamed on the speeders' own fault. But when certain small towns with highways passing through their township use speed traps to generate income to fund their entire police department or paying overtime or bonuses to their court system and law enforcement force, this borders to corruption. When electronic device is used to catch speeder, it is very easy to catch them even just with a fraction of mile per hour over the speed limit, say, 40 miles/hr. When the speed trap is overused or eagerly applied to generate money for the benefit of a small number of people, it is legal corruption. Similarly, when the law enforcement is given right to confiscate valuables and large amount of cash from a traveler under suspicion of drug or illegal activity, possible corruption may occur. The out of town owner often gives up the confiscated money out of fear or inconvenience to go through a lengthy legal process. Then the confiscated money benefits the court or a small number of individuals. These types of laws give incentive to corruptions and they do happen indeed in our country.

The U.S. passed a law, called Foreign Corruption Prevention Act (FCPA), which is meant to punish American corporations doing business with foreign country involving bribery or receiving kickback. This is a Law well-intended to discourage American companies to commit corruption. However, under this law, many foreign corporations having branches in the U.S. are subject to the jurisdiction of this law, thus the Economist magazine termed it "the American Law with a long arm". Foreign companies having business branches have become the major targets of the FCPA law. A recent case is revealed because the victim, Frederic Pierucci, an executive of Alston (French Company) was arrested while on a business trip to the U.S. and jailed for many months in cells for serious criminals simply because Alston had committed bribery when doing business with Indonesia. Pierucci was not involved in the Indonesia business but his name appeared as a recipient on one of the corporate emails discussing the Indonesian deal. The U.S. court under FCPA pursued him and others relentlessly seeking a huge fine. He was released after reluctantly admitted wrong doing. Then, Alston sold its natural gas burning turbine to GE along with this legal hot potato hoping GE will take care of this mess, but FCPA court demanded a fine of $0.775B from Alston, refused GE intervention and rearrested Pierucci again. The case was finally terminated after Alston agreed to the fine. Of course this fine does not include tons of money paid to lawyers, consultants and court fees and the misery Mr. Pierucci endured. He wrote a book in French to vent his grief.

According to a Chinese language blogger, this type of legal pursuant has grown bigger and bigger in penalty size and more and more in frequency on foreign companies because the process generates such a huge monetary reward benefitting the few specialized lawyers, consultants and court judges involved with FCPA. The blogger was afraid of reprimand from the people in this FCPA "business chain", he never published anything in English and never wanted to be named. He also claimed that a small number of people in the FCPA "business chain" always keep a low profile not wishing to be in the limelight to spoil their good business but their zest for FCPA target is growing with the size of the fines they have succeeded in obtaining. According to a list of FCPA cases the Stanford Law School tabulated, eight of the ten top cases were all foreign companies having business in the U.S. The ten with their final fine are shown as follows: Petrobas (Brazil, $1B), Siemens (Germany, $0.8B), Alston (France, $0.775B), KBR (US, $0.58B), Society General (France, $0.57B), Teva Pharmaceutical (Israel, $0.51B), Telia ($0.47B), Dch-Zeffirelli's (US, $0.4B), BAE Systems (Britain, $0.4B), and Total (France, $0.4B). These huge fines of course do not include the costs of hiring and paying lawyers, consultants and court fees.

The U.S. Congress enacted the Iran and Libya Sanction Act in 1996 (ILSA, effective August, 5th). Apparently, an "ILSA business chain" had formed closely patterning the "FCPA business chain" behavior seeking foreign targets to pay huge fines using a long legal arm. The recent case of Chinese companies ZTE and Huawei smell like the same cookie came out of the same cookie cutter and baking oven used by FCPA, except it is a different team wearing ILSA chef hat. Interestingly, these 'legal' people associated with the U.S. justice system armed with politically correct banners, such as anti-corruption under FCPA and endangering national security under ILSA, can extend their arms extremely long to target foreign companies. They can successfully evade the executive branch's notice, because they are shielded by the 'political correct' banners. Therefore, it was not surprising, the ZTE and Huawei cases occurred during the US-China trade negotiation appearing totally uncoordinated even astonished the White House trade negotiation team and the President himself.

The arrest of Huawei CFO, Ms Meng Wanzhou, draws such similarity with the Alston case except this time the ILSA business chain extended its arm even longer invoking extradition agreement with Canada. The Canadians probably acted hastily without investigating the facts or studying the practices of the FCPA and ILSA legal teams, thus aroused the diplomatic objection from China and the White House's attention. Was the Economist correct in characterizing these legal teams having too long arms in handling their cases? Very recently, countries (for example, Myanmar) have announced that they shall use other currencies (RMB) rather than the US dollars to settle their trades, obviously designed to avoid the U.S. long legal arms. Applying the U.S. laws to foreign countries and foreign companies beyond their branches and personnel in the U.S. is definitely stretching our legal arms too long. When our legal procedure uses coercion, threat, and illegal procedures such as jailing foreign executives excessively (for unproven crime and for purpose of extracting big fine) while American executives are rarely putting in jail (for real white-collar crime committed), it makes our legal system and nation looking very unfair and bad.

It is time for us to pay attention and to clean up 'Legal Corruptions' in our country!

Chapter 55
World Leadership Requirement in A Bi-Polar or Multi-Polar World

****

World order is maintained under interplay of properly balancing national security, core interests and foreign relations among nations. Historically, great nations with strong economy and military strength play a dominating role in leading the world. They resolve geopolitical issues and influence regional economical and political problems to maintain a healthy global economy and a peaceful world. In the process of managing world order, conflicts among great nations always exist; the existing and emerging powers will have their own perspectives of national security, core interests and foreign relations which often produce conflicts. The fact that over 193 sovereign nations having multiple races, numerous cultures and different social strata in wealth, classes, religion , sex and gender order all exist on Earth Planet, it is understandable that maintaining world order is a very complex and extremely challenging task for world leaders.

While continents are separated by vast oceans, the world is naturally divided into regions. When humans began to develop maritime technology and naval power, maritime trade became the economic force for great nations to expand and control the world. Great nations, focusing on their national (self) interest, often practice hegemony to expand their influence and to exert control over conquered land (nation) through colonialism. Such expansion naturally leads to competition and conflicts among great nations eventually causing wars between great powers, spreading to world wars. The WW erupted and was confined in Europe but the WW II nearly spread over all continents lasting many years.

Post WW II, two great nations had emerged creating a 'bi-polar' world divided by ideology: capitalism and liberal democracy, valuing individual freedom especially economic freedom, versus socialism and communist governance, valuing communal equality especially favoring a socialist system. This confrontation essentially divided the world into two camps, one led by the U.S. and her allies including the NATO countries and the other led by the Soviet Union and her allies including the Warsaw pact. The bi-polar world did not erupt into another world war largely because the two leading countries each had piled up significant amount of nuclear arsenal capable of destroying each other and the world thus deterring each other from waging extensive war. The situation of 'détente' could not last forever because the continuous arms race required a continuous strong economy to sustain. Ultimately, the Soviet Union collapsed under the pressure of her failing economy. The world then transitioned to a 'uni-polar' world with the U.S. being the strongest superpower, economically and militarily.

As the 'uni-polar' leader post Cold War, the U.S. indeed tried to be the world police to maintain world order. However, the world has advanced further in science, technology, manufacturing, infrastructure, transportation as well as communication (media) creating an inter-dependent but far more complex global world. The leadership required to manage this new world order must expect the existence and/or the emergence of other great nations and be prepared to deal with a world transitioning from a uni-polar to a bi-polar or a multi-polar world. The rise of China and the rejuvenating Russia are two competing great nations; Brazil, India and South Africa are also rising economic powers joining the existing G-7 (Canada, France, Germany, Italy, Japan, the United Kingdom and the United States), now extending to G20. The U.S. as the leader of G-7 had no choice but to deal with the fast developing BRICS and G20.

As the world progressed continuously with advanced communication, manufacturing and technologies, the emerging nations with significant economic power will exert influence on the world stage. During this progress, unfortunately, the U.S. failed to discourage arms build-up and naively believed that her military strength will remain unmatched and be effective in keeping the ever more complex world in order. In reality, not only great nations such as Russia, India and China now possess nuclear weapons even small nations like Iran and North Korea have gained nuclear arsenal becoming nuclear club members capable of using nuclear weapon for bargaining. So in the multi-polar world, proliferation of nuclear weapon is a serious problem which will neutralize the U.S. military power as an effective force to police the world. The world events in the past decades showed us how ineffective it had been to resolve world issues using military force. To avoid a devastating nuclear war, the best we can hope for is that all nuclear powered nations will refrain from using nuclear weapon, and gradually and ultimately transform the whole world into a nuclear weapon free world.

Observing the current world events, one cannot help but worry about the U.S. foreign policy. The U.S. seems to be still adhering to a 'uni-polar' world model and trying very hard to maintain world order ignoring the fact that the world is transitioning to a multi-polar world. In such a world, economic and military powers are necessary but not sufficient to manage the world; the world leadership needs additional political power, which is political wisdom, people and nation governing experience, geopolitical knowledge and inter-nation diplomatic skills backed by economic and military strength. The leaders of the rising nations are there in different ways through different trainings in different political systems. The U.S. is proud to have the most open and democratic political system to elect her national leaders. Unfortunately, the US election process is corrupted by money; the leaders elected are great political orators, media manipulators and fund raisers but not necessarily possessing the above cited political skills to deal with foreign policy and world issues. Even candidates with administrative and foreign relation experience are not scrutinized enough by the election process to ascertain that they have the political power, integrity and a clear vision of the complex multi-polar world.

The Russian leader, Putin, and the Chinese leader, Xi Jinping, have risen to their supreme political positions with a very different scrutiny. Their 'career' experiences speak volume of their political wisdom, geopolitical knowledge and diplomatic skills. Russia's rapid annexation of Crimea and China's long-term 'one belt one road' vision of world co-development plan demonstrated the skillful play of their political power. In contrast, Clinton-Obama's Pivot to Asia policy based on a legacy strategy of containment created more tension and little purpose. The non-cooperative Okinawa and problematic Taiwan make the island chain ineffective to sustain an island chain around China. Anticipating the rising of a multi-polar power structure in Asia, the U.S. needs to develop a new Asia/China policy to collaborate with the multi-polar powers to maintain a more evenly balanced power in Asia rather than creating an unstable Asia eventually dragging the U.S. to an Asian war. The current Trump administration had the opportunity to develop a new China policy but opted to launch a trade war which will not yield any long-term benefit to the U.S. and the world stability.

The current South China Sea (SCS) saga is clearly orchestrated by the U.S. under the containment strategy which heightened the tension there and prompted China to fortify small islands into potential defense bases as unsinkable carriers thus creating an opposite effect to containment. So far the U.S. and China had done correctly in SCS was that they both appreciated the importance of transparency in declaring their military actions to avoid accidents – a necessary behavior to show a nation's wisdom in world politics. The best, of course, is to engage China as a strategic partner (rather than an enemy with no real cause) to manage the stability in Asia. Broadly collaborate with China to take advantage of her huge market and large population not only can ease the trade deficit but also reduce the military burden the U.S. is maintaining in Asia. The lack of clarity and transparency on how and why the U.S. pivot to Asia Pacific matters to her national security and core interests and the inconsistency of her foreign policy treating China as enemy and Japan do not make the U.S. an effective world leader. In world politics, if you want war, you keep secret plans, if you want peace; you make the foreign policy transparent.

Assuming that the U.S. is not planning for war in Asia, it is very important for the U.S. to recognize the emerging multi-polar world. To maintain peace in Asia and world stability, we urge the U.S. and China to have a dialogue to develop a 'transparent' strategy to gain trust, to reduce tension and to work collaboratively for mutual benefits, world peace and prosperity.

Chapter 56
Deeper Analysis Over Events and Media Interpretations on Taiwan Strait Issue
~The Real Reason for a Probable Forced Reunification

*****

In the recent Foreign Affairs, Snap, 2-15-2019 (online), there is an essay entitled, Will China Seize Taiwan? Wishful Thinking in Beijing, Taipei, and Washington Could Spell War in 2019, authored by Prof. Peter Gries and a PhD student, Tao Wang. The paper appears to be a research work on the Taiwan Strait Issue consisting of some close monitoring of the events happened in recent years concerning Taiwan Strait and some reasonable interpretation of media reports including other scholars' assessment on the central issue - how China will unite with Taiwan? The authors took an observer's position to examine the issue from the perspectives of Mainland China, Taiwan and the U.S. The Taiwan Strait issue was historically regarded as a domestic dispute by two sides, People's Republic of China (PRC) on the Mainland and Republic of China (ROC) on Taiwan. Each side claimed itself as the legitimate representation of the entire China, but the U.S. was intimately involved in this dispute by the fact that she first recognized and supported ROC (1911-1979) and later recognized PRC (1979- present) but wished to maintain a formal diplomatic relation with PRC and an informal relationship with Taiwan.

The main conclusion of Gries and Wang's paper is to warn the three sides that there is a danger of war if every side maintains its own wishful thinking: Firstly, China is determined to reunite with Taiwan. She feels a growing confidence in her economic and military strength to do so and use force if necessary. China is witnessing the rapidly deteriorating Cross Strait Relation due to Taiwan's current Administration's (DPP) anti-China Policy making peaceful reunification elusive. An interpreted belief was cited that the U.S. would sit out if a military confrontation occurred. Secondly, Taiwan's current Administration is leaning towards pro-independence. The DPP Leader feels that Mainland China, with too many domestic problems and pressure from the U.S., is too sensible to take a military action to reunite Taiwan. A complacency attitude in Taiwan is resulting in a weakened military force by giving up compulsory military service and relying more on the U.S. military weapon sales. Thirdly, the U.S. is considering America first, not likely to send troops or want to send troops on behalf of Taiwan in the event of a military conflict at the Taiwan Strait. President Trump seems to think he can rock the boat such as toying with revisiting the One China Policy or using Taiwan as a bargaining chip against Mainland China without consequences.

Gries and Wang concluded, the above wishful thinking by the three sides might lead to a dangerous situation. China might think that the Trump era would offer a "window of opportunity" for reunification. China can easily take Taiwan by force even possibly having no bloodshed, but the authors feel it may provoke the U.S. with an unpredictable reaction from Trump Administration. Here I would like to command Gries and Wang for their discussion and warning of a possible military conflict at the Taiwan Strait. However, I would also like to add a deeper analysis than their observations on the Taiwan Strait issue so that the three sides could understand, deal and resolve the root and obstacles of the reunification issue.

It is well known to the scholars who study the U.S. - China relation, including the Taiwan Strait issue, that the U.S. has adopted a "Status Quo" Strategy for Taiwan Issue, meaning to maintain the separation of Taiwan from the Mainland China in a status quo. Under this strategy, the U.S. honors the one China policy, but insists that the Mainland China cannot take Taiwan by force so long as Taiwan does not declare independence. (Gries and Wang termed this as "Dual Deterrence" in their paper) The "status quo" was maintained in the 80's and 90's when Taiwan was having a decent GDP while Mainland China was busy improving her economy. However, this strategy no longer works as China has improved her economy to be the number two in the world making Taiwan heavily depended on Mainland China in trade. This trend started during the Chen Shui Bian Administration (Democratic Progressive Party, DPP 2001-2008) and accelerated during the Ma Yin Jeou Administration (Kuo Min Tang, KMT 2009-2016) while China rised rapidly bypassing Japan becoming the number two economy in the world. Then DPP regained power and leaned towards pro-independence pushing an anti-China movement.

The anti-China movement has its root in Japanese descendants left in Taiwan post WW II. This small population grew and gained power through the party of DPP and had a tie with Japan and her right wing parties (LDP+). The growth of DPP owed to the support of Japan and the tolerance of the U.S. under the "Status Quo" Policy. The current DPP Administration, Tsai Yin Wen, (2016-) just lost heavily in the mid-term (2018) election. Apparently, DPP's anti-China Policy backfired. Mainland China has always been taking a paternal view about Taiwan looking forward to its reunification like expecting a runaway child to return home. Taiwan benefitted from Mainland China's favorable policies offered to the Taiwanese, but Taiwan government behaved like a spoiled teenager taking those benefits for granted. The recent vivid anti-China movement gave Mainland a wakeup call.

Although the rapid rise of China from a poor country ranked in the bottom of the world to her number two position surprised many, but the process was a humble one. As a very poor and weak nation, China experimented with communism and learned through many mistakes, diplomatically swallowing quite a few abuses. As a large country she was modest on the world stage, gradually beginning to appreciate the value of capitalism and market strength. Then China decided to embrace the West, accepting capitalism and trading her market for industrialization. She was cautious and industrious with rigorous economic development planning. In four decades, China had transformed herself and succeeded in her economic development but yet maintaining a governance model and development process of her own. Now China is a major contributor to the world economy with the ability to assist other developing nations.

Barring the evolvement of the anti-China sentiment in Taiwan through textbook revision and education reform, the reunification would be peaceful and smooth since the PRC constitution provides a liberal multiple governance system to coexist in China. (Hong Kong is an example even with her own currency) Clearly, it is the current DPP Administration that has created an urgency ('window for action') for Mainland China to set a timetable to reunite with Taiwan. The "window of opportunity" for reunification perceived by Dries and Wang was attributed it to the fact that Trump Administration might have given China the impression that his Administration will sit out if China would use force to unite Taiwan. Hence, they imply that window is open before the US 2020 election. I disagree with this assessment; rather I believe that the 'window' is really mandated by the behavior of the DPP Administration. Since the majority population in Taiwan has spoken through their 2018 election, accepting the One China Doctrine and willing to increase interaction with Mainland China, it would be logical for the U.S. to sit out the Cross Strait Reunification Process unless the U.S. deliberately wanted to initiate a war.

The "Status Quo" Strategy does not make sense anymore. There is indication that Japan has revised her China policy realizing her interests is really in Mainland China not a wishful thinking of reoccupying Taiwan. Japan is embracing China's One Belt One Road (OBOR OR BRI) initiative for mutual benefits. Japan must have realized that muddling with the minority pro-independence group in Taiwan does not help her relationship with China. The same logic applies to the U.S. China policy. Targeting China as an enemy has little justification, whereas collaborating with China brings mutual benefits to both nations. Especially, when the majority of people in Taiwan has spoken, any interference from the U.S is meddling and cannot be twisted as Human Rights action.

So while we should warn the three sides of the danger of war in the Taiwan Strait like Gries and Wang did, more importantly, we should make a deeper analysis and understanding of the issue to advise the parties to revise their policies to support a peaceful reunification of Mainland China and Taiwan, which not only fulfills the Chinese mandate for reunification but also insures a peaceful Asia and a prosperous world.

Chapter 57
Asian Americans' Dual Responsibilities (I)

****

According to the U.S. Census Bureau, Asian Americans (AAs) consist of people residing in the U.S. coming from or having ancestry from the Far East, Southeast Asia and Indian Subcontinent. However, historically the population of AAs was insignificant in number in 19th century or earlier. In early 20th century, AAs were chiefly Chinese immigrants who came to the U.S. as laborers working in the railroad construction and mining industry. They were referred as coolies and seriously and unfairly discriminated by the white Americans. Despite of the discriminating laws (1920-1940's) more Asians immigrated to the U.S. from India, Japan, Philippines, and South China. Post WW II and after the abolishment of discrimination laws against Asians and especially after the elimination of quota limitation placed on Asian regions (1965), the population of Asian immigrants increased and diversified to include people with ancestry from various parts of Asia. Realizing the productivity of AAs, the U.S. opened the immigration door to Asians especially to Asian students. By the last census in 2010, the population of Asian AAs rose to 17,320,856 and grew to 22,408,454 in 2017 reaching 6.9% of the total American population, becoming the fastest growing minority group in the U.S. They are generally hard working, mainly distributed in the following states: California, 5.6M, NY, 1.6M, Texas 1.1M, NJ, 795K, Hawaii, 781K, Illinois, 669K, Washington, 604K, Florida, 573K, Virginia, 522K, and Pennsylvania, 403K, making significant contribution to the economy of the U.S.

Practiced in the US Census, people with origins or ancestry in the Far East, Southeast Asia, and the Indian subcontinent are classified as part of the Asian race whereas those with origins or ancestry in North Asia (Russians, Siberians), Central Asia (Kazakhs, Uzbeks, Turkmens, Tajiks, Kyrgyz, etc.), Western Asia (Diaspora Jews, Turks, Persians, Kurds, Assyrians, West Asian Arabs, Afghans, etc.), and the Caucasus (Georgians, Armenians, Azeris, etc.) are classified as "white" or "Middle Eastern". For the purpose of this article, it is not necessary to exclude any American coming from Asia or having ancestry from any part of Asia as AAs. In fact, the author agrees with the objection voiced by many AAs that it is unnecessary and somewhat discriminating to further subdividing the AAs, not the Whites, into categories designating smaller regions in Asia. One of the reasons for such objection is the fact that some Ivy League schools practice discrimination in their college admission process against certain groups of AAs. Further defining AAs in subgroups only help such college discrimination, yet AAs are more educated and paying more taxes per capita in the American society.

The U.S. is a country of immigrants, progressing rapidly over two and half century with the influx of capable and productive immigrants. The immigrants are drawn by the liberal democracy and equal justice principles the United States Constitution proclaims. The U.S. had a number of wars of aggression against her neighbors during her early stage, but in the two World Wars, the U.S. stood by the side of justice defending and helping her allies, especially in the WW II when her Allies were attacked by the imperialist Germany in Europe and Imperial Japan in Asia. In the end, the Allies won the war and the U.S. became the strongest nation in the world. Her citizens, several generations of immigrants, are very proud of their country for standing up for justice and liberty and being a defender of democracy. This immigrant American spirit, built on the principles of 'American can do', freedom, liberty and human rights was vivid till 1990, the time the Soviet Union collapsed.

The collapse of the Soviet Union made the U.S. the superpower and the de facto leader of the world, there began a serious change in the U.S. The nation developed divisions, not just bipartisan politics, but divisions on many issues, war, fiscal and social issues damaging the fundamental principle of democracy - majority rules (minorities should yield to the majority so that policies can be established and executed smoothly). The U.S. government became less competent and less effective; the American society became more fragmented and more selfish focusing on applying liberal principles on self-centered interest making the country stagnant in progress in infrastructure, social welfare and nation building. The U.S. economy has transformed, abandoning human and labor intensive manufacturing industries and adopting capital intense financial industries letting printing money, manipulating currency and debt carry the day. American economy drops in percentage of world economy. American foreign policy turns to a selfish hypocritical behavior – saying one thing and doing the other. Take Europe for example, despite of the vanishing Warsaw pact, the U.S. encouraged the growth of NATO pushing member recruitment and more military and weapon deployment. Take Africa, the U.S. engaged with many African countries and involved with their governments but none had become a shining example of liberal democracy with prosperity. In contrast, China's investment in Africa gained more African support in the U.N. In the Middle East, the U.S. policy caused prolonged wars with no peace insight which certainly did not benefit the people in the Middle East especially the countries blessed with rich oil deposit.

The U.S. Asia Policy is of concern to AAs. Instead of taking the collapse of the Soviet Union as an opportunity to rebuild Asia, the U.S. policy tends to divide Asia and create tension. The U.S. insisted on dividing the two Koreas rather than letting them unite and focus on economic development like the Germany did. Now, the world is facing another nuclear threat from North Korea (NK). If the U.S. media would do an honest survey on AAs (especially Korean Americans), not many would believe that NK would ever shoot a nuclear missile to the U.S., not today, never mind a decade or two ago. Asking any Japanese Americans, not many would believe that NK would shoot a nuclear missile to Japan either. People know that regional nuclear war has no winner but committing suicides. What is wrong to let Asian countries to focus on economic development and reach a balance of power on their own? Ask any AAs, how many would believe that only the U.S. can and must maintain peace in Asia, with her current Asia Policy? With China, India, Japan and Russia rising at their own rate, there would be a natural balance of power keeping peace; perhaps the natural course would be better than an outside country interfering and holding the Asian countries with strings to play a balancing act.

The AAs have a serious dual responsibility in this world simply because they would love to see that the U.S. (their home) and Asian countries (their motherland) in peace with each other. As an Asian American, one must be honestly assessing America's Asia policy. The assumption that any Asian country would attack the U.S. today is based on a legacy theory with no concrete evidence. The legacy theory targeted Russia as the enemy, but it took two to tango in arms race. Russia has been wakened since the 90's, but the U.S. military strategists switch target to China and NK. Must the U.S. have a target enemy to maintain her super military power? Assuming that any Asian country is destined to have a war with the U.S. or with its neighbor extending damage to the U.S. is a questionable logic. Japan was the aggressor in Asia attacked other Asian countries prolonged WW II but Japan is now the strongest ally of the U.S. Currently, the U.S. is walking away from globalization, pulling out of disarmament agreement with Russia and increasing military pressure in South China Sea. Where is the logic? The U.S. can leave Asia alone and concentrate on making America great again, but she is not. The AAs have a responsibility to themselves to understand the U.S. Asia Policy and steer it to the right direction. (Part II to be continued in next chapter)

Chapter 58
Asian Americans' Dual Responsibilities (II)

*****

Asian Americans (AAs) are not only a fastest growing group of minority but also have the highest educational qualifications among America's major racial categories. Chinese and Indians have over 50% of their population having bachelor's degree versus 27% for all Americans according to the 2010 census. By 2012 statistics, 61% of all Asian adult immigrants have a bachelor or higher level of education. AAs are the largest group on campuses of some of the best universities in the United States, for example, 28% at MIT and 39% at UC Berkeley. AAs have been regarded as a "model minority," with high achievement in school and doing well overall, particularly at the top of the curve. AAs enjoy also high achievement in employment with 45% of AAs in management, professional, and related occupations, a figure that is much higher than the same categories in the total population. More than one third of AA families earn $15,600 more than the national median income for all households. So AAs are making a significant contribution to the U.S. economy, undoubtedly a key support to making America great again.

However, despite of the hard working culture and mental drive for high achievement, a bamboo ceiling seems to be hanging over AAs as exhibited by some statistics. First, AAs' average life-time earnings are $400,000 less than that of Caucasians which is one convincing data supporting the bamboo ceiling. Second, less than 2% of AAs fills the top corporate C-level positions in Fortune 500 companies; in contrast the number of women leading companies (CEO) in the Fortune 500 has grown to 6.4 percent in 2017 from 2.6 percent a decade ago (but has dropped to 4.2% in Fortune's 2018 list). Third, discrimination practice in college admission against AAs, especially in Ivy League schools (as claimed in a lawsuit against Harvard) is extremely disturbing to AAs. What is more alarming to AAs is that the current U.S. Asia Policy and China Policy are bringing more discriminations against AAs, for example, like restricting admission of Asian immigrants to the U.S. (reducing visa quota), discouraging Asian Immigrants/Americans to pursue hi-tech career (not hiring them in R&D positions) and bringing charges against AAs for suspicion of espionage (apparent increase in cases and false charges). The above data and facts alone should make AAs realize that they have a responsibility to themselves to pay attention to the U.S. Asia and China policies and make their views publically known.

The AAs, came to the U.S. and stayed as immigrants, were motivated to do so because of two fundamental reasons. One is that the U.S. has provided opportunities for work and wealth creation (based on US stable and healthy economy) and the other is that the American Constitution respects individual's freedom and rights (the American value). These two reasons are vitally important not only to Asian immigrants but also to all Americans/immigrants. Therefore, the AAs like all Americans have a citizen's responsibility to safeguard the American value and demand their government to maintain a healthy economy offering sufficient employment opportunities. In today's globally interconnected environment, the U.S. economy is intertwined with other economies, Asia (GDP \$30,220B, 2018 IMF), N. America (\$23,550B), EU (\$21,820B), S. America (\$3,610B) and Africa (\$2,330B). The U.S. trade with the five key Asian regions already amounts to 27.6% of her total world trade with a breakdown as follows: China (Total 15.5%, Export 7.3%, Imports 21.1%), Japan (T 5.1%, E 4.5%, I 5.6%), South Korea (T 3.1%, E 3.3%, I 2.9%), India (T 2.1%, E 1.9%, I 2.2%) and Taiwan (T 1.8%, E 1.8%, I 1.8%). The above data shows that Asia has the largest GDP and is the biggest trading partner of the U.S., thus, it should be obvious to AAs that maintaining peace in Asia would be beneficial to the U.S. and the world. Therefore, it is easy to conclude that AAs, for their own as well as for all Americans' benefit, have a dual responsibility in this world, that is to keep America great with a sustainable healthy economy and to keep Asia in peace so that the Asian economy and the world economy will be stable.

The current trade war initiated by the U.S. against China is obviously damaging the economies of the U.S., China and the entire Asia even the entire world. As we discussed in part I, the AAs may have a different view on the current US-China conflict which is not revealed by the U.S. mainstream media. The AAs' input was hardly sought or considered especially on the assumption that China is destined to be the enemy of the U.S. and Asia must be interfered by the U.S. for Asia's sake. No Asian American wants to see Asia to become a battle ground like the Middle East. The AAs' voice and their opinions must be reported to influence the U.S. administration's policy making. The AAs must make efforts to reach out to the think-tanks on the issue why it is beneficial to the U.S. to keep Asia in peace rather than creating and engaging in wars in Asia.

Unfortunately, very few avenues are made available to AAs to express their concerns in foreign policy. Recently the Asia Society - Center on US-China Relations (Asia Society was founded in 1956 by John D Rockefeller III, initially established to promote greater knowledge of Asia in the U.S., today it is a global institute with a mission to promote mutual understanding between Asia and the U.S.) in partner with UC San Diego -School of Global Policy and Strategy had made a study: 'Course Correction: Toward an Effective and Sustainable China Policy'. The subject is important and timely. However, the entire task force group does not have a single Asian American scholar. It is no surprise that its conclusions and recommendations reflect only the view on what changes in Asia and between the U.S. and China were observed rather than trying to understand in depth why and how Asian countries, particularly China, had changed. It is the rate of change that has frightened the U.S. and caused rash reactions even though the present differences can be traced and understood.

The task force should have investigated what policies have triggered reactionary opposing policies which then in turn triggered further reactionary policy changes. Without making a thorough analysis on the causality relationship of the US Asia/China policies and the China/Asia US policies, one can not suggest any sound course correction. The Asian Americans with their close attachment to Asia and the U.S. can offer a deeper insight to why Asia has changed and why China has changed so fast as well as the reactionary nature of the past policy changes. Targeting China as an enemy rather than a strong healthy competitor is definitely resulted from the legacy strategy used in the Cold War days. Asia is a very different continent, more countries, more people, more diverse culture and a long history available for studies and references. The Asian philosophies are far broader and deeper than the 'Thucydides trap' theory which is apparently influencing the U.S. national security strategy. AAs are assets in the U.S. for understanding Asia, its culture and philosophies as well as the changes happened in the past century. Seeking AAs' input and making an understanding of the cascading policy reactions, the U.S. will be able to make a right Course Correction leading to China and Asian countries to correct their policies. Whining, complaining and blaming the Asian/China changes to unfair competition practices are too naïve not a productive solution to eliminate the economic competition from China/Asia because of their people, culture and drive for a better life. According to a Rand 2018 report, China's behavior over the past two decades does not mark her as an opponent to the post war international order. I urge all AAs carry their dual responsibility seriously by speaking out thus helping the U.S. to make a course correction which will make America great again and maintain Asia in peace.

Conclusions

*****

Both the U.S. and China are facing economic problems. China has been following the U.S. as a successful example in her opening up and developing economy. China's fast rises is not a miracle but simply because of Chinese citizens have been poor for too long thus having a tremendous drive to improve their living standard. As China is successfully removing poverty, they gradually face the similar economic problems the U.S. is facing, income and wealth gap, declining GDP growth, job creation issue and high debt throughout all levels of government and common citizens. Therefore targeting China to make her like the U.S. does not make sense, rather, targeting the U.S. and working with China may solve their problems.

The U.S. has been a superpower since WW II. Post war, the U.S. was leading in science and technology almost in every field making her the most productive nation in the world having her GDP peaked closed to 40% of the world's total GDP at one time. Since 1950's the net U.S. GDP has been steadily increasing but declined as a percentage of worlds GDP, downward below 20%. Of course, this is due to the rise of many other countries' productivity. This is a good thing for the world not necessarily bad for the U.S. either, since the U.S. does not want to be the only prosperous country in the world. The U.S. is still leading in many areas of science and technology then why is the U.S. slipping in per capita productivity and why are Americans nervous about the future? Technology and foreign competition have been blamed as the culprit, but never the U.S. economic model, the U.S. cultural change and never the American society.

The advancement in technology did bring mechanization, automation, large data processing, robots, and artificial intelligence replacing human labor and human brain in our industries and changing many aspects of our society. The principal change forced on human by technology is exhibited in jobs loss/obsolescence, but the technology advance also brings new jobs, however, the nature of new jobs requires very different set of work skills which demand appropriate education and retraining. Dealing with this issue, the U.S. economic model and government policies must bear the responsibility. In an article by Cheng Li of Brookings Institute published in Foreign Affairs, Snapshot, March 10, 2019, entitled How China's Middle Class Views the Trade War, made a good analysis for the U.S. to ponder on. The CPC government is very sensitive to how the Chinese middle class feels about China's economy. The Chinese leadership knows the tremendous and ever increasing political influence of China's middle class to the legitimacy of its governance. Therefore China acts carefully to sustain a long term economic growth and is currently in the midst of a delicate process to transition her economy, balancing manufacturing export, domestic consumption and technology innovation, while dealing with the external pressure such as the trade war initiated by the U.S.. Whereas the U.S. government is only accountable to four-year term election which unfortunately is controlled by the upper 1% rather than the middle class in America, thus only making the U.S. government focusing on short-term policies , stock market performance, and busy reversing policies of the previous administration. Consequently, the U.S. is unable to manage her national economy as well as China does.

The fundamental conditions of a healthy economy are healthy productivity and healthy consumption. While the healthy productivity gain depends on science and technology and skilled workers, the healthy consumption depends on a large employed population who can earn good wages and make spending. This equilibrium condition for a healthy economy can be represented by a sufficient GDP figure and a high enough employment rate. However, the employment rate should be represented by a steady permanent employment rather than a transient short-term employment for supporting a healthy economy, since short-term jobs cannot produce skill upgrade needed for new challenging jobs and innovations. When technology advances, it increases productivity and raises wages not only in a particular industry sector but it has a ripple effect raising wages across all industries. Under a socialistic concept, sometimes, the government will impose a minimum wage policy which automatically raises wages across the board as a means to raise the income level hence standard of living across the entire population especially helping the lower income groups.

When wages are high in an industry sector which cannot maintain high enough profitability to support the growth, the industry is likely to become a low-tech high-labor (LTHL) sunshine industry, for example, textile, furniture, steel making and fresh food industries. These LTHL industries will have to move to low labor cost countries which will be glad to absorb the low tech industries. The developing countries with large populations are generally the target locations for these low-tech migrations. Numerous cases are available to illustrate this trend. The U.S. essentially lost many low-tech industries through this natural process willingly and voluntarily. No one can steal American jobs, because the U.S. is capable of prohibiting it. For example, exporting high-tech in terms of products, corporations and personnel has been strictly controlled by the U.S. government.

Losing low-tech industries is not necessarily a problem since maintaining high-tech industries can generally command higher profitability. There is a saying that a developing country making a billion pairs of jeans makes less profit than a developed country selling one jet plane. This is a true fact but one must recognize another fact that an advance jet plane may require a thousand technical professionals and skilled workers but the billion pair of jeans support hundreds of thousands of low skilled workers, a very much needed job creation industry in a developing country. So the issue in a developed country is how to create enough new jobs, how to educate new workers and retrain workers upgrading them from low-tech jobs to the new Jobs. The new jobs must produce new products having a market demand domestically and in other countries. Why didn't the U.S. follow this simple formula to sustain her technology lead and upgrade industries which can maintain her job and product market base? Hindsight, there is a clue.

The U.S. has enjoyed the highest GDP and led in most advanced technologies. While the above natural technology migration occurred, the U.S. being a capitalistic nation, controlled by the 1% wealthy individuals rather than the mass middle income class, was driven only by profitability in their industry transformation forgetting the above discussed conditions such as to maintain employment to sustain a healthy economy. The U.S. had given up most of her labor intense low-tech low-profit manufacturing industries and focused on high return capital intensive financial industry and high profit advanced high-tech sectors, such as medicine, weapons, and sophisticated IT products. Although these capital intensive industries may have high profitability but they do not support large number of work force, in addition, they reject the low-tech skilled workers, because they are not easily re-trainable for the new jobs.

The U.S. higher education is the best in the world attracting talents from all over the world. There was not an issue of turning up enough talents to meet the demand in the financial and high-tech industries, however, that number is far short of the displaced workers who were not retrained for a new job employment. High-tech High profit sometimes do need low-tech assembly and manual packaging and to be close to the market place to sell. (smart phone is an example) The developed countries can accept the high priced high-tech products but they have less population or cheap labor and they want to protect their own high-tech industries. The developing countries have large population but they cannot afford the high priced high-tech products even they may desire them. China being a large developing country with huge rising middle income population is one of the best country for high-tech products to enter. But the high-tech products are vulnerable to government regulation or import laws and also oddly even subject to the U.S. sanction laws based on national security concerns. Thus the U.S. economic model - driving her capital intensive industries to create high profits good for the few stock holders but not enough jobs to support her replaced low-tech workers - will eventually have problems. Now she does!

The U.S. favored financial products on the other hand do not even need assembly workers thus even less welcomed by the developing countries. So they are hampered by complex local laws and regulations which are designed to protect their citizens from capital taking. Other than investment financing, most financial products such as insurance and money management are simply taking money away from the developing countries where they need their capital for their education and economic and social development. It is perfectly understandable that all developing countries are leery for opening their financial markets to the developed countries, because with capital being controlled by foreign firms they cannot design and control the destiny of their economic development. So they have to put protection laws to prevent the foreign financial industry to rob their capital. China needs huge capital for her economic development. Chinese have a good habit of saving money, but they are vulnerable to foreign financial products offering a little higher interest. It is no surprise that China protects her financial market.

The above description is a nut shell how the U.S. has arrived at her current state of economy – income and wealth gap, declining GDP growth, high unemployment (for more permanent high-productivity jobs), and high debt throughout all levels of government and common citizens. The U.S. has more higher education institutions than any other country in the world and yet they produce more graduates who cannot get a meaningful job. Government must honestly take responsibility for this situation, not inventing half baked stories that other countries stole American jobs, pirated American technologies and practiced unfair trades. Other than trades under the gun point during the 'colonial eras', modern trades are made by two parties voluntarily. The U.S. does not have to buy low priced imports just the same as other countries can refuse to buy high priced imports. Trades are made by needs and demands. Human civilization is advanced by absorbing technologies from each other. Every developed nation has absorbed technologies from other countries before they became a developed nation.

Today, no one can steal someone else's job; it is all initiated by corporations, who own the jobs, by doing transfer, lay-off or merger. Every advanced country including the U.S. practiced copying, learning and pirating technologies at different levels and at different times in different industries from advanced nations, otherwise the world will see far less technological advances. The crux of the matter is how a country manages its economic policy to keep up with the competing and advancing world. The U.S. must visit the ground level of economic theory to employ right policies to make America great again. Not by targeting China or any other country. China has been embracing capitalism, in many ways learning from the U.S. except she was large and poor with very uneven economic condition across the country. China is very much concerned that she will become like the U.S., thus the U.S. China policy to demand China to be more like the U.S. will not go too far unless the U.S. can fix her own economic problems.

China seems to have understood the above discussed scenarios, especially the U.S. industrial migration problems (at least at her present economic development stage); China is rightly concerned that the financial and economic problems in the U.S. may replicate in China. China is taking precaution making ginger steps in opening and reforming her economy from manufacturing export to domestic consumption, especially careful with her financial sector. In Eastern Europe and Latin America, there were ample examples that opening financial market essentially yielded economic development to foreign conglomerates whose goal is nothing but making profit for themselves. China not only has a right to be prudent but also need to have a strong grip on her economy, otherwise, her economy will never be sustained at a high growth rate, more likely to shrink and collapse dragging the world down with her. Christopher Balding has published a paper entitled, What Is Causing China's Economic Slowdown and How Beijing Will Respond?, in Foreign Affairs Snapshot, March 11, 2019. The paper discussed many reasons such as rising wages, mounting debts, and external pressure (trade tariff and interest rate) , not so different from the problems the U.S. has. However, the author seems to have faith in China's government to weather out its problems.

What should the U.S. do for her economic problems? This is an important question, but the answer is not in the simplistic legacy strategy by targeting China as an enemy then China will collapse like the Soviet Union did in 1990, nor is the answer in the sophisticated economic theory. Actually the answer lies in some common sense philosophy and applying which can lead to a few good policy changes. The main objective of any economic policy must be creating meaningful long-term jobs for the citizens and focusing on industries and products not only having a market demand, making profits but also contributing to the positive advancement of human civilization in a collaborative way. The Earth resources are limited. One nation or a few nations cannot dominate the usage of all resources such as energy, food and materials.

Fair usage and fair competition under peaceful regulation and negotiation are the only way to keep the world economy going.

As the most advanced nation, the job loss and job change in the U.S. is only getting worse not better if the government does not target the U.S. to find a solution. With the advancement of AI and robotics, some handwriting is already on the wall. However, stopping advances in technology is to stop advancement in human civilization, therefore, the U.S. cannot stop technology development but must embrace competition as well as collaboration. Recently, China has increased story reporting about many unsung heroes in science and technology profession emphasizing their life-long dedication to their careers with very little financial reward not even recognition. In contrast, China has also increased harsh criticism on the exorbitant income and greed in the entertainment industry. They blame that to the influence of Hollywood and argue from socialistic point of view: Who made more contribution to the society, thousands of professionals working their whole lives devoting to research, for example, converting desert to productive agriculture land versus a few movie stars who made a few movies grossing millions of dollars? This simple question brings us to think what is wrong with the U.S. economic model and her society and what fixes she has to make.

The problem the U.S. is facing is definitely not technology competition nor trade competition; it is in her society and in her culture. The U.S. claims to be the democratic country with the most freedom and liberty, but the U.S. has a society with at least 21.3 % on government assistance program, 20% receiving food stamps and 35% getting some form of government assistance. The income gap can be described as top 0.1%, 1%, and 10% having income equal to 198 times, 40 times and 9 times of the average income of the lower 90% of the population. The social benefits take away incentive to work or to become productive in the society. The income gap accentuates the culture that capitalism breeds in the American society. No wonder we have a poor work ethics. Our democracy cannot make minority yielding to the majority's decision, instead, the minority puts up protests and boycotts to hinder progress be it infrastructure projects or social programs. Our culture worships stardom right from the school age. More kids want to be sports or movie stars to become famous, because they make millions of dollars. The rich and famous are the ones in the news, on TV and mingling with power. Interestingly, China is sensing the same issues worrying American culture happening in her society. Should the U.S. target China to make her become like the U.S. or should we target the U.S. to work with China together to solve the problems? The answer is clearly the latter!

Appendices (I)

Articles related to US-China issues written in Chinese are published in a separate volume instead of being collected here in this appendix.

Appendices (II)

US-China Relations (4/2015)
ISBN 0977159426 ISBN 13: 9780977159420
Publisher
TLC Information Services
3 Louis Drive, Katonah, N. Y. 10532-3122
Available from Amazon.com and Other Retailers and Kindle
Search Example
http://www.amazon.com/U-S-China-Relations-Mainstream-Organic/dp/0977159426

Conclusions

Understanding the U.S and China (4/2016)
ISBN 0977159442 ISBN 13: 9780977159444
Publisher
TLC Information Services
3 Louis Drive, Katonah, N. Y. 10532-3122
Available from Amazon.com and Other Retailers and Kindle
Search Example
http://www.amazon.com/U-S-China-Relations-Mainstream-
Organic/dp/0977159426

Table of Contents of Understanding the U.S. and China

             Conclusions

The Changing Giants – The U.S. and China (4/2017)
ISBN 0977159450 ISBN 13: 9780977159451
Publisher
TLC Information Services
3 Louis Drive, Katonah, N. Y. 10532-3122
Available from Amazon.com and Other Retailers and Kindle
Search Example http://www.amazon.com/U-S-China-Relations-Mainstream-Organic/dp/0977159426

New World Order – The Bipolar View (4/2018)
ISBN 1981506942   ISBN 13 9781981506941
Publisher
TLC Information Services
3 Louis Drive, Katonah, N. Y. 10532-3122
Available from Amazon.com and Other Retailers and Kindle
Search Example
http://www.amazon.com/U-S-China-Relations-Mainstream-
Organic/dp/0977159426

Table of Contents of New World Order – The Bipolar View

Notes and References

In the book, US-China Relations, the author has included a fairly detailed notes and references section for each chapter to explain the special terms and people's names mentioned in the text. From the second book onward, only a few references are listed here for readers' convenience to look up any definition of a special term or a brief biography of a person. The following references will provide the readers either rapid search engines to find information you need or ready information in an organized manner:

US-China Forum, Bilingual, http://www.us-chinaforum.org or
US-China Forum, English Papers, http://www.us-chinaforum.com
Wikipedia, **http://www.wikipedia.org**
Google Search Engine, **http://www.google.com**
Baidu, A Chinese Search Engine **http://www.baidu.com**
Foreign Affairs, **http://www.foreignaffairs.com** Magazine
Foreign Policy, **http://www.foreignpolicy.com** Magazine
Foreign Relations of the U.S. (FRUS),
      http://history.state.gov/historicaldevelopments
New York Times, **http://www.nytimes.com** Newspaper
Wall Street Journal, **http://www.wsj.com** Newspaper
Washington Post, **http://www.washingtonpost.com**, Newspaper
Diplomat, **http://www.diplomatmagazine.com** Magazine
Economist, **http://www.economist.com** Magazine
e-International Relations, **http://www.e-ir.info** Website
Global Politics, **http://global.politics.co.uk** Magazine
Rand Review, **http://www.rand.org** Research on Policies
Tass, Russian News Agency, **http://www.tass.ru/en**
      http://www.tass.ru/world
The Chinese Journal of International Politics,
      http://cjip.oxfordjournals.org

Peer Reviewed Academic Journal

Central News, **http://www.cna.com.tw** Chinese News

Xinhua News, **http://www.chinaview.cn** Chinese News

Xinhua News, English, **http://www.xinhuanet.com/english**

China News, **http://www.news.cn/english**

List of International Relations Journal,
**https://en.wikipedia.org/wiki/List_of_international_relations_journal
s**

www.ingramcontent.com/pod-product-compliance
Lightning Source LLC
Chambersburg PA
CBHW081407270326
41931CB00016B/3402